WONDERFULLY HUMAN

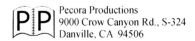 Pecora Productions
9000 Crow Canyon Rd., S-324
Danville, CA 94506

ISBN-13: 978-1-940144-02-3
ISBN-10: 1940144027

First Edition

WONDERFULLY HUMAN

A True Story of Love, Loss, and Freedom

Lea Gambina Pecora

With Love

This book is dedicated to the 5 of us, in remembrance of the many moments we've shared.

Mom, Dino, Julie, Dad, and Me

THE GAMBINAS

CONTENTS

LEA'S ORIGINAL POETRY

CAREGIVING ASSISTANCE

OTHER ORIGINAL WORK

INTRODUCTION

This book is a memoir. It's a true story told by me, a daughter wanting to do justice in preserving my parents' memory. It's not only a tribute to them, but an offering to all those who are experiencing hardship – to those human beings that have lost someone close to them and are struggling with grief, a broken heart, and the realization of their own mortality. I've been there.

I lost both of my parents, back to back, after unexpected illnesses spanning a period of 2 ½ years. I experienced an intense journey. I discovered that a big part of life isn't about the details of what happens, it's about the level of engagement in response to what happens in life, or choosing not to engage at all. I've learned that choosing to engage brings a richness to our lives and inspires an outpouring of creativity and connection with others, if we allow it.

This book is written in story form. It's not a "how-to" book, however, I've included many details of practical things my sister and I did in caring for, and managing the care of, my parents – all designed to keep them living at home. I've included notes from family meetings which helped our family remain on the same page. I included the job ad we used to find caregivers, care notes to guide caregivers, schedules we created, hospital care guidelines for my dad's special needs, a customized live-in agreement we created for our particular circumstances - all of which can be used and modified to help others facing similar challenges.

We succeeded in keeping my parents at home, as was their wish. Neither of them was admitted to a live-in care facility (not even my father, who was a quadriplegic from an accident he had 40 years prior, when I was just one year old.) We also succeeded in leveraging resources and creating a drama-free environment which allowed us to have the most quality time and connection with our parents during their last months of life. For this, I am forever grateful.

Not only did I get through the hardships of the experience of my parents' illnesses and subsequent deaths, I grew and thrived as a result of the intangible gifts I received during the journey. *I learned something.* It took years for me to be able to articulate what I learned, however, I knew – from the depths of my soul – that if I succeeded in my efforts to authentically express my experience, others would surely benefit (including me).

In this book, I also explain how I dealt with grief and anxiety. After my parents died, I remember what it felt like in my chest at the mention of their names and the tears that were impossible to hold back. I remember the thoughts that led me there – the strong feelings of loss. To this day, I allow tears to flow with thoughts of them, but instead of the heavy sadness in my chest, I feel the expansion of gratitude in my heart. My tears no longer come with a dampening of my spirit. They are sweet expressions of love that continue to set me free.

This book is an uplifting, bittersweet, engaging story of real, raw, life. It is not a *sad* story – it's a *real* story – with humor, love, big messes, little messes, and everything in between. My childhood and coming-of-age experiences are memorialized, and what I know of my parents' lives are as well.

My parents' life story is one made for the movies. It's modest, endearing, traumatic, and powerful. My dad's charismatic personality comes across in these pages. My mom's strength and love are undeniable.

My portrayal of their end-of-life experiences, from a daughter's perspective, offers valuable insight into experiences that most of us will encounter during our lifetime, simply because we are all human, living in this world, right here, right now. None of us will escape the transition from this world to the next and the unknown moment that it will occur. I've witnessed my parents' journey, being fully engaged and by their sides.

We are given the gift of life when we are born, and we will all face our inevitable deaths. What do we wish to experience in between? What can we control, and what is beyond our control? We can attempt to avoid the inevitable changes that life forces upon us, or we can face them head-on and allow the beauty of it all to rush in. We do have a choice, and the realization of this fact is not only empowering, it offers a freedom that is truly hard to describe, yet this book is my attempt to do just that.

I invite you to allow this book, in all its depth, to touch your heart and inspire you to also share your story. We all have unique and important perspectives to share as we journey through life. Imagine if we all left this kind of legacy? *The ripple effect would be amazing.* We simply cannot fathom how many people would benefit from the lessons we've learned in our lives. Imagine the understanding we can foster in our existing relationships once those close to us get a glimpse into our world, through the personal perspective of our own words and the stories we decide to tell from our own hearts.

Let's all unite as we go through this experience together…this mysterious event we call Life.

I'll start…

In the Beginning

I had no idea what the weather was like that day.
  Cold, hot, humid, rainy
I wouldn't have known what that meant.

The only care I could imagine was simple,
  comfort - so I could sleep.

Yes, that does sound selfish,
  but I didn't know how to be anything else.
Me, me, me was all I could have felt
  the day I was born.

My mother remembers that day. I was out in 20 minutes flat.
(Dad was still parking the car.)

I was a good baby, she said.
I seldom screamed and cried.

I wish I could remember that long ago
being just a few days old.
  What a fascinating memory to have.

Imagine the moment of truth,
  learning that you're a separate being,
  apart from everything else.
What an awesome discovery that must have been.

The human race is a sacred phenomenon.

We were all babies once
  knowing nothing,
  absorbing everything,
   growing
    thinking
     learning . . . . . .

Part One

Destiny

There was a certain look on my dad's face that day. His expression was one of embarrassment and discomfort, yet he surrendered all resistance. I felt his gratitude. It's amazing how one expression can communicate all this – and to a child of 3 or 4 years old. This was one of my earliest childhood memories. My dad, who was paralyzed from a diving accident when he was 29, was having fun doing "wheelies" in the kitchen (which he often did, and much to my mom's dismay). He flipped up his chair using a bit too much strength, and he and his wheelchair fell backward onto the linoleum kitchen floor. My mom could not lift him up and I remember sensing her stress. I was sitting next to my dad's face feeling worried. Mom gave me a wet washcloth and showed me how to pat his forehead. She told me to stay right there, then she disappeared. (I think she left to get a neighbor.) I don't remember where my brother and sister were at the time. It felt like it was just me and my dad.

I remember feeling very small with a strong sense of responsibility as I wiped my dad's forehead with the washcloth. Forty years have gone by, yet I recall his expression so clearly. He didn't say anything. I could tell by his slight smile and his averted eyes that he was embarrassed. By the sweat on his face, I got the sense that he was uncomfortable and worried. Through all this, I could feel his gratitude. He was relieved that I was there next to him. I didn't dare move from my post. I felt lost as to what to do anyway. I just stayed there like my mom asked me to do and I took my job very seriously as I patted his forehead gently with the wet washcloth.

Memories are so interesting. They are like small snapshots of time. Pictures in my head with feelings attached. My parents are now gone, yet my memories keep them present. Then I think about memories from childhood, or "before the news" of my mom's illness, when life was normal. Then I feel almost normal again. Almost.

Growing up, my mom was always in motion. She was cleaning, cooking or doing maintenance on the house most of the time when we were home. If she wasn't standing and doing, then she was crashed on the recliner or on the couch, exhausted. I enjoyed lying against her on the couch. Even though she was usually half asleep, it was very cozy there. I felt cared for as a child, but a bit wistful – always waiting for that moment when I would gain her undivided attention.

"That's very nice," my mom said gently as I reached up to give her the wildflower I had picked from outside. It must have been winter because I had a thick jacket on with a hood and I felt "bundled up", almost uncomfortably so. I clearly remember that the flower was very small, and that I had held it up with both hands as an offering to my mom. She was in the kitchen and she turned around from the sink to acknowledge me, briefly. She then said, "Now go back outside," and she put her hands on my shoulders and gently turned me around. She never took the flower. Yet, I remember feeling good because I liked the soft tone of her voice and I walked away admiring the flower I still held.

My mom was an excellent caretaker. Whenever one of us kids were sick, she took such good care of us. I almost liked being sick, because she would bundle me up on the couch, and give me a new coloring book. She would cater to me and give me juice and soup, and tell me when I should try and sleep. Then she would gently wake me up to give me medicine. Having fevers was a horrible feeling. I didn't like how spacey I felt. My mom was always right there, and I remember her calling the doctor too and making notes as she cradled the rotary phone between her chin and shoulder.

I recall times throwing up as a kid and mom would spring into action, swishing me up and onto the kitchen floor. She would have me and the floor cleaned up in no time. I felt very secure when I was a kid. I knew my mom was the one who would always care for me. She proved it time and again. Even when I became an adult, the little girl in me knew who had my back. As fun as my dad was, my mom was the hero in our house.

I remember feeling confused and sad one day when I was riding in the car with my mom. She was upset. I remember this incident clearly because my mom rarely complained. She really didn't talk much unless asked direct questions. She did tend to yell quite a bit and us kids would scamper away when she was in her moods, but complaining – no, that wasn't something she normally did.

This day in the car though, for some reason, she was visibly upset and said something like, "I'm always the bad guy and your dad is the fun one." She was kind of crying when she said this. As a kid, I just didn't have the words. If I did, I would have expressed my view of her – she was everything to me. She was awesome and beautiful. She was strong and did her best. I loved her more than anything. She was MY mom. She was my hero. Even as a kid, I could sense she didn't know this. She didn't know how incredible she was. I did. I just didn't know how to tell her being such a little kid, so I stayed quiet. It wasn't until many years later that I would begin to understand the level of stress she was under.

****

Classic

Picture the 1960's…a background of black and white, black leather jackets, skirts and ducktails, 1950 Chevys, coolness…straight out of a timeless movie! That was when my parents were in their prime.

My dad was 100% Italian. His name was Henry Anthony Gambina, but he insisted on being called "Hank". He was born in 1939 and grew up in Oakland, California. He was an "oops" baby – meaning his parents didn't plan to have another baby. My grandma was in her 40's when she gave birth to my dad. My dad had a brother, Joe, who was 15 years older than him, and a sister, Ann, who was 10 years older. He was surrounded by family, and his Aunt Nina helped raise him because his mom struggled with asthma and other illnesses. My dad had fond memories of going to church with Aunt Nina – sometimes 7 days a week. He was raised Catholic and even though his spiritual views changed quite a bit over the years, he always remained Catholic. (My dad's little first communion sport jacket from the 1940's is hanging in my closet. My mom had kept it safe, and now I will as well. It still has his little first communion pin on it!)

My grandfather (my dad's father) was a gardener who took great pride in his work. He and my grandma migrated to the U.S. on a boat from Italy to New York, and settled across the country in the West in Oakland, California, in a neighborhood with mostly Italian families. Both of my dad's parents spoke only Italian. My grandfather was from Palermo, Italy, and my grandmother was from Messina, Italy. Some day I will visit those cities. I never had the opportunity to get to know my dad's parents before they died, although my mom did say that my grandmother held me when I was a newborn baby.

My dad was the "life of the party" wherever he went. He had only one serious girlfriend before he met my mom. She was a neighbor of his, and I remember him saying she was a really nice girl and had long, black hair. He seemed to have fond memories of her. After this girlfriend, my dad dated a lot. My dad's friends would tease him whenever he would bring a girl around. They would make bets on how long my dad would stay interested in a girl because apparently they would see a girl once, maybe twice, and then my dad would introduce them to a new one.

My dad was very attractive. He had those Italian good looks – a muscular physique, dark skin, and dark hair, and was around 5'10" in height. He told a story many times about when a group of girls drove by him one day when he was on a rooftop working with his shirt off. It was a very hot day. The girls yelled, "Woo hoo!" and waved hello as they drove by in a convertible. My dad was very surprised and flattered by this. Apparently this didn't happen much in the 1950's.

My dad loved cars and always took very good care of them. He loved motorcycles too. He liked to have fun, and treated people very well. He would come to the defense of others as he saw fit. He was assertive, kind, confident and cool. The girls adored him!

Then there was my mom. What a beauty. My mom was 100% Portuguese. Her name was Brenda Joyce Gambina – named after a famous movie star from the 1940's. My mom was born in 1945 and grew up in Honolulu, Hawaii. When she was in high school, her parents moved the family to Hayward, California, to be close to my mom's sister, Doreen, who had moved there earlier – apparently as a solution to some troublesome teenage years. My grandma missed Doreen so much that she was able to convince my grandfather to make that big move.

My mom was a quiet person and strived to be a "good girl" growing up in her volatile home. (As I understand it, her parents, especially her father, were heavy drinkers.) My mom was beautiful, with dark hair and dark eyes. She was 5'3" in height and petite. She enjoyed roller skating in the skating rink when she was young, and even competed for a while when she was a teenager. My mom wouldn't say too much about her childhood. She always said her parents did their best. She did say that she looked just like her father and that her father seemed to really like this. Her personality was on the shyer side and she didn't offer up information too readily. She had a smaller circle of friends. She loved to dance. Music and dogs were her two favorite things, along with her 1969 SS Chevelle.

My mom did very well in school. She liked academics, however, had a hard time socially. She said her nickname in school was gorilla because she had fair skin and the hair on her legs was very dark. My grandma wouldn't allow her to shave them. She was one of the only Caucasian kids in her class and felt a bit like an outsider.

My mom enrolled in a community college after high school. I remember her saying that she didn't like college because it wasn't structured enough for her. She didn't like all the choices of courses and having to walk around all over campus to change classes. She quit college and got a job as a bank teller at Bank of America. She really enjoyed the job. For the first time she was earning her own money and felt a sense of freedom.

Below is an excerpt from my mom's memoir. (My mom wrote an 18 paged memoir when she was 50 years old. I remember our family eating together at a restaurant called Black Angus to celebrate my mom's 50th birthday. She brought along 3 beautifully wrapped gifts, one for each of us kids. Each box contained a copy of her memoir. I'm so thankful she took the time to write down her memories!

1963 was an eventful year—not only graduating from high school, but I became an aunt for the first time—Gordon was born. I started college—Cal State, Hayward. I was honored at a basketball game for winning the Bank of America Achievement Award in Business administration and welcomed to Cal State as the first freshman class. I majored in Business and minored in Math. There were only two tall buildings on a large campus up the big hill. I didn't have my own car but Dad was carpooling to work so I was able to use our '56 Buick if I scheduled it right. Didn't like college much, not like high school. It didn't have the structure, too much idle time in between classes. I know that was supposed to be for study but unless there was a deadline, it was hard for me to just study. Met this guy, Larry, and we hung out in the library sometimes. I think he was in my calculus class—that was where all the guys were! I was the only girl. I didn't mind. Hank met me at school once and wasn't too excited when he met Larry. He was just a friend, but I liked that Hank was jealous. I barely made it through my freshman year when I decided college wasn't for me. I wanted a job and some independence and I knew what my goal in life was, and it wasn't a career. In those days, women and careers were not compatible, but I don't think society's attitudes had much to do with my decision. It seemed raising kids would be much more fun.

I love knowing that my mom really wanted to raise kids. I'm sure this desire really helped her survive the hard times that were yet to come.

****

Greased Lightening

It's always fun for me to hear about how couples first met. My parents' story is a great one. My dad was asked to be the Best Man in his friend, Frank's wedding. My mom was asked to be the Maid of Honor for the same wedding by her friend, Judy. Frank asked my dad to do him a favor and pick up a girl named, Brenda, from her house and take her to the rehearsal dinner. My dad agreed.

I recall my dad saying that he drove up to the house and my mom walked out and got into the car with a shy smile. He thought she was so adorable! He said he kept glancing at her sitting next to him in the car and that she didn't talk much. He said she looked so cute quietly sitting next to him. He pretty much adorned her with attention and affection. My dad has always been the romantic type. He swept her off her feet and they were together ever since. Here is an excerpt from my mom's memoir about meeting my dad for the first time:

The Friday before the ceremony at All Saints Catholic Church, there was the rehearsal. Judy said to be ready and they will pick me up. About 7:00, a 1958 white Impala drove up in front of our house and I walked out to the car. Frank and Judy were in the backseat and the best man was in the driver's seat. Judy introduced me to Hank. Now this was a good looking hunk! He had bulging biceps and was older (23, I was 17) and Italian. His hair was slicked back with dixie peach with a duck tail in the back and sort of curl in front. He reminded me now of John Travolta in Grease. He purposely did not wear his glasses even though they were required for driving. We started dating immediately.

The history of our family was in the making! My parents' journey together had begun.

I remember my mom talking about going on a trip with her family in San Diego during the time she and my dad were dating. She said she missed my dad so much while she was gone. She also mentioned that because her father was a drinker, that she never wanted to be with someone who drank too much. She was a bit disappointed the first time she saw my dad buy beer. My dad did like to drink and have fun while doing it. My mom said she developed the taste for beer, but she was never much of a drinker. They had a great time dating in the early 1960's, and even though my mom wasn't comfortable with my dad drinking, she was in love.

My parents got married in 1965. I remember my dad reminiscing about their honeymoon and how it was the happiest day of his life when they left their wedding reception, got in his car, and drove down the California coast to the Madonna Inn. He said he had $100 cash in his pocket and was on Cloud 9. I love looking at my parents' photo album with all their black and white photos from this time.

I recall only a few details about my parents' early years of marriage based on what they talked about. My mom said that they didn't have a phone in the house on purpose. They wanted their alone time. However, when my mom had a miscarriage (before my brother was born), they quickly realized the value of it. My mom was home alone when it happened.

My mom started having babies when she was 21. She gave birth to my brother, Dino, in 1966, me in 1968, and my sister, Julie, in 1969. They moved into a home in Newark, California, when I was 1 year old and stayed living there until the day they died. Just prior to buying the house, my dad's mother had passed away and they received a $3,000 inheritance which they used to make a down payment on the home. The home was their 2nd choice, because their first choice was a few thousand dollars more – which was too expensive for them. Here's another excerpt from my mom's memoir which I found interesting about their search for a home:

> *We had looked at several homes. A flattop off of Cherry St. in Newark. I remember it was a little weird—you walked into the living room, then through the kitchen, to get to the bedrooms. So you would have to go through the kitchen each time to get to the bathrooms or bedrooms. We seriously considered buying it because of the price – $18,000.00. We also looked at the brand new homes just being built at the Newark Lake. The cheapest model was $26,000.00. Hank wanted to buy it but I couldn't see how we could possibly manage it. We only had $3,000.00 for a down payment and could afford $180.00 a month maximum. We compromised on another home. I was so impressed with the kitchen, bar and family room. I was still concerned that we couldn't afford it. It appraised for $23,000.00 and had been on the market for over six months. The couple that owned it was in the service and*

was moving out of state. He gave it to us for $20,600.00. It was unheard of to buy a house for under the appraisal price. I guess we were lucky.

My parents did love their home – even though it wasn't the one my dad wanted near the lake. They always took good care of their house. With my dad's father being a gardener, my dad was very particular about the yard. The house was on a large corner lot, and my parents mentioned more than once that the home was originally owned by the builder of the neighborhood. The home was painted yellow. It was a ranch-style, 3 bedroom, 2 bath house with a small backyard, and a very large front yard. It was 1,400 square feet. My parents liked to have parties at the house. For the longest time, there was a pool table in the family room. My mom was an awesome pool player!

After my parents passed away many, many years later, I was very happy that we were able to present their home for sale in a way that they would have been proud of. The yard and garden were pristine. The carpets were pulled up and the hardwood underneath refinished. The interior was painted fresh. We even had it staged with a few pieces of furniture and accents in the family room and dining room. The minimal improvements we invested in made a big difference. We received multiple offers, and the people that bought it were very excited about their home and thankful we chose them.

I cried when I signed the papers selling the home, and cried again the day I closed my parents' checking account. I was surprised by this because it was "all business" up until that point. Deep down though, it was more. It was another goodbye – a goodbye to a home that held so many memories.

I ended up writing a letter to the new owners just to let them know how much love was in their home in the past. They actually wrote me back and was so appreciative of the little bit of history I gave to them. It felt good to write that letter, and even better when it was well received and the new owners actually took the time to write me back. It meant a lot to me. It was the closure I needed which helped reconcile my feelings saying goodbye to my childhood home.

****

Trickle Down Effect

Following are some memories I have of my extended family. I'm still in touch with some of of them. I am so grateful for this, and also for the fact that I hold no ill-will toward anyone in my family, whether I'm in touch with them or not. I say this only because I've heard so many stories of strife amongst families and I realize with gratitude that I do not carry this type of burden.

My clearest memories of my mom's dad (my grandfather), was smelling the alcohol on his breath whenever we would see him, although I didn't know what the smell was at the time. I just remember being grossed out by it. I also remember my grandfather had mushy lips when he kissed my cheek. I liked him though – he smiled a lot and always brought my brother and sister and me bags of M&M candy so we were very happy running up to greet him. I wasn't particularly close to him, although I enjoyed having him around. We didn't see him that much.

My mom's mother is the grandparent I remember most. She used to take either my brother or sister or me for a day at a time. She never took us all together. The 3 of us were too much for her. My grandma was afraid a lot of the time. I'm not sure why, but she was an anxious person. Whenever I was out in public with her, she would hold my hand so tight it would literally hurt. She didn't drive because she was too afraid.

I loved where my grandma lived. It felt like a neighborhood of doll houses. She lived in a manicured trailer park in Hayward, California, with black tar, curvy streets. I remember the asphalt was so black and perfect looking. She would serve me Eggo Waffles for breakfast and put butter and syrup on them. It was so good. My mom rarely put butter on our food at home, so it was a treat. Grandma also made me tuna sandwiches with lots of mayo on white Wonder bread. My mom's tuna sandwiches were much dryer and she used wheat bread, which didn't taste nearly as good.

My grandma always wore Hawaiian "muumuus" and thong san-dals. She really missed living in Hawaii. She always had red painted toe nails. At night, she would sit and drink her tall glass of chocolate milk, and for some reason, she didn't allow me to have any chocolate milk. Maybe it was because it was right before my bedtime. I just remember watching her drinking it and wishing I could have it.

I was sad for my grandma when my grandpa divorced her. She al-ways held out hope that he would come back. As I understand it, my grandma didn't like leaving the house, and my grandpa wanted to go out. Apparently while out, he met a nice woman whom he ended up mar-rying. When his new wife passed away, I remember overhearing my mom saying how my grandma really thought my grandpa would go back to her. He never did. He always took care of her financially though. As far as I know, my grandma never worked a job in her life.

Both my grandma and grandpa were heavy smokers, and spent a lot of time at the local bars in Honolulu during my mom's childhood. My mom remembers being in the bars as a little girl, and also sleeping in the back seat of their car with her sister, Doreen, when my grandparents stayed in the bar late. My mom started smoking at age 15. I remember her saying it was hard to smoke because she would cough and didn't re-ally like it, however, her cousin was a smoker and was teaching her. My mom always thought her cousin was cool, and she thought smoking was cool, so she eventually mastered it, and smoked for the next 15 years ev-ery day, many times a day. Here is an excerpt from my mom's memoir about her first experience with smoking:

> *Carol and I learned how to smoke at the gas station bath-room over at Tennyson Shopping Center. I was 15, she was 14. The first puff I took, she told me to swallow it. I couldn't stop coughing. So I figured I must not be doing it right. Well, that's all the encouragement I needed to think I wasn't doing something right meant the challenge was on. So after some practice, I learned how to "do it right". That was probably one of the biggest mistakes of my life. I became addicted al-most immediately and really missed out on great opportuni-*

*ties, I think. Mainly in the area of sports. I loved P.E., volley-
ball, skating, running, dancing. Can't really pursue physical
activities if you're a smoker. It became much easier to light
up rather than practice hard in sports to relieve the same tension. I was not allowed to smoke at home when my parents
first found out. But that didn't last long since they were smokers; I'm sure they felt guilty about their example. By 16, Mom
was buying cigarettes for me. I couldn't legally buy cigarettes
so Mom became my enabler and my smoking habit quickly es-
calated. I think Mom secretly liked my keeping her company
and having something in common with her.*

My mom's sister, Doreen, smoked a lot too – it was pretty common
for people to smoke back then. Aunt Doreen owned a bar in Hayward,
California, and had a motorcycle. She was married and had 2 sons, my
cousins, Gordon and David. Then she got divorced and married again
and had a daughter, my cousin, Jenny. I named one of my dolls after
Jenny – she was so cute with blue eyes and blond hair. Aunt Doreen
got married a few more times. Her lifestyle was so different from my
mom's and they didn't spend much time together, or even talk much.

I know there was some stress between my mom and my Aunt Doreen when my grandma got sick with lupus and ended up in a nursing
home when she fell and broke her hip. My mom always insinuated that
Doreen was my grandma's "favorite". My Aunt Doreen didn't visit my
grandma much in the nursing home, and when my mom would visit, my
grandma would often ask where Doreen was. I remember my mom feeling bad about this.

As a child I visited my grandma in that nursing home with my
mom. It had an odd smell. There were also people living there who
were not in their right mind. I remember thinking how awful it must be
for my grandma, who was very clear-headed, to have to listen to all the
moaning and yelling of some of the people there. During one visit, I remember being in my grandma's room and hearing in the hallway a man
yelling, "Give me someone who cares!" I looked around and no one reacted. Then I heard the man say again, "Give me someone who cares!"

There was still no reaction from any of the adults. Finally, the man yelled, "Give me someone who doesn't care!" That made me laugh a little and I tried to muffle it since no one else was laughing or even paying attention. Another man was yelling, "My shoe! My shoe! My shoe!" Nothing made sense to me there. My grandma passed away in that nursing home.

Even though my mom and Aunt Doreen weren't particularly close, my mom was at her side when my aunt became ill with liver cancer. My mom held her hand as she passed away at the young age of 54. I remember my mom saying that in the days before she died, Aunt Doreen expressed sadness that her doctor hadn't come in to see her, even though she could hear him talking in the halls. My aunt felt she had a friendly rapport with her doctor and thought of him as a friend. She expressed to my mom that she thinks the doctor must not be comfortable seeing her anymore because he knew she was going to die. I'm not sure why this memory stuck with me.

My aunt had a lot of friends. I remember her funeral service. There were so many people there and they could not all fit in the church. A lot of my aunt's friends also had motorcycles. They did a procession on the bikes at her funeral. I'm sure my aunt loved that!

Even though I don't recall a lot of family over the house growing up, and even less as I got older, I do remember Thanksgiving holidays at my Uncle Joe and Aunt Betty's house. I remember my Aunt Betty being fiery. She "talked" really loud. She made delicious food and seemed to enjoy having everyone over. My dad's brother (my Uncle Joe) was funny. I liked being around him. He would make us balloon animals – any one we wanted. He carried balloons in his pocket wherever he went. I remember him as a lively person. He passed away suddenly one afternoon from a heart attack in his family room. After that, we didn't get together much with extended family.

I remember my Auntie Ann, my dad's sister, very well. I'm told I look a lot like her. She and my Uncle Don lived in Sacramento, a 2 hour drive from our house. My parents always seemed happy when we were driving to visit them. Apparently, my Auntie Ann helped my parents a lot, and watched my siblings and me so they could go out and spend time together. I remember my Auntie Ann liked my curly hair and I would sit still on a bar stool and she would take the time to make my curls really smooth. She also made dresses for my sister and I, and she was the one who taught me how to put tights on my legs. It took a while for me to get the hang of it and she was very patient.

Uncle Don was a more serious type. I remember when I was very young, I accidentally wet my pants while I was on his couch. He got so upset with me that he started throwing the sofa cushions at me. I was so startled. I don't recall being upset. I felt more shocked because no one ever did something like that to me before. I never peed on any of his stuff again!

It was very sad when my Auntie Ann got sick with lung cancer. She was always a heavy smoker and I recall overhearing someone saying that when Auntie Ann asked if her smoking is what caused the lung cancer. The doctor said, "Not necessarily." My aunt continued to smoke despite her diagnosis. My parents watched how much pain my aunt went through.

After spending time with Auntie Ann during her illness, my mom was inspired to quit smoking, and she did – "cold turkey". I clearly remember when my mom quit smoking because our home turned into a forest of plants. Apparently my mom needed to keep her hands busy to avoid smoking. After a couple of years, she scaled down the amount of plants and we were freed from the jungle.

My dad also quit smoking, however, it wasn't as easy for him. He loved his cigars, or "stogies" as he called them. He had a catalogue that he would enjoy looking through and he would choose his stogies. He would sit in the front yard and puff away for an hour or two on one cigar. He loved it. I remember as a little girl I would watch him and I could tell how much he enjoyed his cigar. I was asking him a lot of questions about it and he put the cigar up to my lips and said, breathe in. I did as he asked, then started coughing and crying. My mom got so mad at my dad and started yelling at him. In his defense, he thought he was doing something good. He thought if I had a bad experience, that I would never smoke. I never did, however, who really knows if that incident was a deterrent. I don't really think so.

My dad said I was the one who inspired him to quit smoking his beloved stogies. One sunny day I was hanging out with him outside as he was puffing away. I asked him when he was going to quit (because I knew he was cutting back since my auntie died). He said, "I only smoke one cigar a day." Apparently I said, "Yeah, but when you smoke cigarettes, it only takes you 5 minutes to finish one. It takes you over an hour to finish a cigar." Something clicked with him when I said that and he quit. Chalk another one up to common sense out of the mouth of babes.

****

Hint of Legacy

I wonder if my mom would have died as young as she did if she didn't smoke. She lived a healthy lifestyle for many years after she stopped. I guess we'll never really know for sure, although it's likely smoking for so many years was a contributor. The more I think about it, and after my experience with both of my parents at the end of their lives, I really think it was simply their time to go. The way they went was the way they were meant to go. They lived their lives and faced the end just like we all are going to have to face the end of our human lives at some point – a point in time that we have no way of knowing the details of. We are all in the same boat on this earth.

I packed a lot of recollections about my parents' earlier years together for a big reason. This book is largely a tribute to them. They have left a legacy in me, my brother and sister, and our children, and their legacy lives on through us all. These stories are in my head and heart. I wanted to bring them to paper. Actually, I felt compelled to bring these memories to paper so they live on. I don't want all the stories that are so clear in my mind to die with me.

I treasure my mom's memoir. She has no idea what a gift she left for us. This got me thinking. I bet most people have no idea what a gift their story is. Whether we view our past as good or bad or somewhere in between, we each have a story to share. I guarantee the telling of that story will impact others. We simply cannot know the massive impact we can make by putting our memories on paper. Those memories that flash in our minds are meant to be known at our discretion. Those childhood memories, for example, that I hold in my 40 year old mind, are the same memories I had when I was 20, 15, 10, and younger. For some reason, I have certain memories. I don't question them. They are what they are. It's kind of interesting what sticks in my mind and what doesn't.

****

Obstacle Course

In a lot of ways, my parents were a normal married couple. However, there is one very unique circumstance to my parents' relationship – my dad's disability. Often the first question that people ask when they meet my dad or hear about him is, "What happened? How did he get in a wheelchair?"

I can totally understand why this question comes to peoples' minds. After all, how many quadriplegics do you know or see around town? One time a little boy in our neighborhood walked up to my dad and asked, "What happened to you?" My dad said, "I broke my neck." The boy paused thoughtfully and asked, "How did they get your head back on?" My dad started cracking up, laughing. He laughed a lot. Even with his disability, my dad knew how to have a good time.

In September of 1969, my parents had rented a house boat with some friends for the weekend. My brother, Dino, and I stayed with my Aunt Doreen. My mom was 6 months pregnant with my sister, Julie. At the time of this trip, my dad really disliked his job. He was a furniture buyer for a store called Capwells. He had given up his prior job, working with juveniles, because he felt he needed to get a "real job" to better support the family. He hated dressing up and wearing a tie to work every day. At his previous job, he enjoyed working with young adults, and he was good at it. They respected him. My dad had a motorcycle and he lifted weights, and was not that much older than the kids he worked with. He'd take them to "field trips" on Sunday to go to church, which they liked because it was the only time they were allowed to leave the detention center. They behaved well in church because they knew if they didn't, they couldn't go back out the next week.

The night before my parents left the houseboat to go back home, my dad had been partying and drinking, which wasn't unusual. Everyone was getting ready for bed and my dad was sitting on the top of the houseboat staring into the darkness above the lake. He was really bummed because he and my mom had to leave earlier than everyone else because he had to go to work the next day. I remember my mom saying my dad always dreaded his first day back to work after being off. My dad made the split-second decision to dive head first into the water. What he didn't know is that the boat had drifted, and the water was only a foot and a half deep. Here's my mom's account of what happened that night:

> *Hank was working at Capwells in Fremont. A brand new store. He'd ride to work occasionally on his Honda when I needed the car. He'd be in his suit and tie on the bike—no helmets in those days. That was the only thing Hank liked about his job, was the location being close to home. Other than that he hated his job.*
>
> *Joe and Carol organized a fun weekend for a bunch of us to rent a houseboat and cruise the San Joaquin Delta. So it was four couples--us, Larry and Angie, and Gary and Joyce (Carol's sister). On our way up to the river, we came across an abandoned school bus in a field. Joe (the brains) and Hank (the guts) decided to go for a joy ride. Joe hot wired it to get it started and Hank started driving it. They were having a good ole time. I remember feeling panic—that we were all going to go to jail for stealing a bus! I guess the bus died again and it became too much work to keep it going, so they finally gave up and we went on our way. There were always a lot of pranks when the guys got together; it was entertaining. We arrived at the Delta and boarded our boat. It was so neat. With an open porch in the front, a small living area with kitchen, and bedrooms in the back. Angie and I were busy putting away our dishes and food we brought. I felt like we were playing*

house. It was very hot and we would get in the water to cool off. We cruised under a large drawbridge, don't know exactly where that was, but we started to have some boat trouble. Joe was the engineer—captain of the ship, you might say. Before long, we were sailing again—I was concerned we wouldn't make it back though. We were really out in the "boonies". After spending the whole day cruising, swimming, drinking and eating, we docked for the night. They threw out the anchor towards shore and we remained in the middle of the river continuing to swim even though it was getting dark. Hank was really bummed because he had to go to work the next day, Saturday, for a couple of hours and there was no way he could get out of it.

It was about 9:00 at night, still pretty hot and pitch dark out. There was no street lights in the Delta. Larry had his shirt off and was letting a mosquito feed on his chest. He was being weird and laughing and Angie was yelling at him for being stupid. We heard a loud splash from the porch. I don't remember who yelled first, saying Hank dove over the side. Joe and Carol were on top of the houseboat making their bed for the night. They were yelling for Hank and he was not responding. Joe shined a spotlight down to the water and we saw him floating face down. Larry said he was just fooling around, but Carol yelled "HE'S NOT KIDDING". Joe scrambled down the ladder and jumped in the water. When I saw the water did not even reach his knees, I realized how shallow the water was and that this was serious. What none of us realized, is the boat had drifted to shore in the couple of hours since the anchor was dropped. Joe picked up Hank and the other guys then jumped in to help get him back in the boat. I started screaming. Larry yelled at Angie to get me in the back and keep me there. We were praying Hail Marys but I had to be with Hank. They got him on the boat and turned him over on his back. He wasn't breathing. Carol yelled at them that she knew CPR and proceeded to give him mouth to *mouth. He started coughing up a lot of water and came to. He was not able to move and kept saying his neck hurt. He had a lot to drink and was very intoxicated. Nevertheless, Joe knew we needed emergency help. He and Gary took some flashlights and climbed up to shore to get help. Of course, there were no cell phones then. They were gone for hours. Hank kept saying he loved me and that he was sorry. It was close to midnight before help came. It was amazing to me now how they were able to find their way back. I'll have to ask Joe about that sometime.*

The ambulance transported us to the closest hospital which was San Joaquin Community Hospital. Joe and Carol came with me—the rest were left to get the boat back and drive our cars back home. The medical staff had no idea what to do with this emergency. It seemed like hours before an emergency doctor came in. The most they did was cut off his wet swimming trunks. It was there that I first heard the word "paralysis" and they decided it was better to transfer him to a larger hospital with the proper equipment and staff—St. Joseph's Hospital, Stockton. By the time we got there, it was 7 or 8 Saturday morning, September 27, 1969. I was a complete basket case and seven months pregnant.

The doctors put screws in my dad's head which were connected to a frame so my dad couldn't move and his body could be kept straight. The nurses were able to flip this contraption so the pressure on my dad's body would be relieved. My parents were married just 4 years prior to my dad's accident. My mom was 23 years old, and my dad was 29. His condition was serious. They first told my mom that he was likely going to die. He broke his neck at the C5 level, and was a quadriplegic. He was paralyzed from the chest down. He could not move his fingers either, and had some range of motion in his arms, so he could at least push his own wheelchair.

Something that always stuck with me after hearing the story of my dad's accident – I thought to myself, "Well, I guess he got his wish."

Meaning, he hated his job and really didn't want to go to work that next day. My dad told me that he was thinking about his job just before he made the decision to jump in the water for one last bit of fun before leaving. I always wonder how different all of our lives would have been had my dad felt empowered to make the choice to start another career as an able-bodied man. After all, he did end up making this choice, although it was under much harder circumstances. What if he decided to get his Master's Degree in MFT and begin a new career *before* that day on the house boat? Well, the "what-ifs" are endless on this point.

My dad was in the rehabilitation hospital in Vallejo, California, for 6 months. During that time, my mom gave birth to my sister, Julie, alone. She wanted it that way. The doctor at the hospital called the rehabilitation center to get a hold of my dad to tell him the news of the birth of my sister. My mom told me that she remembers the doctor calling and he must have received resistance because the doctor started yelling in the background to put my dad on the phone. He was adamant that my dad should be able to talk to my mom after she just gave birth. My parents were able to connect over the phone. Here's my mom's account of my sister's birth:

> *I was getting closer to delivery and my doctor didn't like me driving to Vallejo every day, so he suggested inducing labor. He felt that was in my best interest as well as the baby's.*
>
> *I drove myself to Kaiser, Hayward. I didn't want anyone with me if Hank couldn't be there. I had a great doctor, Dr. Klooster. He gave me the shot to induce labor I think around 10 am or so then he left for breakfast or something. I couldn't believe he left! I told the nurse that it wouldn't take long and he needs to get back here. Of course, she said don't worry I had a ways to go before delivery. I told her "you don't understand, I've been here before...." Well it took another hour or so and the doctor did make it back in time. When will the medical profession ever listen to the patient??*
>
> *Julie was 5 lbs. 8 oz. and so pretty. She was smaller than Lea in weight but looked more filled out, not as petite. She*

was strong and healthy, thank goodness. I was concerned with all the emotional upheaval that there could have been a problem. But we were blessed. As soon as Julie was born, Dr. Klooster told the nurse to call Vallejo and get Hank on the phone. The nurse came back and told the doctor there weren't phones in the rooms in Vallejo. Dr. Klooster firmly replied that they can wheel his bed to a nurses' station and get him on the phone now. Coincidentally as I lay there with the phone, another call came through for me. It was Nita wanting to know how we were doing. So she was the first to hear of our brand, new daughter. It took a while to get Hank on the phone and we did finally connect. I could barely get out "It's a girl" and we both started crying and never spoke again except to say goodbye. Yes, it was such a bittersweet time.

****

Responsibility

My dad carried a lot of guilt over his accident. He always took 100% responsibility for it. He told me a story about his visit to the psychologist at the rehabilitation center. My dad was under the impression the psychologist was attempting to get him to let anger out. He would ask my dad questions like, "Are you mad that this happened to you?" "Are you angry with God?" My dad wasn't really reacting and kept telling him, "No," quietly. The psychologist persisted, "Aren't you angry?!" Finally, my dad raised his voice at the psychologist, "No! I'm not angry at God! It's me that made the stupid decision to jump in that water. It's my own damn fault."

One thing I have to say about my parents is that they were people that took personal responsibility for their lives and did what had to be done.

My mom would visit my dad often at the rehabilitation center in Vallejo. She had a lot of people offering to watch us kids. We spent a lot of time over Joe and Carol's house. My mom told me that at one of her visits, she confided to my dad that someone they knew made a pass at her. From what I understand, this person offered that she could come to him if she ever wanted to since he assumed my dad would not be able to have sex anymore. My mom said that my dad cried when he heard this. My mom wanted him to know. She didn't want any secrets.

My dad would get depressed, understandably so. My mom was very clear with him. She told him that she could handle having a disabled husband, however, she could not handle a depressed, disabled husband. My mom really gave my dad hope and true support. I really believe she inspired him to not only survive, but to be the man he knew he could be.

Some things I remember my dad talking about from his time in the hospital after his injury was the way the nurses and doctors would interact with him. He felt lonely a lot and would really be bothered when the staff would talk in his room as if he wasn't there. He also talked about how much he really appreciated when a nurse would do small things for his comfort. He remembered in particular what a huge difference it made when a nurse changed his pillow case to a fresh one. He said he could still remember the wonderful feeling of the clean and cool, new pillow case when it would be placed underneath his head. I think this time in the hospital really educated my dad on the healing effects of having a good "bedside manner". I'm sure it helped him when he interacted with the patients at the VA hospital he worked at years later.

After 6 months of rehabilitation, the hospital discharged my dad and sent him home. A friend of my parents built a ramp in the garage that led up to the back door, and that's how my dad entered and exited the house from then on. A friend also installed a large picture window in the family room so my dad could see outside easily. Fortunately the house was all one level and only slight modifications were needed for my dad. Light switches were lowered so my dad could turn lights on and off. My parents felt very fortunate that their home was wheelchair accessible.

By the time my dad was back home, my sister was a tiny baby, I was almost 2, and my brother was almost 4. My dad said it took him 5 years to accept his situation. In that time, my parents really struggled. My mom said my dad would throw his food in frustration sometimes. They were on food stamps and government assistance. I found it interesting that my mom did not write much in her memoir about the experience when my dad first came home. Here is all she said about that time:

> *After about 3 or 4 months, Hank made some trial weekend runs home. The first one was a disaster. He had to be sent back by ambulance late at night because of a bladder infection and high fever. But later weekends were good practice – still have support and respite of the hospital come Sunday night. Hank was finally discharged after 6 months of inpatient care, which was very unusual even back then to be hospitalized that long. I don't think I want to relive the next several years of adjustments. Suffice to say, it was very difficult and we took one day at a time and made it through.*

Like I said, my parents approached life with the mindset of personal responsibility. My parents stuck together, and because of this, we had a pretty normal childhood. Well, I always thought it was normal until I got in elementary school and realized my dad wasn't "normal". I'm sure all of us were affected growing up in such a stressful environment – money and health concerns, as well as caregiving needs – on top of the usual strains of raising a family. As kids, we were just along for the ride. We just absorbed the stress as part of normal life, and I can honestly say, I have positive memories of childhood. After all, my parents were always there, and this felt good. I didn't know that it wasn't normal for parents to be home all the time, and that usually one parent was gone working. Both my parents did work eventually – but we were older in middle school by that time.

****

The Power of Humor

I remember fun in my childhood. I must agree with my mom – my dad was "the fun one". I admire him just as much as I admire my mom, for different reasons. My dad had a huge personality and a great sense of humor. Sure he had some undesirable traits. He could be self-centered, often focusing on his own needs. I do consider the fact that he was a quadriplegic and confined to a wheelchair, so perhaps that had something to do with his focus on physical needs. His other qualities more than compensated for that trait for me.

My dad never got embarrassed. He loved cracking jokes and "throwing people off." He told me once while he was at a staff meeting at the VA Hospital where he worked that someone put a box of donuts in front of him and asked if he wanted one. He saw a few old donuts in the box and said, "No thank you," as he lifted the box and flung it over his shoulder. It landed on the floor. He went on writing in his tablet like nothing happened. True to character, he waited for the reactions, then started laughing. His co-workers were stunned at first, then started laughing and shaking their heads. It's not every morning at a staff meeting that someone throws a box of donuts in the air.

My dad's disability wasn't much of an issue for us kids because it was all we knew. My memories of my dad when I was a little girl was that he was not only physically there with us, he was paying attention to us.

This was also one way he could help my mom. He couldn't help with chores or anything physical, however, he could keep an eye on us kids and play with us.

My dad LOVED to tease us and joke around. Here's a classic example. I remember him offering me a cookie when I was little, which I happily accepted. Then he would ask if he could have a bite. I remember not really wanting to give him a bite, but I would hold it out to his mouth, since he couldn't grasp it on his own. He'd then bite it and eat the whole thing in one gulp, then watch in anticipation for my reaction. I'd start yelling and got very mad, and he would just laugh, enjoying my reaction. Then my mom would scold him and bring me another cookie. I soon realized that I got a new cookie every time he would do this, so I wouldn't react so much, which of course meant it wasn't that fun for him anymore. This cookie routine soon ended.

My dad complimented my mom often on how pretty she looked. I really believe this is one of the reasons she stayed so young looking and enjoyed dressing nicely. Every time she came out of the room after getting dressed, he would comment on something specific about what he liked about what she was wearing, such as, "Hun, you look really good in that color. Wow." He was very complimentary when it came to food too. He so appreciated his meals. He would say, "This is the best omelet I ever had!" At almost every meal he would say, "This is the best ever!" I do remember one time my mom getting mad at my dad because she found out he didn't like peanut butter and jelly sandwiches. My mom said, "It's been 10 years that I've been making you peanut butter and jelly, and now I find out you don't like it?!" My dad just mumbled that it wasn't his favorite.

The whole family usually ate dinner at the kitchen bar area. In the 1950's, when their house was built, open rooms weren't so common. The bar height was perfect for my dad's wheelchair to fit under, and he had his spot at the corner of the bar. I would sit next to him, my mom next to me, and my sister and brother across from us. Sometimes it was a pain sitting next to my dad. He liked to poke me with his fork. He would laugh when I would yell, "Stop it!" This was literally a daily occurrence. He just liked poking me in my upper arm.

As long as I can remember, I've had this minor and strange phobia about little round things. Peas are the worst. Anything the size and texture of a pea, just grosses me out. It's like blood and guts to me and I literally almost throw up at the sight. I have more of a handle on this weird phobia in adulthood, however, as a child, it was pretty bad. In fact, if we had peas for dinner, the lid had to be kept closed so I couldn't see them, or I couldn't eat. Everyone would try to hide the peas on their plates, and the absolute worst thing is if I saw a straggler pea – a pea that wasn't in the pile with the rest. My dad used to have fun with me about this. (I should say, it was his fun, not mine!) One time I sat down for dinner and there was a pot cover on my plate. I lifted the cover and there was a lone pea sitting in the middle of my plate! I started screaming, jumped up and ran out of the room. My dad would laugh hysterically, and my mom would scold him. (Honestly, he was like another kid sometimes.)

Equally as entertaining for my dad as bugging us, was that he liked embarrassing us too. Before my dad's shoulders "gave out" which forced him to start using an electric wheelchair, he used to have a "push" wheelchair. This required the strength of his arms to maneuver. We were at the mall once when I was a kid. Most people don't pay attention to slight changes on floor surfaces, however, for my dad it was always an issue. The slightest incline on the ground would be a challenge for him to push his chair over. My dad asked me if I could help push him up an incline in the mall floor. This was a normal request, so I immediately started to push him.

Then he started yelling out, "Help! Help! She's kidnapping me!!" I was so embarrassed! I immediately stopped pushing him as he laughed and laughed, and told me, "Okay, okay. I won't do that again. I promise. Can you please help push me up this incline?"

I was frowning, but agreed. Then – you guessed it, "Help! Help! Stop her! She's kidnapping me!!"

"Dad!" I yelled, "Stop it!"

"Okay, okay, really now. I'll stop. I won't do it anymore. Really. Trust me."

Well, I didn't trust him, however, he really did need help, so I cautiously started pushing him again. He did yell help one more time and laughed, but then he stopped. Thankfully!

Another embarrassing mall memory: I was walking along next to my dad and coming toward us was a mother and her tiny baby in a stroller. I noticed the baby – he was very odd looking – or let's just say, you couldn't help but notice this baby. He had spiky hair sticking straight up all around his head and a scrunched up face and squinty eyes. He was very young, so it must have just been that newborn look. Anyway, no sooner did the mother and stroller pass us, my dad couldn't help but blurt out a drawn out 'god' - "Geeeyawwd, what an uuugly baby!"

"Dad!!" I yelled in a whisper. "I'm sure she heard you!"

I have to say, I think he felt a little bad. He just couldn't help himself. I figured my dad was so used to making fun of people he saw on TV that he just blurted it out without thinking.

At his core, my dad is a kind person. Many people describe him in this way. In fact, one of my dad's favorite quotes is: *"My religion is kindness,"* by Dalai Lama. It didn't quite translate for him that day at the mall. No one is perfect.

****

Assertiveness Trumps Disability

My dad could be really tough on people. He had high expectations about service – especially in restaurants. He made a waitress cry once. It was awful! Our family was out for dinner at a restaurant that was "order by number" on the menu. My dad didn't order by the number. He just asked for what he wanted. I think the waitress was new. She just stared at him blankly and asked, "What number is that?" My dad, who is not known for patience in certain situations, got really frustrated and said, "I don't know what number!" He ranted a bit and the waitress started crying, then he must have realized he went too far and calmed down a bit. He felt bad after, but still didn't want to look up the number for his meal.

My dad also believed that strangers should not come to our door at home – especially "sales people". In those days, it was common for strangers to come to the door trying to sell things. Our dining room table was next to a window that was open to the front porch. People who would come over could look into our house through that window. One night, we were eating at the kitchen table. A man walked up and knocked on the door. I started to get up, and my dad said, "No, don't answer it. We're eating." Well, we were very embarrassed because the man saw us through the window ignoring him. He eventually just walked away. I can still remember how awkward that moment was.

My dad would do this over the phone too. He'd be at his desk – his normal spot in the house. The phone rang one evening and he answered it. The person calling was a telemarketer. I remember looking at my dad from behind (because his back was to the room when he was at his desk). He didn't reply to the telemarketer and just put the phone down, face up, and ignored the person. The person just kept talking and talking, then finally stopped at one point. My dad continued to ignore him. Eventually the person hung up. Now that I look back on this, it was very mean! They were just doing their job. My dad didn't look at it that way. He felt like his privacy was being invaded, so he decided to mess with them.

I believe my dad's assertiveness is partly why he lived so long with a disability as severe as his. By the time I was old enough to remember, he was quite used to his circumstances and I always saw him as an independent, capable man. He was responsible for getting the first handicapped curb cuts in the City of Newark. He just kept going to the city and speaking with the mayor. One day, he gave the city an example of how he'd be trapped on his block and couldn't get down the driveways with his chair. I think people just figure that wheelchairs can go down driveways, however, my dad showed them he could not. He demonstrated attempting to get down the driveway, and showed how he got stuck because of the lip in the cement as it met the asphalt in the street. The city did put handicapped curb cuts on each corner of the sidewalks in our neighborhood, making the cement flush to the asphalt. My dad was ecstatic! He could then cruise along to the local shopping nearby.

He was also vocal at restaurants and other business establishments demonstrating the challenge of getting in and out of doors and through hallways and bathrooms. The City of Newark sure knew my dad. I was always proud of him when I witnessed his assertiveness because he was so skillful and people would respond to him usually quite positively.

My dad is a hero of mine. He took action to defend his kids. Here is a perfect example. We lived just a few short blocks from a neighborhood shopping center. I remember the first day my parents allowed my sister and I to walk by ourselves to the shopping center. My sister strapped on her favorite puppet, which of course embarrassed me that I had to walk with her while she pretended she had a live animal on her hip. Despite my protests, my parents allowed my sister to take along her puppet.

We walked over to the shopping center and approached K-Mart. We went in there for a little while and as we left, there were 3 teenage girls I noticed out of the corner of my eye sitting and hanging out in front of the store. We walked past them, and one of the girls shouted, "Hey!" I ignored them, however, my sister and her puppet turned around. I pulled my sister's arm and said, "Come on." Well, this got the girls' attention. They got up and started following us.

We didn't speak to them. We just started our short walk home, and all the while they were swearing at us, pushing us, and harassing us. They even took out their chewing gum and put it in my sister's hair. I remember thinking as we entered our neighborhood that they had no idea which house was ours. I was surprised they kept following us. I thought, 'Weren't they nervous to get caught harassing us?' One of the girls seemed nervous. In fact, she kept trying to get her friends to turn around and stop bothering us. She was the only one out of the 3 girls that didn't join in the taunting. My sister and I didn't know what to do or say, so we did nothing. We just kept walking toward home.

Finally, about a half of a block from our house, the girls decided to turn around. We ran all the way home at that point. We burst into the house and started talking over each other telling my parents what happened. They calmed us down and I remember my dad sitting in front of us in full attention and asking us to tell him the whole story. We did so, in detail. He got so mad. He zoomed out the front door and down the ramp and told us, "Come on!" He got in his van and we did too. I remember feeling pumped up. He wanted to find those girls and we were going to help him! We found them easily. They were walking in another shopping area nearby. My sister and I saw them and yelled, "That's them! That's them!" My dad pulled over and talked to them out the window. I remember the really mean girl – the one who did most of the harassing while her friends followed – was very verbal. She was saying that we "started it". My sister and I found our voice in the protection of our dad and yelled at them as we defended ourselves. I don't remember what my dad said to them at all, but I do clearly remember feeling so good after we confronted them.

If I sound proud of my dad, it's because I am. He wasn't perfect by any means, but he was a good dad. He did his best, as did my mom. Sometimes when I feel anxiety about something, I think about my parents – my mom for the overwhelming responsibility of 3 kids and a disabled husband – at just 23 years old. Then I think about my dad – how it must have been for him to have to depend on others to get out of bed, eat, bathe, etc. He couldn't even scratch himself if he had an itch. Or how it must have been when he got stuck in his chair and just had to wait until someone came around to help him.

A good example of my dad having to wait for help is the time we were at the nearby shopping center. My dad went on ahead in his wheelchair to head home. About 10 minutes later, as the rest of us were walking back, we saw in the distance quite a sight. I remember doing a double-take. It was my dad flipped backward in his wheelchair with his knees over his head. It was weird seeing him stuck like that. We ran to help him. (Apparently he used too much power in his wheelchair and hit a bump in the street that spun his chair up and flipping it backwards to the ground.) Turns out, he wasn't hurt. He had no choice but to just wait until someone came to help him back up.

****

More than a Man in a Chair

Growing up, my dad was kind of like a celebrity. He was noticed wherever we went. It's not too common that you see someone in a wheelchair living so independently. He was very open, and it wasn't uncommon for strangers to talk to him and he also would engage easily with people. He really wanted to de-stigmatize being disabled. He was a person with thoughts and desires just like anyone else. He took many opportunities to show this to people. He was very skillful in relating to others. People may say it's because of his Masters Degree in therapy, however, he related well with people long before that.

One day I was near a man who was looking at my dad. I remember overhearing this man say, "What happened to him?" I then remember hearing the man say, "If that happened to me, I'd want someone to shoot me. I'd rather be dead." I had a reaction to this as a child. I didn't say anything. I didn't have the words. I just remember that I felt like crying. You see, my dad was important to me. He was my dad. He loved me. He paid attention to me. He played with me and laughed with me. I remember a physical feeling inside me when I heard that comment. I must have been pretty young because I couldn't articulate my feelings. I just couldn't understand this man because in my mind, if my dad felt the same way, I wouldn't have had a dad growing up.

Now, as an adult, looking back on this, I understand that this man couldn't relate. He really misspoke because he couldn't know what he would do in that situation if he ever had to face it. As a child, I was so confused. I really, truly didn't understand what the man was talking about. You see, my dad was so great to me. The fact that he was severely disabled didn't have any impact on me whatsoever as a child. It was just the way it was. I didn't see it as a bad thing. My dad was my dad and I loved him. Here is a poem I wrote when I was younger that sums up my feelings:

My Foundation

His hair is almost completely gray
      It scares me
      He's showing his age.

Knowing looks, sensitive tears
      and familiar smiles
      I know him.

He insists on pushing his own chair
        since he was 29.
I've never seen him stand.
            Not that it matters.

He can move his wrists, shoulders and arms,
        but not his fingers or hands.

        He's paralyzed
        from the chest down.

He's always been around
        complimenting and encouraging
            helping me grow.

At 52 years old
        he's tired,
            I'm scared.

He's deteriorating, slowly
        yet I see it clearly.
        His muscles and bones are weak
            from 23 years
            in a chair.

My mother didn't want to be a nurse
        at 23 - with three kids
            She's tired too, at age 46.

I usually push the thought from my mind
        but it gets harder
        as the years go by.

If I were ever asked to cry on the spot
        I could very easily with just one thought
            of the day that I know will have to come -
                that swallowing, dark day
                when my dad is gone.

I never showed this poem to my dad. I didn't want him to feel bad that I was thinking so morbidly about him. I did show my mom. Who knows – she probably told him about it. It's so true. Every word. If I ever wanted to cry on the spot I could very easily with just one thought…

****

Our Powerhouse

I feel so fortunate to have memories of a safe environment growing up and feeling loved by both of my parents. The fact that my parents together created a better life for all of us is truly amazing to me. My dad seems to get the most credit. After all, he lived in a wheelchair and stood out. While my mom, his support in the background, was more of a hero in our home. Without my mom, my dad wouldn't have been able to accomplish what he did – or at least not in the same way. My mom provided my dad and our family a home together. She stayed with my dad, despite devastating and extremely challenging circumstances.

I was my mom's shadow. Apparently I followed her around when I was a young child and acted like her too. If she was taking a picture, I wanted a camera to take a picture too. If she was sweeping, I was sweeping alongside her. I'd wear her shoes around the house. I watched her <u>every</u> <u>move</u>. My dad was the fun one, however, my mom was the rock. By her example, she taught me to be non-critical of myself. I don't pick myself apart. I just never saw my mom do this. Meaning, she didn't complain about her appearance, or say things like, "I look awful today." "I'm having a bad hair day." "My thighs are fat." "I'm looking old." She just never did. I really appreciate this about her.

My mom also didn't complain about our "misfortune". We didn't have much money growing up. I noticed only because I would rarely get new clothes. Even though I was older than my sister, my sister grew faster, so I would wear her clothes when she grew out of them. I never heard my mom, or my dad for that matter, talk about money problems. She didn't say, "We can't afford that." "We don't have enough money." I have a vivid memory of being in a store with her one day and I really, really wanted a doll I saw. I could tell by the way she looked at the doll and at me, and the fact that she picked up the doll to look at it, that she was actually considering buying it! I began to get hopeful because I didn't usually get something I saw and wanted from a store, especially something like this doll. She finally said, seeming a bit disappointed, "Not today." I didn't argue.

Another thing I greatly admired about my mom – she looked pretty. What I mean by this is, she made reasonable efforts to look pretty. Even with all her life stress, she didn't let herself go. She didn't wear much makeup, but she did wear a little. She wasn't a big shopper, but she did enjoy getting new clothes and dressing in a variety of ways. She got regular haircuts, but she never colored hair. She had a little grey coming in, but she didn't mind. She ate reasonably and loved to exercise. She exercised much more when we got older. She would get so excited about a run in the morning that she said sometimes she couldn't sleep well the night before!

My mom loved animals – especially dogs. We always had a dog in our household. First there was Brandy, the Irish Setter. Brandy was the "not so smart" dog. I remember when my mom took the dog away to put her "to sleep" when the dog got sick. My mom cried as she sat at the kitchen table when she got home, but only briefly. My mom never indulged long in self-pity.

Then there was Saint, the German Shepherd who my mom had to give away because it bit someone when it was tied to a tree after the person kept teasing him. My mom cried again as she put the dog in her car to take it to the vet to be "put down". She felt forced to because the person threatened to sue my parents.

For a short time we had a cocker spaniel, Buffy, that was technically my sister's dog, however, she couldn't take care of the dog properly so my mom gave it away. I don't remember her shedding tears over this dog. I recall that Buffy was a bit of a menace.

Then came Sheena, a Golden Retriever. This one lived a long time. She was an excellent watch dog because her bark was ferocious. Of course if anyone came up to her she would just lick them, but at least she was able to instill some fear in strangers coming to our door.

As Sheena got older, my mom decided to foster a rescue dog named Max. Sheena tolerated Max. My mom soon adopted Max and realized she could no longer be a foster parent to dogs because she wouldn't be able to let them go.

Next came my mom's favorite dog, the one she called her "best friend" – Tyler – another Golden Retriever. My mom was hooked on this breed now. Tyler didn't live very many years. He died one beautiful and quiet morning playing Frisbee with my mom at a nearby park. He jumped to catch the Frisbee, got it, then when he landed, he died on the spot. Not sure what happened there. My mom was devastated. Tyler was an active, lovable companion for my mom and she simply adored him. A man who was nearby helped her put Tyler in her car. It was way too early for the vet to be open so she drove around not knowing what to do. She decided to stop by my sister's house and told her what happened and gave her the chance to say goodbye to Tyler.

After my mom healed from this experience she decided to get another puppy - Emma – another Golden Retriever. Emma was the dog that stayed with my mom up until her final day. Here's sweet Emma:

My mom had one other puppy, Yogi (the golden boy) for a short while, which I'll talk about later. Yogi brought love and joy to my mom during a time when she needed it the most.

Dogs truly were my mom's best friends. People were much more challenging for my mom to be around, which she would openly admit. This may sound strange. My mom just felt most at peace when she was in nature with her dogs – more than anywhere else, or with anyone else.

My mom loved this quote, and had it framed on a wall in her house:

"I want to be the person my dog thinks I am."

(Author Unknown)

My mom. Oh, how I miss her. In many ways, I miss her more than I miss my dad. With my dad, I feel like I've experienced him more fully. I *saw* him, and he *saw* me. Our personalities meshed without much effort. He was a treat. My mom – she had some mystery to her. There was so much more to her than I ever experienced. I missed out on her gift. I benefited from her strength, courage, discipline and love, yet I didn't learn during her lifetime to draw her out more. I was her daughter and grew up in her care. She died too young and I hadn't matured enough – my heart didn't open enough – to understand how to create a connection with someone more quiet and private. I feel sad about this. Then I cry and tell myself it's okay. I did the best with what I knew how, as we all do.

Part of my inspiration in writing this book is to encourage people to create that space for connection with the people in their life. If my mom hadn't written her memoir, I wouldn't know certain things about her. My mom, with all her stress and challenges throughout her life, took the time to write a memoir. I'm sure she didn't realize what a gift she was giving – *a true legacy*. She chose certain memories and wrote them down to share. I want the world to know something about my mom – about the woman who kept our family together and gave to us so much. She was a light in my life and I never got to tell her that.

I wish I understood life enough during her lifetime to realize how important it is to SAY IT – to think about those I love and what I appreciate about them and *SAY IT*. I know she knew that I loved her. I've done many things to express it, however, there were so many more little things I could have said and done that would have been easy to say and do.

I truly learned the gift of giving and receiving when my parents were dying. The kind of connection that happens between people who are engaged at this level of relating is of another world. Nothing on a superficial level even comes close. It's the different between feeling a sense of meaning in life versus a sense of emptiness, and varying degrees in between. Even with death knocking at the door, life felt clear and beautiful during many, many moments. During my parents' illnesses, there was a life enhancement that is really hard to describe in words.

I have to be careful not to be so hard on myself when I am wistful about my mom because it blocks me from being how I want to be. It blocks me from expressing appreciation right now with the people I love that are with me here on earth. My parents are feeling only love now where they are, yet the people –myself included – living on this earth, are not feeling it fully. I want to do my part to deliver a message while I'm still alive *with my mom as my inspiration.* She was my mother – an imperfect, beautiful, lovable woman – a real woman who has experienced life and death.

I will experience death too, and before I do, I want to do my part to make sure my mom's contribution to this world will never be forgotten. *What was her contribution?* She was an honest, persevering wife and mother who never gave up, even during hardships. She created a loving and safe home environment for our family. She showed her love by her strength and willingness to be there for us. Who she was on this earth was inspiring. *She was our superstar* and this book is one way to shout it to the mountaintops.

Part Two

Reality

At some point in the first few years after my dad's accident, he decided to go back to school to get his Masters in marriage and family therapy (MFT). My mom would drive him to and from his classes at Cal State Hayward, which was about a half hour drive from our home. I was very young during this time. My memories include my dad reading a lot, and my mom typing on her manual typewriter as I lifted my hand up to try and touch the keys. She gently moved my hand away. I found out later that she was typing up his Masters Thesis.

My dad became a counselor at a local counseling center for a few years. I remember him telling me how much he learned there. He first learned very quickly not to try and counsel someone who was under the influence of drugs. My dad wanted to, and his mentor let him try it so he could have his own experience with it. At one point, the man who my dad was counseling jumped up and lunged at him. That's when his mentor stepped in. Lesson complete.

I clearly remember the day my dad got his position at the VA Hospital in Palo Alto, California. I overheard some talk between my parents about "the job." I didn't know the details until I was much older. Essentially my dad met Russ who worked at the VA. Russ referred him to his contact for the job opening for a Clinical Social Worker in the Spinal Chord Injury Unit. My dad was granted an interview. I remember my dad saying he was nervous as he wheeled into the room in front of a panel of people. He acknowledged his nerves right away to the panel and said something to break the ice. Then he smiled his handsome smile. My dad's strength was his personality. Even in a wheelchair, he was able to put just about anyone at ease.

My biggest memory of this time was the waiting period between that interview and the "phone call". My dad talked a lot about the job. I can tell he really wanted it. He followed up consistently by calling the VA. I remember him asking my mom, "Am I calling too much? Should I wait to call again?"

The day the "phone call" came was very exciting. Again, I was very young, but I remember my dad hanging up the phone and the feeling of excitement. He got the job! His dream job! The whole family jumped around in joy. Being little kids, my brother and sister and I just followed our parents along in their excitement. I had no clue what this job meant for our family. I sure understand it now. My dad had landed a job not only doing what he wanted to do, but it included a salary high enough to support his family, with full benefits, including medical and retirement. This was a big deal. Especially considering my dad had a severe disability. He and my mom were so thankful for this opportunity and the security of working for the government and having medical benefits.

For the next 28 years, my dad performed his function at the VA as a Clinical Social Worker. He was well-respected, helped countless patients with spinal chord injuries, and their families, gain hope. They felt understood seeing my dad function in the world with his level injury. My dad's main role was to help the patients find a proper residential situation upon discharge from the VA hospital after their rehabilitation from their new spinal chord injury. He was a true advocate for his patients and their families. He was there for people in a real and practical way. Not only did he help them emotionally adjust to their new lives, he helped guide them to the various resources to help them with their day-to-day living. He was the best example anyone can give to a newly injured spinal chord injury patient. The patients could never say, "You don't understand."

****

Bubble Top Treasure

In the beginning of my dad's career, it was my mom who got him up and out of bed at 5:30am, helped him with his personal care needs (bladder care, cleaning him, dressing him, getting him up, etc.), and fixing his breakfast. When my parents could afford it, they hired a caregiver to come every morning to help my dad with his morning routine. My dad commuted an hour every day across the Dumbarton Bridge to and from work in a specially equipped van that he drove himself.

I was too young to recall all that went into the process of getting my dad a vehicle he could drive with his physical limitations. What I was told is that my dad got a specially equipped van that was paid for with government assistance. (Some years later, my parents purchased the van from the government when they decided to no longer seek government help.) It was white and had a "bubble top" so when my dad got in with the wheelchair lift, he didn't have to duck inside. It was very exciting when we all rode in the van, even though it wasn't very cool looking.

My dad was really into cars and had some cool cars prior to his accident – he would sell and buy different cars – a Porsche, a Chevy, etc. He would keep them in pristine condition. I remember my mom saying she hated the Porsche because it was so loud when they were driving she couldn't hear my dad and felt like she had to yell to have a conversation. My dad also used to ride a motorcycle. He missed these things, however, he was very happy to have the independence to drive again. He wasn't picky about what he would be driving. This was good because he didn't have many choices anyway.

The wheelchair lift to get in and out of the van was very exciting to watch. Anybody could get into my dad's van, if they knew the trick. He used a magnet and held it against a certain spot on the right rear tail light, and the door would slide open. Then he would touch the magnet to another area, and a metal platform would swing out the door. With another touch of the magnet, the metal platform would lower to the ground, then another metal piece would fold down, creating a ramp. My dad would then roll his wheelchair onto the lift, and then that metal piece that created the ramp would fold up for safety in case his wheelchair rolled backwards. Another control swung the whole platform inside the van, where he would then move his wheelchair under the steering wheel. Then he would press buttons on a raised center console to close everything up.

There was no driver's seat in the van. My dad could not move his fingers or his legs, so there were special hand controls to drive the van. His left arm slid into a control that operated the brakes – he simply had to push his arm forward and the van would stop or slow down, or pull back on the control and the van would go forward. His right arm slid into bars attached to the steering wheel so he could steer. It's pretty amazing when I think about the level of my dad's disability – a C5 quadriplegic – and he was able to drive.

My dad's ability to drive helped my mom so much because she no longer had to struggle to get him in and out of her car and drive him around. To get my dad into her Chevelle, she used a wooden board and would have to slide him across it into the front passenger seat of the car. Then she would fold up his chair and put it in the trunk. This took some time and quite a bit of physical exertion on my mom's part. Then, when they reached their destination, she would have to get the wheelchair out, unfold it, and help my dad slide over into the chair. Did I mention my mom was a petite woman of 5'3"? This was a lot of work for her.

Once my dad was in the car, then we would all help get him comfortable, i.e. help pull up his pants from the back because they would slide and twist when he was slid across the board. It was a hassle we were all very used to and had to allow time for. There was no jumping in and out of a car to go anywhere. It was a production each and every time.

Here's my mom's account of the experience driving with my dad in the van. She was very excited!

1976 something good happened! Hank started driving. What a milestone! Following him in his new Dodge Van home from San Leandro was so exciting. We just couldn't believe this was happening. This was the greatest thing since childbirth! It was like being born again actually. Finally, independence. A big load was lifted off my shoulders. It was nice sitting back as a passenger for a change and letting someone else do the driving until I realized this person was paralyzed, plagued with muscle spasms, and blind in one eye—I thought, Oh My God, are we nuts? Of course, that attitude was reinforced by the mechanic on duty where we picked up the van when he was adjusting the side view mirror for Hank. Hank explained he needed it just right because he was blind in the right eye. The guy looked petrified and asked "Do they (the State of California) know that?"

My dad did not use his disability as an excuse. The way he conducted himself in the world was more able-bodied than some able-bodied people. What I mean is, my dad spoke to people, joked with people, engaged with people, was curious about people, and put others at ease in his presence. Besides the very real physical limitations, he "forgot" about his disability.

I remember something funny that I observed much later in his life that proves my point. My dad was around 68 years old and was at his desk reading over his driver's license renewal form. He said to me as he was looking down at the paper, "I can save $25 if I go to the DMV and retake the driving test. I think I will go do this." I looked him up and down and started laughing. Picture this: He is an "old man" – he looked older than his years – with white and grey hair, wheelchair bound, and blind in one eye with a cataract in the other. I told him, "Dad, don't go near the DMV! I'll pay you $25 NOT to go to the DMV!" He realized immediately what I was inferring and started laughing.

Not to worry. My dad didn't commute to work anymore at that point in his life and only drove locally around town. In fact, I don't recall him ever being in an accident. He was fine driving, and very clear-headed. I'm just not sure the officials would agree. (Or the general public for that matter.) I didn't want him showing up at the DMV and risk losing his driving independence. Needless to say, he heeded my advice and stayed clear of the DMV office.

The white van wasn't my dad's only vehicle. Years later, the van got quite old and unreliable. My dad started referring to it as "the white sickness". He was finally able to get a new van – a baby blue Chevy with more modern hand controls and a smaller body. He liked the looks of this one much better. It was no Porsche, but he took the time to find someone who could put pin-striping on it to customize it. It was a cool van. Well, as cool as a handicapped-equipped van can be.

****

The Lucky Gorilla

I have many memories playing growing up. My mom was so busy most of the time and we were home a lot because it was challenging getting my dad out with 3 kids in tow. I remember playing around the house and in our neighborhood for most of our childhood.

I also remember playing with my dad a lot. My dad could not physically help my mom with things, however, he could make phone calls for her, and he could keep his eyes on us kids while she cooked and cleaned and changed light bulbs and took out the garbage, and mowed the lawn, etc. My dad was a good entertainer.

As we got older, we were able to help out a lot by picking up things my dad dropped and getting him items from the refrigerator, and water, etc. We were the TV channel changers – there were no remotes in those days. We had chores when we were very young. I remember needing a barstool in front of the kitchen sink to be able to reach it to wash dishes. We also took turns cleaning out closets. My mom had a piece of paper posted on the inside of the bathroom closet where we would sign our name when we cleaned it. This is how we all knew who was next in line to clean out the closet.

I definitely preferred indoor cleaning versus outdoor yard work. I really disliked being dirty. I didn't like sweeping up leaves or pulling weeds. My parents had all 3 of us do all chores. I knew my mom liked it when it was my turn to clean the bathroom and kitchen. I did a good job because I liked to make the sinks and counters all shiny.

When we were older kids, my dad would take us to the store so he could help my mom with shopping. By taking us, we could push the shopping cart and take things off the shelf, etc. I have a very clear childhood memory of shopping at K-Mart one day with my dad. We went down the toy aisle and I looked up and saw a big stuffed animal. It was a hairy gorilla. It had big, doggy eyes and a belly sticking out. It was so cute! I pointed it out to my dad and he also really liked it. I managed to get it down and I wanted it so badly. He let me put it in the shopping cart! When we got to the cash register, we were literally counting out change to scrape up enough to be able to also buy the gorilla. Food stamps couldn't be used for things like that.

My dad didn't care that we were holding up the whole line and we were intent on finding enough money for that gorilla. We were both working hard counting the change, and I kept fishing in the back of his bag (he had a bag that hung on the back of his wheelchair where he would keep his wallet, etc.). I found some more loose change at the bottom of his bag. I was sweating because I was getting very worried that we didn't have enough money for the gorilla. A woman behind us put down a $5 bill and said, "This is my good deed for the day." I was in awe! We thanked her so much. I got my gorilla!

I named him Lucky because he almost wasn't able to come home with us. My dad and I loved this stuffed animal. I still have Lucky. He wears a hat and has a t-shirt on that says Lotza Motzarella. He's falling apart a bit after all these years, but he's as cute as ever.

****

Happy Dose of Rivalry

Growing up, my sister and I played a lot together. We also fought a lot. There was really not much in between. Either we got along or we didn't – in dramatic ways. I was pretty bossy about what we played. If it were Barbies, then I chose which ones I wanted and which clothes, etc. I always got the Ken doll and the house, and my sister was always the single mother. (We only had one Ken doll and one house). I let her use my rock collection to create an outline of a house. One thing she refused to give up was her Barbie car. That was the only thing that would stop her from playing, so I reluctantly agreed to let her have the car.

Julie was so accommodating to me. I think she just wanted to play so she just let me have my way. I was kind of mean to her when we were young kids. I just remember getting so mad at her. I don't even know why. Like I said, it seemed like we were either playing and having the time of our lives together, or we were screaming and fighting with each other. My poor mom! She said we couldn't go a day without fighting over something. She sat us down once and said that if we didn't fight for 3 days straight, we could have our own rooms. Wow! Were we excited! We really wanted our own rooms. (Now, logistically, this would only be possible if my parents did a home remodel. We clearly weren't thinking about logistics.) We only lasted a couple of hours not fighting anyway, which I'm sure my mom figured would happen. At least she had a couple of hours of peace that day!

One thing my sister and I liked playing a lot was factory. We didn't watch TV much, except for Saturday morning cartoons, and home computers didn't exist, so we constantly thought up things to do. For factory, we would find all sorts of things and line them up in 2 rows and pretend we were working on a factory line. My brother liked to watch us play this for some reason. Usually he left us alone when we played, however, the factory interested him.

My brother also enjoyed watching us get into screaming matches. He actually instigated many things. He would do things like whisper in my ear, for example, to tell me something Julie was doing, such as, "Julie took your doll and hid it." That's all I needed to hear and I would jump up and start running to find her screaming at the top of my lungs. Dino would laugh. We provided my brother much entertainment.

My sister and I would play secretary too. My mom gave us an old phone and we loved to play with it because it was a real phone. It didn't matter that it didn't work. We also got to keep her old appointment books. We would tape names of famous actors we liked such as Scott Baio, Leaf Garrett, Rob Lowe, John Travolta, and Shaun Cassidy, with a separate name on each door of the rooms in our house. These were their offices. Then we would use the phone and pretend we were setting up appointments. This would keep us busy for a long while.

Our favorite pastime was playing doll house with small wooden dolls, which were mostly Fisher Price toys. The dolls had round heads and round bodies, and some of the dolls had plastic hair. All of their bodies were different colors. These little dolls would be considered choking hazards now, but we never had a problem. I don't recall ever putting any in my mouth, or even considering it. We had a whole town of toys such as a hotel, houses, a cabin, a treehouse, a light tower, a Sesame Street replica, and cars. We had a school bus and a van, and furniture for the houses. All of these items were given to us over time, or my mom got some at second hand stores. We would lay out all of these items in the living room of our house and my mom would let us keep everything up for sometimes as long as 3 days. We would play all day with it. It was so much fun. My brother didn't really join in on the playing much. He liked to observe.

There is one vivid memory of my brother where he was not the observer, but the entertainer. I probably remember this because his entertaining resulted in a 911 call. Dino was stomping his feet on the couch in the living room to the beat of the Monster Mash song. My sister and I were laughing watching him. The couch had a wood base and as my brother was stomping, his foot got stuck in between the wood on the base of the couch. This stopped the action. I remember his face getting really red. He didn't cry. (I always remember my brother had a high tolerance for pain.) My mom attempted to get his foot out, and she couldn't. It was getting very swollen and more stuck.

The most exciting thing happened! Real firemen showed up. I don't remember my mom making the call. I just remember them coming in. Those fireman looked gigantic. They were so nice and calm and they got my brother's foot loose almost immediately. My sister and I sat quietly watching it all unfold. Usually day-to-day life was pretty uneventful, so this was very exciting to us.

As I mentioned, my sister and I played a lot together, but she also really knew how to push my buttons. She has always been very sharp and clever. I remember one time when my parents held "family court" because my sister and I were in a dispute over a purse. My sister said it was her purse, and I knew it was mine (and so did she). Well, she won her "case" and got to keep MY purse! I was livid, and she smiled a certain grin as if to say, 'Hah!' I recall we had a family outing right after "court" and my parents took a picture of us before we left. I wasn't smiling, was looking miserable, and my sister was smirking as she carried MY purse over her shoulder.

Here is another story that my sister is probably tired of hearing me whine about. I loved my dolls and would keep them nicely in order in my closet. One day, my sister had to clean out her closet at my mom's insistence. Well, she got to the point where it was all cleaned out. She had these empty shelves now and had the idea to start a doll collection.

She asked me, "Can I put your dolls on my shelf? I won't keep them, I just want to put them on there." I hesitated. Finally, after her repeated requests and assurances, I allowed her to put all but my 3 favorite dolls on her shelf. (Thank goodness I didn't give all the dolls to her.)

I don't know the details leading up to the garage sale that happened later. In fact, I don't know how many days had passed since I allowed my sister to put my dolls on her shelf. It could be that they were there for months. I just remember that I wasn't home at the time of the garage sale. I remember coming home and realizing that all of my dolls that my sister had in her closet were sold. I started raging! In my typical loud and reactive fashion, I complained to my mom about the unforgivable thing my sister had done. I was extremely disappointed when my mom exasperatedly replied, "Well, there is nothing we can do about it now." I don't even recall my sister getting in trouble for it, although she probably got some sort of punishment.

Even though my sister had the power to trigger me, I felt mostly annoyed with her. After all, she was my "little sister". I remember when I wrote a fan letter to John Travolta who was popular at the time for his TV role on Welcome Back Kotter. My sister decided to write a fan letter to Horshack – a goofy character on the same show. I remember saying to her something like, "You don't know what you're doing. You're so immature." I thought she was dumb for writing to a goofball, whereas I was writing to a very handsome, and much more famous young man.

Well, my sister got the last laugh. I received zero response from John Travolta. In contrast, my sister received in the mail a bunch of fan club memorabilia from that clown Horshack. What made things worse, is that she proudly taped up a huge poster of him in our room, alongside all my teenage idol posters. Talk about annoying, me having to look at that goofball every day.

What can I say? Well, one thing is for sure – I wouldn't trade my sister in for the world. She can bug me for the rest of our lives if she'd like. She can do no wrong in my eyes. I love her.

What to say of my brother? Of course I wouldn't trade him in either. He is a breath of fresh air with his humility and honesty. The simple life suits him. I love him.

Words about myself? I'm the social butterfly who keeps us all together, a role I happily embrace.

✳✳✳✳

Energizer Bunny and the Gang

I recall feeling safe and happy during my childhood. I was fortunate not to have experienced major conflict or trauma. Having said this, it wasn't all puppies and rainbows. My mom had a temper and yelled a lot, and my dad would be a bit dismissive of her feelings and could be self-centered and even a bit manipulative, which triggered her, resulting in more yelling. Observing this cycle was no fun. I'm thankful that my personality allowed me to view my mom's yelling from the perspective of, 'She's acting crazy again. I'll go away until things settle down.' I didn't internalize it or make it personal. For some reason, I always thought of it as 'her issue'. Overall though, my childhood memories are more positive than negative, and the bottom line is – I felt like I belonged and that I was important in the family.

I do have one vivid memory of feeling very scared – like nothing I'd ever felt before. I don't recall why, but I was sleeping on the couch. I had a nightmare and when I woke up I wasn't aware that my foot hit a lamp. I saw the lamp seemingly pull apart in mid air, as if it happened on its own. I remember screaming and screaming and my mom came running in to console me. She figured out what happened almost immediately. My heart was pounding and I was so glad she was there to comfort me.

The only other time I remember feeling more than a little scared as a child was when I heard something about nuclear war. I don't remember if I saw something on TV, or overheard something, but I was scared for many, many months that there was going to be a nuclear war. I thought about it every day. I had a hard time sleeping during this time. I never talked about it. It was as if it was fact. It seemed very probable in my mind and I didn't know how to deal with it. Eventually I must have matured because at some point I was no longer scared about it.

I was a pretty cautious kid. I never broke a bone. I wasn't a big tree climber or an outdoorsy kid. I liked socializing – talking, talking, talking. I also had a lot of energy and would bounce around a lot. My parents called me the energizer bunny. The name came from a commercial about a battery-operated bunny that kept hitting a drum, and kept going and going and going.

My biggest injury was in middle school when I spent the night at my friend, Erin's house. We were hiding and spying on her big sister who had a school dance that night. We watched her and her friends make fondue. (They boiled oil and dipped bread and cheese in it). After they all left for the dance, we wanted to try the fondue also. Erin heated up the oil and we starting dipping our bread and cheese in it.

I was sitting across from Erin eating the delicious fondue. The bowl with oil was almost spilling over. Erin realized this wasn't a good thing, so she got another bowl and tried to carefully scoop out some oil. She accidentally scooped it out and onto my forearm. Oh, the pain! I jumped up and screamed. We didn't know what to do, so Erin called my mom who immediately drove over. Fortunately she was only 5 minutes away. I'm not sure where Erin's parents were. They were probably driving her sister and her friends to the dance. My mom immediately put my arm under water. That burn was the worst pain I ever felt. It was pain that wouldn't go away. All night long it persisted. I ended up with these large, gross blisters all over my arm that we had to clean and bandage daily. To this day, the skin on my arm is extra sensitive. Fortunately, the scarring is barely noticeable and some of my hair grew back.

On another memory track, I recall a humorous story involving my mom. I remember when I was a child, my parents invited the priests over for dinner. We attended the local Catholic Church, went to school there, and later my mom worked there. It was considered a privilege to have the priests over and my mom, who was a very good cook, made a special dinner. She set the kitchen table very nicely. The priests were sitting at the table with all of us and talking with my dad as we waited for my mom.

I remember looking at my mom with her back to us as she was tossing the salad at the bar. She seemed to be taking a while so I walked over to her and noticed her face was in a panic.

I said, "Mom, what's wrong?" I watched her frantically tossing that salad.

She whispered, "My Band-Aid fell into the salad!"

I put my hand to my mouth and muffled an "oh-no"! Then I started to laugh because she was tossing like a maniac desperately trying to catch a glimpse of the band aid. She was muffling laughs too. She couldn't serve the salad with it in there! Thankfully, she found the band aid and fished it out, and yes, she still served the salad. It was delicious, even though, now that I look back, that's really gross.

Even though my dad was known for his humor, my mom had her moments too – although sometimes it didn't work out as planned. For example, one day, when my sister was little, she was quietly playing in her room. She was talking to herself as she did imaginative play with some toys on the carpet. My mom was in the backyard where the bedroom window faced. She thought it would be funny to stand there with a rubber mask on until my sister noticed. The mask looked like the face of an ugly, old bald man. My mom was smiling underneath the mask as she waited for my sister to notice.

My sister finally looked up toward the window – probably sensing something was there – and started screaming. She jumped up and ran out of the bedroom, crying and screaming. My mom ran inside to console her and felt so bad. We laugh about it now because my mom said, "But I was smiling!" (How would my sister have known that?)

My sister will probably remember this next story better than me. After all, her face was the one my mom spread corn all over. I just remember being at the kitchen bar with the whole family eating. I don't know what preceded it, but my mom walked around the bar to where my sister sat, and spread food all over her face. I remember the fun energy surrounding this moment. My sister was resisting, just a little, as she tried to block the food fight. We were all laughing.

I have many good memories of eating together as a family. That's where the dynamics can be seen. I do remember my mom saying more than once to me, "Let your sister and brother have a turn to talk." During dinner time, my dad instigated a lot of things, my brother would watch and laugh, my mom would protest, my sister and I would talk and argue, we would then attempt to quiet it down when asked – which never worked – and this would happen night after night. Our family dinners were less than picture perfect, and I hold lots of good memories. We all had our place in the family and felt a sense of belonging.

Some of my fondest memories of childhood were when other families would come over and all of the kids would play together. The "quiet game" – the loudest game ever – was so fun. My parents would initiate this game during dinner time when they had company over in an attempt to have a more peaceful dining experience. However, as soon as one kid was "out" during the game, things would get boisterous and the volume went up.

The rules of the game were simple. Whomever could stay quiet the longest won. Well, this game provided literally only a minute of silence, at the most. We just couldn't stay quiet long. For example, if someone threw a pea at me, I would scream and be "out". Or, some kids would make goofy faces, making others laugh, or just start laughing as soon as the game started. Any time we were supposed to stay quiet, the humor in everything intensified, so even when we heard, "Mark, get set, go!" some of us would start laughing right then.

We also had fun putting on skits for the adults. I remember this one skit our cousin, Michael, starred in. (Well, technically he isn't our cousin, but we grew up with him, so we've always referred to him and his siblings as cousins. In fact, his mom, Carol, was the one who saved my dad's life that day on the houseboat.) Back to the famous skit. Each kid ran into the room saying, "The viper is coming! The viper is coming!" Then Michael ran in holding a roll of toilet paper up as if flying a kite, and said, with a vampire accent, "Anyone want a vipe?" I remember the adults roaring with laughter.

As far as vacationing, I recall only a few. I remember just one camping trip, and my mom said "never again". I don't blame her, now that I think about it. There is so much work involved with camping, and with 3 little kids and my dad, there was simply no vacation experience there for my mom.

I clearly remember our first experience staying in a motel room as children. It was a Motel 6 type place. We ran through it, all excited, checking out the bathroom. We couldn't find my sister at one point. My mom found her next door saying, "We're your new neighbors!" The poor guy at the door looked like he just woke up, as he stood there looking down at my sister. I still remember what he looked like – bald head, hairy, with a white t-shirt that was too small to hide his protruding belly. Apparently my sister knocked on his door to introduce herself. I don't think he was as delighted to meet my sister and she was to meet him.

Our most favorite vacation was when we rented a little cabin somewhere. I don't recall the exact location, but it wasn't too far from home.

We pretended it was our own little house. My sister went missing again, and my mom found her running out in the pasture to greet the cows.

Our family had dysfunction just like many families. There was screaming and fighting – my mom and I were the loudest. We were spanked as kids for disciplinary purposes. My parents had a wooden paddle with our name on it. I never remember the exact reason we got spanked. I'm sure it was when my sister and I were fighting about something. My mom would tell us to go in our room, then she would call us out after a few minutes, have us bend over, then she would swat our butts. It hurt, but it didn't resolve anything. The fact was, I couldn't help fighting with my sister. I just didn't know any other way to handle my frustration with my sister, other than to fight with her. No amount of spankings would have changed this.

I do remember growing up in a cloud of stress, although I didn't have a term for it as a kid. My mom called herself a realist. I remember her saying, "Bad things do happen." My dad would balance it out with his ability to find humor in just about anything, and his belief that, "It'll all be fine."

Even though my family didn't have much money, didn't go on many vacations, or experience different events out in the world, we had a childhood filled with imagination and play, albeit with a backdrop of anxiety. My parents did have quite a lot to deal with. They did the best they could for our family, and I really appreciate their dedication. My childhood would have been drastically different had my parents not teamed up and persevered like they did. I do realize my good fortune to have had the kind of childhood I did.

****

Studious Shenanigans

My school memories were more about social interactions than academics. This is a bit ironic because I was a very good student and fit in well with the system. I took self-initiative and had a personal sense of satisfaction if I did well in school. I only recall one time getting in trouble during school, and that was in the 2nd grade. I was distracted by Eugenia who was missing her two front teeth. She was showing me the gap and I was so intrigued because I was looking forward to losing mine. I couldn't wait until I could sip on a straw through that gap. I started daydreaming about me and my missing teeth, and was reprimanded in front of the whole class for not paying attention.

I do recall having some anxiety around homework and schoolwork. I was the type of kid that liked to get a jump start on classwork because the stress of not feeling prepared was too much for me to handle. I remember one time in the 6th grade when I forgot my homework. I had a panicky feeling as I sat at my desk searching. I'll never forget when my teacher, who must have sensed my anxiety, came up to me. She placed her hand gently on my shoulder and asked me what was wrong.

I quickly answered with wild and frantic eyes, "I forgot my homework."

She responded by gently asking, "What do you think will happen to you?"

This threw me off for a moment. Then I got back into the comfort of my anxiety as I thought, 'She must be crazy.' I said again, "I forgot my homework!" My statement had much more emphasis this time because she clearly didn't understand the seriousness of my problem.

Yes, I was a bit high-strung as a kid.

I detested attention on me. I was fine giving answers in class and raising my hand, but getting in front of the class was a dreadful experience. I remember being so self-conscious during elementary and middle school in particular. I went to the same Catholic School from grades 1st through 8th. I didn't like the way I looked with my short, frizzy hair. During that time, the popular hairstyle was Farrah Fawcett's "feathers", and there was no way my hair was going to do that. It was really coarse and curly. I remember wishing I needed braces so I could get headgear so my hair would be mashed down and not frizzed out all over the place. I was actually envious of the couple of kids in class who wore headgear for their braces.

By the time high school came around, I was feeling better about my hair. I knew how to work with it. Also, curly hair was "in" during high school. When everyone was getting "perms" to make their hair curly, I was the one envied by many for having that look naturally. Yes, I went to high school in the 1980's.

Back to my self-consciousness which was magnified in school. One day, we had an assembly in the hall in elementary school. We had brought our lunches to school that morning, and they were handed out to us by the staff during the assembly. I don't know what happened, but the chocolate chip cookies my mom baked were given to me in a brown paper bag as my lunch. I took one look into the bag, realized that I didn't have a normal lunch and quickly closed it up. I could feel my face getting hot in embarrassment. Some kids would have been thrilled to have been served a bag full of homemade chocolate chip cookies (which, by the way, are still my all-time favorite dessert), but I was upset. I quietly gave the bag to a parent. I don't remember what they gave me to eat, but I remember feeling relieved that the bag of cookies was gone.

My classmates voted me valedictorian in 8th grade. I had no idea at the time what an honor that was. My parents were thrilled. I came down with the chicken pox the week before graduation and missed all the festivities of the last week of school. I managed to make it for my speech as valedictorian, pale-faced and chicken pox scarred. I don't recall what I said as I stood at the podium on the church altar, but I made it through.

Because of being named valedictorian, I was invited to the Catholic High School that I would be attending to meet up with other teenagers that were in a leadership role. I remember having a lot of fun that day, and then feeling a bit intimidated by the end. The school was huge compared to what I had experienced the last 8 years. I was going from 30 kids in my class to several hundred. Also, the anxiety over switching classes was definitely there. Will I find my class in time? Will I be able to open the lock on my locker? Will my hair cooperate?

My first day of high school came, and it turned out to be quite eventful for me – and not in a good way. By the time 2nd period came, I was feeling a bit nauseous. I remember the room feeling warm and stuffy. The teacher asked us to turn our desks so we could face the person next to us, and then we were supposed to introduce ourselves, etc. As I was turning my desk, I was feeling really woozy. I must have felt really bad because, otherwise, I never would have called attention to myself by getting up in the middle of class. I walked up to the teacher's desk and whispered to him that I needed to go to the bathroom.

From this point on, everything felt like slow motion. The teacher slowly put up his finger as if to say 'just a moment', and then he slid a pad of paper across his desk and started writing me a pass. I recall zoning in and out, looking at his ring and stubby fingers. Then, I barfed in the garbage can next to me. I remember seeing my teacher's hand and stubby fingers flap around sporadically. He said, "Oh! Oh!" Then he said, "Who do you know in this class?" Still in slow motion, I held one hand against my queasy belly, and pointed with my other hand toward my friend, LeeAnn. She looked at me in horror as if to say, 'How could you embarrass me like this?' LeeAnn quickly and gracefully came to me and took me by the arm as she dragged me out of the room.

As we stumbled down the empty hall, it got comical. We watched two teachers in the distance strolling and chatting. They noticed Lee-Ann and me. They must have thought I was going to throw up again. I must have looked in pretty bad shape. The teachers started running toward us, grabbing a huge garbage can along the way. They were tripping over each other to grasp it. This was all still in slow motion for me. It was so surreal watching these teachers. It was like a movie scene with their long hair flying behind them as they ran with that garbage can. My only memory after this was sitting in the nurse's office, feeling miserable, waiting for my mom.

High School was actually quite fun for me overall. I laughed a lot. I'm still in touch with many friends that I met there. I wasn't quite as studious as I was in elementary school because I was more interested in my friendships and boys, however, I did okay. I don't recall my parents ever being "on me" about grades. I do remember, however, that they did not allow me to take any class other than academic classes. I really wanted to take "home economics" and learn cooking, but they refused.

I still studied and applied myself in school. I remember thinking Algebra was fun. I liked the process of figuring out an equation and penciling out my work over 3 pages, and coming up with the final answer: 2. I was good at Algebra. I didn't much care for math word problems though. I would read a question and think, 'Who cares?' I always enjoyed writing, especially creative writing, and doing book reports and papers.

While I did have an anxious side to my personality as a kid, I also had a comical side. I love jokes and watching funny movies. My dad and I joked around a lot. We have similar personalities, including a silly side. Even when I grew up into adulthood, we would often call each other whenever we heard a good joke. Here are a couple of my personal favorites. I wish I knew who the creative people were who thought these up so I can give them the credit they deserve.

Joke #1:

A man walking along a California beach was deep in prayer. All of a sudden he said out loud, "Lord, grant me one wish."

Suddenly, the sky clouded above his head and in a booming voice the Lord said, "Because you have tried to be faithful to me in all ways, I will grant you one wish."

The man said, "Please build a bridge to Hawaii, so I can drive over any time I want to."

The Lord replied, "Your request is very materialistic. Think of the logistics of that kind of undertaking. The supports required to reach the bottom of the Pacific! The concrete and steel it would take! I can do it, but it is hard for me to justify your desire for worldly things. Take a little more time and think of another wish, a wish you think would honor and glorify me."

The man thought about it for a long time. Finally, he said, "Lord, I have been married and divorced four times. All of my wives said that I am uncaring and insensitive. I wish that I could understand women. I want to know how they feel inside, what they are thinking when they give me the silent treatment, why they cry, what they mean when they say "nothing" and how I can make a woman truly happy."

After a few moments, God said, "You want two lanes or four on that bridge?"

<u>Joke #2:</u>

A little boy, Billy, after playing outside for a while, opened the back door of his house and yelled, "Mom! Hey, Mom! Come here! I have a question!"

His mother yelled back, "Please don't yell across the house! I'm in the living room! Come inside if you want to talk to me!"

The little boy complied and ran through the kitchen, across the dining room, and into the living room. As he stood dutifully in front of his mom, she said, "Thank you, Billy. Now, what was your question?"

Billy replied, "I stepped in a ton of dog poop. Do you know where the hose is?"

****

Relationship Dynamics

My parents' relationship wasn't ideal. Of course there were challenges with my dad's disability, but I'm talking about their relationship as a whole. It seemed my mom was mad at my dad a lot. I remember feeling really bad once as a kid when my mom made a comment to the effect of, "If it were me that was disabled, he wouldn't have stayed with me. He wouldn't have been able to handle it." This made me sad because I thought he would have taken care of her. In my young mind I thought, "Of course he would have!" I really believed it. However, I was just a kid, and I simply could not possibly have understood the complexity of their situation. Again, I didn't know what to say, so I didn't say anything. I just remember feeling very sad that my mom didn't think he would have stayed with her. What a terrible thing for her to live with and believe about him. It wasn't fair really, although again, I had no way of understanding the complexity – even now as an adult. My mom's life is not my life.

I also remember my dad having a lot of guilt over his accident. Until the day he died, he continued to feel bad that he did such a dumb thing like jumping in that lake and because of it, my mom was "forever burdened by him." There was such a dynamic between my parents. My mom was my dad's primary caregiver, and there was a lot that went into caring for someone who could not do basic things for himself. My parents did get more help when all of us kids grew older and left the house. We were the "gophers" for my dad and helped a lot when we lived at home. When we were gone, my mom had even more to handle, so they started the journey of finding caregivers to help. They were fortunate to find very good caregivers, however, it was always so stressful when one of them quit and it was time to find another person.

I have to say, my dad was very skillful at orchestrating his care. He was helped by people who were truly dedicated and really cared about him. My dad really cared about others too, despite his self-centered tendencies. Or was it obsessiveness? Perhaps this trait was how he survived so long as a quadriplegic for over 40 years. My dad knew how to treat people. He was kind and complimentary and a good advocate for people. My dad was generally in good humor, as a way of being, which I believe made him more fun to be around and caregivers more amiable when helping him.

As an example, here is a story about my dad interacting with his caregiver. I believe it was Jessica's first day on the job. She was at the house helping my dad get up and ready for work. My dad was still lying in bed and she got him dressed. He then asked her to comb his hair. She got the comb and starting combing his hair, while my dad said to her, something along the lines of, "Thank you. It's important that I look good because the women at work really like me and I don't want to disappoint them." Jessica didn't know my dad yet, so she just kind of said, "Uh, okay…" Then my dad started cracking up and she realized he was joking. She started laughing in relief. I think it was a good ice breaker.

It's not like my dad was joking 100% of the time, however, if you ask anyone, I'm pretty sure most people would mention my dad's sense of humor when reminiscing about how he was.

When my sister and I were older in our 20's and out of the house, my mom would open up more about her frustrations with being married to my dad. She'd confess about the hard time she had with his disability, and while other couples their age were traveling, she and dad were not, due to the extreme challenges. She also complained about normal relationship-type things, like my dad's self-centeredness. I think she talked more to my sister than me about things like this, so for me, it was interesting to hear. I remember both my sister and I asked her why she stayed with him. We wanted to be supportive and it did appear extremely challenging living with and caring for my dad because of his disability. His care needs were, and would always be, intense.

My mom seemed very unhappy at times. I remember when we asked her why she stayed with my dad, she paused for a moment, then she sighed and said, "He's a nice guy." (There was much more to their relationship, of course, than I can ever assess an accurate description of.)

My mom was a woman of few words. I found an email from her that she sent to all of us kids dated just a year and half before my mom's diagnosis. The email was written during one of those stressful times when my parents had challenges with a caregiver for my dad. This is when my siblings and I started getting involved. We started helping my parents when caregivers would give notice that they were leaving. My parents were just too emotionally drained after so many years of dealing with it, and we began to step in to assist. There is the reality that finding quality assistance for someone in my dad's condition was challenging.

What I like about my mom's below email was that she was reassuring us kids that she was happy most of the time. I never really viewed her as a happy person, so it was nice to hear her say it. Another part of her email I found interesting was about her relationship with my dad. After so many years, there was still that wistful wish of getting more of a certain type of attention from my dad. What I've observed of my parents over the years is that their problems were very normal relationship-type problems, such as miscommunications, misunderstandings, challenges with expressing their true feelings, etc.

> From: Brenda Gambina
> To: Julie Thomas; Lea Pecora
> Cc: Dino Gambina
> Subject: attendant follow up

> The above subject title would have been quite different had I done this write up this morning. It would have said something like. "Venting-read at your on risk". I have since picked myself up by the boot straps as has been done thousands of times before.
> Yes, another disappointment on two counts, of course, Lea, you already heard all this but I am just laying the groundwork for the other two. Our new attendant left out pertinent information during the interview process that she had another job that interfered with every other Sat. night schedule. Had it been revealed we certainly could have talked about flexibility if things worked out. But instead she chose not to mention it and it really hurts her credibility, which of course, is most important. Then this morning she did not show up or call at 5:30 am for training with Jessica. Did show up at 7:00 am very contrite and apologetic. (Overslept from her other late night job). The disappointment was greater this time since it has happened with the last 4 attendants in the last 6 months.
> So Lea, I just want to thank you so much for taking on the initial interview process. It saves us so much, you have no idea, especially emotionally. Please keep in mind, however, that Dad has been doing this for a very long time, over 10 years. Not to mention what he does at work. I know you want to make sure we have done our part correctly. I do get involved with the details that Dad might miss and I am still a pretty good problem solver. This episode prompted me to share some of my thoughts with you all.

It comes to mind that you all see both Dad and I in a different light and it is very understandable now that I think about it. My complaint with Dad has been how others at work, and the outside world for the most part, get the best of him.... happy, alive, smart, jokester, caring, loving, advocate on and on. That is a fact I have to live with to a degree because he is almost 68 years old, paralyzed, blind in one eye, trouble sleeping (but luckily in good health!) and is doing the best he can.

And then, there is me. I do have to remind him that I am here and need a little bit of the good stuff too. It also occurred to me that you guys do not see my good side much either. You may be surprised to hear I am happy most of the time, excited about aspects of my life, able to run/bike, and enjoy my job, even though I do complain about some stuff. But like Dad, I come home from work pretty darn tired, and still have dinner, laundry, cleaning, food shopping, house, dog, car, backyard cleanup and maintenance, pay bills, check email, etc.,etc. I know I am forgetting something. So when I am asked why we do not have company much, that's why. I would never refuse any of you coming for a visit because I don't see you or the kids that often, but usually the times, after work especially, you may translate my being in a bad mood when I am just plain old tired. I guess I am doing the same thing Dad does.

That is enough for now. Could you please respond to this e-mail so I can get a feel whether this is helpful to you or whether you just as soon not have all this detail. This did take a half hour to do and my dinner is getting cold!

Love, Mom

My mom was 61 years old and married to my dad for 42 years when she wrote the above email. While their marriage had many challenges, they chose to stay married. My thoughts on why are: They appreciated their history together. They came together and overcame extreme challenges. They each did their part. Not only did they love each other, they liked each other. I also think at the time they were married in 1965, thoughts about marriage were different. They went into marriage with the mindset of "forever until death do we part". They were also Catholic. So when challenges came, they just didn't "go there" so easily with thoughts of separating during the tough times. (I wish I could ask my parents if my thoughts are in the ballpark of their reality. I would so appreciate knowing their insights.)

I, for one, as their daughter, am so appreciative that they had the presence of mind to work on their relationship and were able to provide a nice home life for our family for so many years.

****

The "Whatever" Period

My sister and I shared a room until we moved out of my parents' house. I moved out at 19, and my sister moved out at 18. My brother moved out at 22. As teenagers, my sister and I gave my parents a lot of grief. They couldn't really deal with both of us at the same time. Whenever my sister was in trouble, I kind of liked it because my parents wouldn't pay as much attention to what I was doing. Then when they had her seemingly under control, they would start paying attention to me and would get on my nerves. We were pretty good teenagers as far as the more serious things like drinking and drugs. We were never into that. My brother wasn't either. I tried drinking and would drink a wine cooler here and there, but I never got into it.

I remember when I learned the lesson of not mixing different types of alcohol. It was my 22nd birthday and my friends and I rented a limo. We had a great time in the limo, but I sipped part of a wine cooler, some Peppermint Schnapps, and some Bacardi and Coke. Then, as we went to different dance clubs, I was given free drinks for my birthday and would sip them also. I got so sick that I threw up on the limo driver. Poor guy. I remember my friend, Judy, asking the limo driver if she could do anything to help, and he said, "Yes, can you wipe my hand?" (Gross!) I was in bed by 10pm that night and on my couch all the next day. I remember the timing clearly because at 4pm the next day, my friend, Angela, banged on my door. She came in and said, "Guess where I just was?"

I mumbled from my couch, "Where?"

She said, "On a date with the bouncer who kicked you out of the dance club." Apparently I fell asleep on a chair in the club, and it wasn't good for business, so we were asked to leave.

I never drank much after that. Sometimes I would drink one too many glasses of wine, and would always regret it. That sick feeling is the worst.

I'm happy we went to a Catholic school, for a simple reason: We had to wear uniforms. I was very glad about this because I rarely got new clothes and didn't have much to wear. The uniforms kept me in a "level playing field" where I wasn't judged on my clothing by other students. I dreaded "free dress day" once a month in high school. Again, I didn't have much to wear, and I would see all the trendy outfits on the girls and I felt like I didn't measure up. I still think it's pretty amazing that my parents managed to send all 3 of us kids to a private Catholic School. In my mom's memoir, she clearly states how much she had wanted to go to the Catholic School in Hawaii when she was young, and she said that when she had kids one day, she would send them to a Catholic school. The power of intention!

My dad's sister helped pay for our school at one point, and we were also on the tuition assistance program which involved me staying after school to clean the chalkboards. I disliked doing that. It was embarrassing when kids would peek in from the hallway and see me there cleaning. I would complain about it to my parents. My mom said that if I got a job, I wouldn't have to do that anymore.

I heard about a job opening for a File Clerk at a law firm from my Office Practice class teacher. I interviewed one day after school after my parents drove me there. I got the job! I think the fact that I already was able to type 45 words a minute really helped because I overheard the manager saying, "She can help with typing." My parents were much more excited about this job than I was at the time. I think they realized what an opportunity it was for me. I was just happy not to have to clean chalkboards. (I was around 15 years old when I started working at the law office).

My sister and I had major attitudes around the house growing up – especially from the ages of 15 to 18. I remember that I didn't understand why my mom wanted me to hang around with them. After all, I did all my chores. I just wanted to be with my friends. We didn't have cell phones back then. I used to drag the phone and long chord into my room to have privacy when I talked to my friends. Good luck if anyone tried to call my parents. I loved talking on the phone with my friends whenever possible, and I would be on the phone every single day. My dad could never understand this. He would ask my mom, "What could she possibly still have to talk about?"

Rolling my eyes at my parents was a frequent occurrence and I was a master at it. Remember the phrase, "Whatever?" That was my response to a lot of things. If my mom would scold me about something, I would say, "Whatever," then walk away. When she asked if I could sit longer at the dinner table, I would say, "Whatever." I must have been very annoying to them.

I remember one time I apologized to my mom for something. Her reaction was amazing to me. She actually stopped and stared at me in shock. Then she almost started crying and said, "That's all you have to do." Thinking back on this now, I have a lot of empathy for my mom and what she was feeling. She had very little control over my sister and I and I'm sure she just wanted to know we cared. It's sad to say (but perhaps normal?), during my teenage years I didn't care about much except being with my friends and doing what I wanted to do. I don't recall having much empathy for my parents. I had a lot of empathy for my friends. They were my world when I was a teenager. My parents, on the other hand, were my parents – people that I definitely took for granted a lot of the time. We had our moments of fun and togetherness as a family during those teenage years. I just recall having other interests that were a priority, so to corral me in the family was challenging.

There was a memory I have that makes me feel bad whenever I think about it. Mainly because I know I really hurt my dad. I was 19 and dating someone (let's call him Jason). Jason was cute and fun. I met him at a gas station. At that time, it was common to have attendants help fill up gas tanks in cars, especially for my dad because he was disabled. Jason flirted with me and was really cute. He had blond hair, a stocky build, and a friendly smile. I recall the owner of the gas station warning my dad about Jason not being the best choice for me, but my dad couldn't really do anything about the mutual attraction.

I discovered in a fairly short amount of time that Jason was irresponsible, and lied a lot (but not to me, or so I thought, so I didn't put much significance on this fact in the beginning.) He lived at home with his mom and step dad. I soon realized he had a problem with alcohol. When he asked me to forge his AA attendance slips so he could turn them into the Court, I started feeling very uncomfortable. I remember telling him, "No way! I can't do that!" I still really liked him though. After all, he was cute and fun, and "had so much potential."

I don't remember all the details, but I remember leaving my parents' house with Jason and the plan was that I would stay with him at his mom's house indefinitely. My dad was crying softly at his desk when I walked out. I remember almost crying too when I saw my dad, but I still left. I wish I could remember what led up to this point. I think I just wanted to get out of the house. This adventure was short-lived.

One night Jason scared me. I was attempting to leave his house because he was acting strange. (He would never drink alcohol in front of me, but I soon learned what he was like after he drank – not his normal self.) He didn't want me to leave. He yanked me by my long hair so hard I fell to the ground. It totally shocked me. He seemed surprised too and didn't touch me again and apologized. I got up and called my friend, Judy, and walked outside and down the street to meet up with her when she drove up. He was yelling apologetically and trying to get me to stay as I hopped into Judy's car and left.

Things got pretty dramatic because Jason was trying to block the car. He wasn't in a good state of mind. Judy screamed out the window, "You scared her!" and sped off. That was it. I was so turned off. I liked guys that were attentive and kind. (Like my dad always was to me.) I had no more interest in Jason and resisted his attempts to win back my affection. It was tempting because he was such a charmer, but his attempts didn't stick.

I must have went back home because I clearly remember officially moving out for the first time into an apartment after an incident with my parents. My mom had the nerve to start charging me $300.00 a month in rent because I decided to skip a semester of college when I was working full time. (I'm being sarcastic here.) I was still working at the same law office that I started working at when I was 15. I moved up to a legal assistant position by age 19 and was going to school and working full time.

When my mom told me about having to pay rent, I freaked out. I yelled, "How am I supposed to save money to move out if you charge me rent?!" I recall that same surprised look on my mom's face that happened a lot in response to my terrible attitude when I was a teenager. She mumbled something like, "I guess I should have said something sooner…I thought it was obvious if you weren't going to school that naturally you would help out…"

At this point, I wasn't listening to her anymore. I was just fuming. I moved out within 3 months and moved in with Diane, who was a law clerk at the same office I worked at and was working her way through law school. When I moved, my mom handed me $900 cash – the rent she was charging for those 3 months. I realized then my parents' plan. They intended on holding that money and giving it back to me at some point. Wow.

I soon realized that it cost a minimum of $1,000 per month to live on my own and every $5 I had to think about spending. I had a small TV that sat on a cardboard box. But I was free.

****

Sweet Independence

I matured pretty quickly after being on my own and fully responsible for myself. It was hard to make ends meet, but I did it. I never moved back home. At one point, I stayed with Judy's parents for a few months after a roommate moved out suddenly. That was nice of them to take me in. I soon found a new living situation with a roommate again that I was happy with.

I had a lot of freedom during this time living on my own and making enough money at the law office to take care of myself. I ended up going back to college and became a Certified Paralegal when I was 23 years old. I was also supervising the office staff at the law office. I really enjoyed my job. It was never boring because I was able to learn a wide variety of areas of law. My favorite was Family Law and Probate because each case was a different story about real life relationship issues. I enjoyed writing up declarations, and was very good at listening to clients and the attorneys and writing up declarations based on notes. I enjoyed knowing that I was really helping people. Being able to explain the legal process to people confidently and being "on top of" their cases made the clients feel more at ease during a time in their life that was extremely challenging – getting divorced or dealing with the passing of a loved one. For some reason, I was able to be calm and reassuring regardless of how emotional the clients became. Looking back, this is a strength of mine that I didn't recognize at the time.

By this point in my 20's, my relationship with my parents was much better. I wouldn't say we ever had a "bad" relationship. I just think once I had the independence I wanted, there wasn't anything to have friction about anymore. I also matured. I visited them a lot and we got along great. I was always welcome. I would help them and even help clean the house. In fact, on one of my mom's birthdays, I gave her a "gift certificate" that I made myself saying I would come and clean the house for her once every 2 weeks for a certain amount of months. I followed through and enjoyed doing it too. For my dad, I spent many hours working on a cartoon poster consisting of over 60 different cartoon characters that I drew. I cut out a picture of my face and put it in the middle, then drew a Santa hat on my head. It was a Christmas present in 1990 for my dad. He loved it. It was a funny picture. I didn't really think about the fact that it was HUGE and maybe they wouldn't want to hang it up in their house. It ended up in a closet.

I made a similar picture for my mom later – much smaller – and that one hung in their house for years. Lesson learned. (I now have that huge picture I drew for my dad framed in my office in my creative space. I don't mind how big it is!)

My parents' home was open to all of us kids to visit whenever we wanted. We didn't have to call and could just come by, although usually we were in communication about it. I always felt welcome. In fact, I remember just assuming that my parents would want me to join them in whatever they did – even their anniversary dinner. I called them and found out where they were going to dinner and I said, "Great! I'll meet you there." Now that I look back on it, it was really presumptuous of me to impose myself on them any time I wanted. I don't really think they minded, but I could have at least asked.

Those years I worked at the law office were my single and dating years. I did have one boyfriend in high school that I really liked, but he dumped me for a car. What I mean is, he was on the older side for his grade so he was the first to get his license out of all of his friends. He had a VW bug and as soon as he was able to drive it, he became "Mr. Popular" and broke up with me. I would see him driving around Newark in his VW with a bunch of friends seemingly having the time of his life, and I felt devastated. I remember being in my parents' room on the phone when he broke up with me and my mom was trying to console me. She said, "You'll meet someone else." I cried and said, "But not like him!" Well, of course my mom was right.

Throughout my 20's, I moved apartments just about every year or so. They were the type of moves where I could call my friends and my dad would come with his van and it would take only a day to move. I traveled light in those days.

I wish I had the presence of mind to buy a property and find roommates to live with me, versus moving to places where people were seeking roommates. I just didn't have a mentor or anyone who could guide me in this kind of risk-taking activity. I got close once. One of the attorneys I worked for introduced me to a realtor. This realtor showed me a 3 bedroom, 2 bath home close to my work at the law office. I still remember the house. It had refinished hardwood floors, and a nice family room with a fireplace that opened to the kitchen. I really liked it. I remember the price was around $230,000. I took my mom to look at it and she liked it too.

My parents were actually talking it over and were thinking of buying it together with me. It was totally affordable, if I got roommates. But, my mom started getting nervous about maintenance on the home and other possible unexpected expenses that could come up. This made me nervous too because I was taking her lead. I remember the realtor trying to encourage us because the home hadn't gone on the market yet and he felt it was a really great opportunity. This realtor knew my boss, and it was one of those situations where I had "first chance" at it. Well, I didn't buy it. Too bad I didn't. Not too many years later it was worth over $700,000. California had a real estate boom and Fremont is a popular area because of Silicon Valley.

Oh, well. This is just one example of how important I believe guidance is in life – to teach what we learn, and guide and encourage others that are eager and interested. For example, I believe I would have taken the risk and purchased that house on my own, had I had someone I trusted mentor me and "show me the numbers" and calculate for me how it could work, i.e. get 2 roommates who pay "x" each month, set aside "x" for future maintenance, etc. It's okay. It was a passed opportunity, but there are always other opportunities in life, and I've taken advantage of many since.

My brother and sister and I didn't have a lot of contact during these years that I first moved out on my own, other than with my parents. We were all growing up and doing our own thing. My sister did come along with my friends and me for certain events. I also remember visiting her when she was waitressing. She waitressed for a long time and was really good at it. My sister is beautiful with long, very dark hair, porcelain smooth skin, and big, dark doe eyes. She'd make massive tips at the restaurant when she was in charge of the "shot booth" on Thursday nights. She'd just stand there in all her beauty and smile as she asked the men who would pass by, "Would you like a shot to go with that beer?" Much more often than not, they would say yes.

****

Fun and Heartbreak

I had such good times in my late teens and 20's with my friends. "Cruising" was a big thing. Susanne and Judy and I would drive certain boulevards which would be packed with other cars – other young people out cruising and socializing. The cruising strip went from the Carls, Jr. to the Burger King. We also enjoyed going dancing, more so in our early 20's. I also dated a lot. The young men I dated had several things in common – cute and fun of course, however, now I was more interested in what they were doing with their lives. I guess I was maturing a bit.

I was the type of young woman that preferred to be in a relationship versus dating multiple young men at one time. Also, if I didn't believe the young man had the potential for a long-term relationship, I lost interest. I remember at the law office, everyone was pretty entertained by my dating experiences. They had a hard time keeping track of who was who.

Even though I met and dated many different young men, there were only 3 that I really, really liked – to the point that each time I thought "could this be *the one?*" They weren't. I experienced major heartbreak with each one. (Perhaps I was heartbroken because THEY were the ones who decided to break-up with me instead of the other way around? Hmmm…could be.)

One of them I refer to as my "favorite ex-boyfriend" because it was the only time that I had a breakup where we both were the first to know. Meaning, we talked and decided to break it off because of his focus on his career, which sent him all over the country at a moment's notice and we never knew when we'd see each other next. We hadn't dated all that long and I didn't want to wait for him until he got a different job (which he had no immediate plans to do), and obviously he didn't want to wait for me either.

Number 2 of my 3 more serious relationships seemed to become disinterested at one point. We had a long-distance relationship for many months and then he moved to California. Things fizzled fairly quickly.

I was very disappointed, to put it mildly. What made it worse is that he ended up living 2 blocks from me, and not only that, I had to drive by his apartment every single day whenever I left mine. There was no other route to travel because my apartment was at a dead end street.

Number 3 just changed his mind, as if a light switch went off. This particular boyfriend was particularly devastating because we were talking about marriage. In fact, we broke up shortly after I declined to move in with him. I thought I was doing something good for our relationship by saying no and explaining why. It was actually my mom who influenced my change of heart about moving in with him. I was moving out of my apartment because my roommate was moving out. I was talking to my mom and telling her that my boyfriend (I'll call him Daniel) and I were talking about marriage. My mom simply said, "But he hasn't proposed yet, right?" Hmmm. That was correct. He didn't actually propose but he wanted me to move in with him.

I remember talking to Daniel and explaining that I felt it would ruin our relationship if we moved in together. In hindsight, I'm really glad I didn't move in. One day not too long after, he just stopped talking to me. He'd get moody sometimes, but this was extreme. I'd be over his house and he would just sit there quietly. He wouldn't talk and I wasn't able to engage him in conversation. I asked him if he wanted to break up and he just didn't answer. So I left his house and said, "I guess we're broken up because I don't know what's going on if you won't talk to me." It was the weirdest thing. He never called me again and didn't respond to my attempts to reach out to him. My sister went over to Daniel's house some days later to pick up a few of my belongings, and had the pleasure of meeting his young secretary who was over there, appearing quite cozy. Well, that answered some of my questions.

I remember crying and telling my dad about what happened – that Daniel just stopped talking to me and he is seeing another girl. My dad said, "He sounds like a jerk to me." My dad wasn't very empathetic to my feelings about this, but his matter of fact attitude did help me somewhat. It wasn't so much what my dad said, but I could sense that he was thinking, "Why would you want to be with someone who does that?" I felt discarded by Daniel and never got closure in that relationship, however, I did come to terms with the truth that I only wanted to be with someone who wanted to be with me.

Heartbreak! Uggggg….tears, loss of appetite, sadness, obsessive thoughts…oh, how I can empathize with heartbreak. It's so hard to wade through and get to the other side, and it's all so serious and devastating at the time. Now, with 2 kids and 14 years of marriage, those dating memories all supported me in growing up, and I'm thankful to all the men I've met in my life.

****

The Big Smile and the Red Shirt

Before I met my husband, Oliver, I had only dated someone for a year at the most. I have to admit though, I was pretty fickle when it came to dating. I got turned off so easily. I was so immature really. One time when I was on a health kick – I was eating very healthy and I didn't eat any cheese or butter or mayonnaise, etc. – I was at dinner with a young man, and he started spreading a lot of butter on his bread. That was it. I never went out with him again.

I have so much compassion for men dating. It must be so hard for them to remain confident and to take risks with women. But for those who do, they will always win – eventually.

At the time I met Oliver I had went out a couple of times with a man that owned a house boat, and he had visions of living on a house boat one day. Well, as much as I liked this person, I did not see myself living on a houseboat, so I was losing interest fast.

When I met Oliver, he met my usual baseline criteria – cute and fun – so it was promising. We met as a result of a little matchmaking effort. One of the attorneys at the law office, Lee, got very interested in flying and was taking pilot lessons. I remember how excited Lee was about these lessons. He would just be getting back from Court, and he would change his clothes and practically run out the back door on his way to the airport. His flight instructor, Keith, was Oliver's friend. Oliver has his pilot's license and learned to fly from Keith also.

Lee and Oliver met one day at the airport and became friends. Pilots enjoy hanging out together as if they are in a club of their own. They just enjoy being around planes and aviation, and they would have barbeques and music bands at the airport for fun. One day, Lee asked Oliver if he was single and Oliver said yes. Lee told him about me. Apparently Oliver wasn't sure about meeting me, or anyone, because he was only in California visiting. He lived in Germany.

One day at work, I remember Lee yelling out to me, "Lea! Italiano!" I was running around the office like usual (at this time, I was managing the office). I glanced down the hall and I saw Lee motioning me over. There was Oliver next to him with a big grin and a bright red shirt on. Lee introduced us by saying, "Italiano!" as he motioned to me, and "Italiano!" as he motioned to Oliver. I said hello and got back to work.

Next, I remember Lee inviting me on a flight with him and Oliver, and I said yes. It was my first experience being in a small Cessna plane. We flew to a small town nearby called Twain Harte and had an Italian feast prepared by Maria, a friend of Lee's. It was awesome. I love Italian food. At this point, I liked Oliver, but I was well aware that he lived in another country, so I wasn't thinking anything serious. I was just having fun. I remember though at Maria's house when she asked what each of us wanted to drink – soda or juice or beer – we both said "water" at the same time. Turns out we were both major water drinkers, which I really liked.

There were a lot of things I really liked about Oliver. For starters, like I said, he was cute and fun. He also was a curious person and enjoyed doing a variety of things. He was good at a lot of things too, probably because he tried a lot of things. He spoke 2 languages, German being his first language, which I thought was really cool. He talked a lot, which was sometimes tiring. I remember when I mentioned this to my mom, she said, "Uh, oh. Another one bites the dust." I think she got used to the fact that usually when I pointed out something I didn't like about a guy, it was a sign that I was losing interest. Well, with Oliver, he had so many good qualities, I wasn't deterred.

I met Oliver in September of 1996, and he ended up extending his stay in California until after his birthday at the end of November. We had a couple of months of fun together – motorcycle riding, going dancing, going on picnics, flying. I remember my parents weren't too sure what to think. They asked, "Does he ever work?" Well, little did they know how much he worked. He was part of a consulting company in Frankfurt, Germany, that he and his cousin formed with some other college graduates focusing on the area of quality management. Part of the reason Oliver came to California that summer though was because his stepfather had passed away recently, and his mom who lived in California was planning to sell her house in Castro Valley and Oliver was considering buying it.

He also missed California and the sunny weather. Now, with meeting me, he had even more of an incentive to move back. A little background on Oliver: He's ½ Italian and ½ German and looks much more Italian than German, taking after his father who lives in Southern Italy. He was born in Germany. His mom and dad divorced and his mom brought Oliver and his sister to the United States when he was 8, with his uncle's assistance.

Oliver lived in California until he was 20, went back to Germany for 10 years and in that time, completed his studies in mechanical engineering and helped form SIC Consulting in Germany. When I met Oliver, he was 29 years old and transitioning back to California. All these things about Oliver helped solidify my interest level. I felt he was "going places", which was very attractive. He also had integrity of character, was thoughtful, and kind. Jackpot!

The night before Oliver left that summer to go back to Germany, I really didn't know exactly when he would come back. He set up my first home email account (back then, it wasn't that common to have email at home). I'm so glad he did because we were able to keep in good contact. I'm not sure we would have made it without this ability. Germany was 9 hours ahead, and expensive to call. I took 3 weeks off from work to visit him in Germany in January, which was good timing because his face was getting fuzzy in my mind. I remember being sooooo excited when he picked me up at the airport. He was so cute with his dark hair and black leather jacket. The trip was cool because I got to see his apartment and meet all of his friends and really get a feel of what his life was like there in Germany.

I remember my boss, Bob, giving Lee a bad time after I planned that trip to Germany. He said jokingly, "What were you thinking introducing Lea to someone from another country!" I did a lot at the law office. I was there for years and was very appreciated for my work. I could understand the attorneys being a little nervous about my new interest.

I could tell that Oliver was pretty special because of my own actions, or inactions. I was a big "gym person" at the time. I was in really good shape – I ate well, and I worked out 4 to 5 days a week. I had my routine. Right after work at the law office, I'd change my clothes and go across the street to the nearby gym for a workout. I usually did free weights and the treadmill. It wasn't unusual for guys to talk to me and/or ask me out. In fact, most of my dates I first met at the gym. I was there most often and wasn't interested in going to bars or meeting people in dance clubs.

One day at the gym, a really cute guy was flirting with me and I was flirting back. Well, he ended up asking me out to dinner, and I remember feeling bummed for a minute because I knew I wasn't going to go out with him because I was committed to Oliver, who was in Germany at this time. I was bummed only because I would have liked to go out with this guy, and I never turned someone down that was cute and fun. Well, there is always a first time. I was honest with him, telling him about Oliver and he understood, and was quite gracious. He gave me a big, cute smile as he walked away.

I was at work one day about a month after my Germany trip, checking the fax machine, and there was a paper showing a flight itinerary coming through the machine with no cover page. I noticed a picture of a champagne bottle at the top. As I examined it further for names to see which attorney it belonged to, I realized that it was Oliver's flight itinerary. I saw his one-way flight from Frankfurt to San Francisco landing the day before my birthday. Oliver has always been a romantic and still is. He loves giving surprises.

This was an exciting time.

****

Snapshot

I can write a whole book about our life together from this point. The marriage proposal in Venice, Italy, starting our IT business, remodeling our home, having our children, the ups and downs in our marriage, etc. However, I'll leave those details for another time. If I start writing about our kids, Dominic and Sophie, it would probably become a book in itself. I really enjoy being in their company. Just thinking of them in this moment makes me want to tell so many stories. I cannot resist... here are a couple.

Dominic Story #1:

I was getting ready for work one day. I was standing in front of my full-length mirror putting makeup on. Out of the corner of my eye, I saw Dominic walk into the bedroom. He was around 5 years old at the time. He started laughing out loud.

I glanced over at him and saw that he was pointing his finger toward me as he giggled and said, "Silly sweater!"

I looked at myself in the mirror. I had a turtle-neck sweater on with thick tan and brown stripes. I couldn't help feel-

ing a little self-conscious. I decided to use this situation as a teachable moment for Dominic.

I said to him gently, "Dominic, it doesn't make me feel good when you point at me and laugh. You know, women especially, they like to be told that they look pretty."

He stopped laughing and his expression turned pensive. He then walked over to me, looked up at me and said, very sincerely, "Mommy, you look very pretty in that silly sweater."

Dominic Story #2:

I was driving Dominic to school one day when he was 10 years old. He had a test that day, and I asked him, "Aren't you glad that you studied for your states and capitals test because now you know it really well."

Dominic didn't respond. I looked in the review mirror and was surprised to see him plugging his ears with his fingers.

I asked, "What's wrong, Dominic?"

He said, "No, Mommy, I'm not glad I studed because now you'll want me to do that all the time and I don't want to spend my life that way. I only have 90 more years to live."

Sophie Story #1:

Our whole family was playing the Ungame. (It's a conversation board game.) Sophie, 6 years old, landed on a "comment" space which meant she was supposed to say a comment out loud. She said giggling, "I love Daddy."

On her next turn she landed on a "comment" space again, and said giggling, "I say again, I love Daddy."

I was curious to hear something new from her, so I asked,

"Can we hear a different comment this time since we already know you love Daddy?"

She said, "Okay." Then she paused and said, "I want to marry Daddy!"

Sophie Story #2:

We were visiting Germany one summer when Sophie was around 7 years old. We banned her from the room where we were all trying to watch the Olympics Gymnastics because she kept doing cartwheels in front of the TV, blocking our view. It was getting quite annoying, and for some reason, she just wouldn't stop doing it, even after repeated requests.

After about 5 minutes of her being alone in the other room, I went in there to talk to her. I asked, "Sophie, why do you think you kept doing cartwheels in front of the TV when the whole family was trying to watch the Olympics?"

She immediately replied, "Where else can I do cartwheels, watch the Olympics, and annoy you all at the same time?"

Oliver and I have been married 14 years now as I write this, and while we've had some very challenging times, we appreciate each other more than ever before. We've learned so much by being together and at times not wanting to be together, but choosing to work things out.

The most difficult time in our marriage was when the kids were 2 and 4 years old. Neither of us felt close to the other. We were both lonely and spending our energy on work and tasks and caring for the kids. Oliver was the one who initiated the possibility of a separation, and the drama of that time period shook me up to the point I actually "saw stars" for a week as the realization sunk in that I may not have an intact family anymore. When I "came to", I realized that I also definitely didn't have the relationship that I wanted and I was just too exhausted to do anything about it. After all, managing a business, and being the primary caregiver for 2 small kids was simply too much to balance out with my mindset at the time.

I realized the fantasy of what I thought marriage was supposed to be was the beginning of the string of disappointments in our relationship. I was faced with that moment of decision. What now? A part of me wanted the relationship to be over (although when I look back, I think what I really wanted was relief from the constant strain and pressure I was feeling). I decided to figure out what I could do to improve our relationship. That started with taking a serious look at my life and how I was living and what I was doing day in and day out, then making real changes.

I believed that I had no right to leave our marriage – a marriage that included two small children – unless I can say, with 100% honesty and confidence, that I did all I could to work things out. Oliver had the same thoughts as I did. We both felt, 'How could we in good conscious leave each other and break up our family knowing that we didn't do our part?'

The tension in the air was thick, and I knew the kids felt it. I have a vivid memory of one particular evening. I was sitting on the couch and Dominic took Oliver by the hand and brought him to the couch to sit down next to me. Then, Dominic sat in between us and took our hands and put them together. He didn't say anything – he just held our hands together as he sat in between us.

Here is another memory that inspired change in me. I was angry with Oliver and yelling at him. Oliver walked away. Dominic couldn't find the words, but managed to say, "Mommy, why you talk mad? Now daddy is sad."

I had to do something to change this energy.

It's quite an interesting experience working on a relationship with someone that I could barely look at and didn't particularly like at the time. I knew, though, that how I was feeling was all due to so many mis-understandings and built-up hurt feelings. I did have hope.

Part of why I believe we succeeded in improving our relationship is that we both wanted to the same things in a relationship and we both believed in our ability to succeed. After all, we recognized how much we built together up until this point. Why couldn't we apply the same te-nacity to our relationship?

Bottom line – and what a windy road to get there – we each are in-dividuals, with our own thoughts and feelings, and we are changing and growing at different paces. We agreed, through marriage, that we want to build a life together and raise a family, yet we are individuals within our family. This fact cannot be ignored. We realize when we're acting immature and we take responsibility for our own actions and do not be-lieve the other is responsible. What this means is that we simply get past disagreements and arguments much more quickly. Often what would put us in a spin for a couple of days, and add to a steady stream of built-up resentments, we can often sort out within 10 minutes. Meaning, we can go from being full-blown angry, to "I'll be down in 10" and then cud-dle up and watch a movie. (If it takes longer than 10 minutes to shift, it just means that we want to pout a bit longer. At least now we're aware of what's happening.)

I can write a book on marriage. I don't have all the answers, but one thing I tell myself when there is an air of conflict in our relationship is: TELL THE TRUTH. That may sound simple, but for me, it's not so simple. First, I have to have the presence of mind to stop and sort out what the truth is. I have to ask myself, "Why am I reacting? What is re-ally going on here?" Then, the even harder part is mustering up enough courage to tell Oliver my truth, *without being attached to him respond-*

ing in a certain way. What I've learned is that just because he doesn't always respond to me initially in the way I'd prefer, doesn't mean he doesn't care. The important thing is he does come around.

Oliver and I still have the ability to "push each other's buttons." I'm glad we're both willing to look at ourselves and what we contribute to our relationship. During the challenging times, I think to myself, "Well, here's a good opportunity to practice." I mean this sarcastically. These times are not that fun, however, all the effort is worth it. It feels good to live true to myself. *The storms do pass.*

When I feel frustrated because Oliver is not behaving the way I want him to, or behaving the way I think he should, I think about this:

> *A great trick to getting what you want, fast, though one requiring a deep level of understanding, is "insistence." Not the kind, however, that expects "life" to behave a certain way, but the kind that expects you to behave a certain way.*

> *Yours truly,*
> *The Universe*

> *(Quote by Mike Dooley)*

I just keep coming back to the clear and simple fact that I cannot change anyone. I can only work on changing myself, and that takes quite enough effort. In fact, it's one of the most challenging things I've found – to be how I want to be despite how others are behaving, or despite what circumstances I find myself in. The paradox I've learned is that the more I succeed in being how I want to be, the more Oliver is the way I wish him to be. (This is the same with people in general.) When I have a certain energy, it seems to permeate through them. I don't even have to say a word.

When I was in my 20's, my mom gave me the below quote. I carried it with me in my wallet for a long time. When she first gave it to me, I didn't really understand it. Now I do.

"There is a place for hard work in a relationship. It's in facing yourself, admitting your needs, anticipating your weaknesses and summoning enough respect for the outcome to be your staunchest advocate. And, it's in having the courage to be patient with the process."

(Author Unknown)

When I'm struggling, I say to myself often, "I'm my own best friend." I do for myself what I'd do for my best friend. *I don't give up on myself.* I do what's important to me. I'm my staunchest advocate – because I know that I cannot give to anyone what I cannot give to myself, and it feels really good to be able to give. The receiving part is more challenging for me. I'm aware of this, so I can practice. If I'm not able to receive, then my energy gets depleted, and the flow in life cannot be. I do love the flow. It feels like heaven on earth.

****

The Calm

My parents were supportive during the time Oliver and I were having our challenges – especially my mom. My dad was cordial, but he wasn't as accepting of Oliver during this time. I think it was just really challenging for him knowing what a hard time his "little girl" was having. I was open with my parents – not about all details – but I would cry in front of them and they were there to comfort me. I admired my mom for how she interacted with Oliver. She would give him big hugs when she saw him and treated him very well. I think she really understood what both of us were going through, whereas my dad was a little more biased. He never said or did anything inappropriate. He was just a bit more aloof with Oliver during this time. He came around after Oliver and I worked things out.

In 2008, life was smoothing out again after all our marital troubles and a couple of years of focused hard work on our relationship. We were living the life that most people aspiring to have families of their own would like to live. We had healthy and happy kids, a lucrative business, a nice home, material comforts, and the flexibility to travel. We socialized with our friends and family. I saw my parents on a consistent basis. Although I didn't realize it at the time, we did socialize quite a bit together.

My parents still lived in the home I grew up in. I was very comfortable over there. My mom usually had her favorite music playing, the windows were open and the house was always clean. Her dogs were hanging around, content. My parents, with all their history, spent a lot of time together – going out to eat, meeting at the local coffee shop after my mom's morning runs, seeing a movie, and relaxing at home at the end of each day. Sure they got in their moods and it wasn't always picture perfect over there, but it was definitely home.

I never thought much about one of my parents dying, although I knew it was bound to happen one day. I felt like I was part of a strong family unit. I liked how I was included in this unit. Looking back, I was a grown-up kid with kids of my own, and my parents were my parents. I didn't think about how I would feel not having them around. It was simply not something that was on my mind. I was living life and I had my place. I enjoyed the comforts of home that I could feel even when I was not with my parents. They were always just a phone call away.

I underestimated the connection I had and to the intoxicating feeling of being totally loved and accepted by my parents. I held the belief, which was confirmed by their actions again and again, that my parents were interested in me. They were genuinely excited for me when any good fortune came my way. They welcomed me at any moment that I chose to reach out to them. They complimented me and praised me. What a grand gift I had that I connected with two people that were my parents. They were my foundation, and in many ways I took them for granted. I don't blame myself for this. They were just always there from day one, and I had no sense that they would be going anywhere – at least any time soon.

Part Three

Launch

I noticed my mom was reaching out more than usual. For Christmas, she actually invited us all to come over to celebrate. The reason I say this as if it was surprising is that as my parents got older, my mom wasn't as interested in hosting events at her house. She felt it was a lot of work and had other interests like being active and outdoors in nature. This particular year, I'm so happy she initiated a gathering. We didn't know it would be the last one before "the news". I remember driving up to my parents' house on Christmas with my whole family and we saw my parents looking out of the large picture window (the one that was put in after my dad's accident many years prior.) They were smiling with goofy grins, and they both had a huge red Santa hat on. They were waving in unison and then I noticed my mom was holding up her middle finger. I started laughing. It was the funniest thing watching them standing there acting so silly.

After Christmas, my mom was putting effort into coordinating regular game days. We really enjoyed playing Nerts together as a family (a fast-paced card game), and Charades, Pictionary, etc. I remember telling my mom that I wasn't sure how often I could commit to game days (she wanted them on Sundays in certain intervals). I told her I would calendar the game days and see if I could work it in. (I wasn't sure I really wanted to drive all the way to their house so regularly, which was a 45 minute drive.) Little did I know that soon, not only would I be driving to their house 2 to 3 times a week, for 2 ½ years straight, but life as I knew it was about to change forever. A force of nature – called life and death – was about to barrel right through all of our lives.

I did attend a game day. I remember it clearly. We played Cranium and my mom and I were acting out something. I forgot what we were acting out, but I remember that she was supposed to sit there while I moved her around while others guessed. We were laughing so hard! When my mom laughed, it was so fantastic. She was definitely more of a serious type, so it was music to our ears to hear her laugh – especially when she laughed so hard she had tears in her eyes!

****

Unexpected Halt

When my mom told me she was having a CAT scan done on her brain, it was over the phone. She was very calm, and made it sound like no big deal. She said she'd been having headaches for the last couple of months at the base of her neck that were affecting her workouts. She would run about 3 miles then would have to stop and it was really bugging her that her exercise was being interrupted. Since her headaches weren't going away and she mentioned she had blurry vision at times, the doctor wanted to do a CAT scan to "rule out anything bad", then go from there. I wasn't worried at all. You see, my mom was a healthy and strong 62 year old woman. She took great care of herself and looked 10 years younger than her age.

My mom paid attention to what she ate, loved her early morning exercise routine – whether it was cycling class, yoga, swimming, or running. (Running was her favorite.) When my mom was a teenager, she used to do competitive roller skating, and after a few years of doing jumps in the rink and landing on one foot, her knee was weak and painful. She used to run 5 to 6 days a week, and was down to a couple of times a week because her knee couldn't take it. She actually had knee surgery hoping to make it stronger so she could run more, however, it didn't work out that way. After healing from her knee surgery, she accepted her fate, and decided to take up bicycling with friends.

My mom would always say she really enjoyed bicycling, however, it was second to running. So when she talked about her headaches and it affecting her once-a-week running routine, I knew she was bummed because she lived for those runs. I wasn't surprised that she was diligent about getting rid of her headaches so she could resume her normal active lifestyle. It didn't even sound like the headaches were that bad from the way she casually mentioned them. I wrote down the date of her appointment because I wanted to make sure I didn't forget to call her and see how it went. This was how unconcerned I was.

I remember getting a phone call the day of her appointment. I don't remember who called me. Was it my sister? I remember being told of the legions found on my mom's brain and that further testing would need to be done. My parents had called the Chief of Neurology, who was a friend of theirs, and he took a look at the scan and said, "Well, the lesions don't look particularly angry." I didn't know what that meant, however, it did provide us with some hope.

I had confided in only two friends of mine at that point. After the phone call, I continued in my food preparations for the 11 women who were going to be coming over. I was hosting my first Bunco game at my house. I was mixing the salad and tears just kept running out of my eyes. I wasn't crying. Well, I was, however, I was making no sound – the tears just kept flowing and I would wipe them and keep mixing the salad.

My friend, Jamie, was one of the friends I called and told about the news. She was also in the Bunco group and she said that I can just cancel it and that everyone would understand. I didn't want to cancel on 11 people, and I thought it would be a good distraction, and it was. I always get energized spending time with people.

At the end of the evening, as people were leaving, one of the women asked me about my mom. Word must have got around. My tears immediately started to flow again. I remember the look on her face and could tell she felt really bad and didn't know what to say. I mumbled something about the lesions on my mom's brain and her expression went from bad to worse. This was my first experience with other people's reaction to this kind of sobering news. It was uncomfortable to see someone stumbling for the right words. I didn't know how to console her, or myself.

****

Fuzzy

I have a clear recollection of the day with my mom, my dad, and my sister to see about my mom's most recent test results. (After the awful CAT scan results, my mom had a CT scan and an MRI done so doctors could figure out where the brain tumors originated from.) I have a very vivid memory of sitting in the small exam room waiting for the doctor to come in. I don't even remember my mom calling me or how I found out that the doctor wanted to see her in person. I just remember that day we found out the news.

The doctor walked in looking somber. My mom really liked her doctor. She had the same one for years and was diligent with her annual checkups. She always said he was thorough, direct and competent. He had x-rays with him that he put up and he pointed to the tumors that were found in my mom's kidney, chest and lymph nodes. He said he believed the tumors originated in her kidney. We asked the obvious questions as the news started to sink in. "What does that mean?" "Can't she just get her kidney removed?" Somewhere along the line the word 'cancer' was mentioned.

What I do remember – extremely clearly – is that my sister was sitting in a chair to my left. I was also sitting in a chair. My dad was on my right in his wheelchair, a little in front of me. My mom was sitting on the patient bench with the white paper underneath her and was higher than the rest of us. I could see her profile.

The doctor said he recommends my mom consult with an oncologist as soon as possible for treatment options and he said he would give her a referral. My mom asked him if she could wait a little while, and he said, "No." We were surprised by this answer. My mom asked him to be straight with her and she wanted to know what would happen if she waited and did nothing. He said, "You probably have a month, at most."

My dad started to cry softly. He leaned over in his wheelchair and reached out as far as he could to put his arm on my mom's shoulder. I remember my mom's face – her head was tilted slightly down and she looked pensive. She was frowning thoughtfully. I remember putting my arm on my dad's shoulder, and looking down at my lap. Out of the corner of my eye, I saw my sister's hands in her lap. We were both very still. I just remember looking at my sister's hands and thinking 'I want to reach out and hold her hand', but I simply couldn't move. It was so surreal. My thoughts were slow and fuzzy.

My mom said, "But I've never been sick." No one responded. Then, abruptly, my dad's social worker skills kicked into high gear. He said, "I want a copy of her medical records so I can get a second opinion." The doctor said, "Yes, of course." He told us where the medical office was. We all filed out and it was quiet in the nurses' area. I could tell they knew what our appointment was about by the way they acknowledged us – with sadness or maybe compassion – whatever it was, it didn't feel too good. It was making it all more real. I wasn't ready for this to be real.

My dad was zooming ahead of us in his wheelchair while my mom, sister and I were huddled together walking in a zig zag, slow manner following him. I remember feeling amazed by my dad. He was so focused and sharp. I was not thinking clearly at all. By the time we turned the corner following him, he already had someone open the door for him to the medical secretary station, as we trailed in after him. He was assertive with the medical secretary and refused to come back for the records. He wanted them right then, and he got them right then. He then zipped back out of there with the folder, and we all got up from our chairs and stumbled behind him again as we left the building together.

I recall one other comment from my mom that day. She said, "I wonder who this is worse for – me or your father?" I remember thinking, 'What?! Of course YOU!' What was she talking about? She was the one with cancer! Little did I know that I would learn exactly what she meant. She knew my dad so well.

From this day forward, there wasn't one day that went by that I didn't talk to my parents – often multiple times a day. I was 100% "in".

****

Punchy

I was visiting my parents a couple of weeks after "the news". My mom and dad and I were sitting at the kitchen bar talking. My mom and I were being light-hearted and joking around. My dad was somber and rubbing his forehead with the back of his hand. Usually he was the one that joked around. Not today. My mom and I were "punchy". We found humor in everything we were saying.

My mom told me that a friend of hers in her bicycling club had loaned her a book a couple of months prior. My mom saw this friend earlier in the day, and after their bike ride they went back to my mom's car. My mom said she wanted to return the book to her. She opened her trunk and got it out to give it to her. Her friend asked if she read it, and my mom said no. Her friend went on to say how good the book was and talked about the story line, mentioning something about cadavers and how interesting it was. At this point, as my mom was relaying the story to me, I stopped her and said, "Mom, you didn't!" I was thinking, 'This isn't the time to tell your friend about your news!' My mom started laughing as she continued relaying the story.

She told her friend, "Well, my doctor said I have legions on my brain and it's cancer and I didn't feel like reading a book right now about cadavers."

Oh my God! Her poor friend! I asked my mom what happened after she said that. My mom said that her friend burst out crying and was apologizing about the book and was horrified and grabbed her and hugged her and was pretty much hysterical. My mom and I were both laughing so hard we were crying. It was completely awful and funny at the same time. My dad did not see the humor at all. Poor guy. He just sat there with his head down and his hand over his eyes.

I cannot explain why we were able to laugh so much during this time. Maybe the news was still so fresh and it hadn't sunk in yet. We didn't know really what was going on at that point even though we knew my mom had cancerous tumors in her kidney, lungs and under her breast bone and in her lymph modes and scattered throughout her entire brain. She would be starting whole brain radiation treatments immediately because the body organ the doctors were most concerned about was my mom's brain. I wasn't educated on cancer and so I didn't know my mom's situation was so dire. I was hopeful that there were treatment options. My mom probably knew the seriousness of her condition because both her parents and sister died of cancer. I'm pretty sure my dad knew also because his sister died of lung cancer and he worked at a hospital. I still had a lot to learn. I was optimistic.

What I knew at this point is that I loved my parents no matter what and I was completely comfortable in their presence. I soon learned how important this was for them – for people to be comfortable and normal in their presence. Unfortunately we found that it's very hard for some people to do this, and even with the best of intentions, some people made it harder for my parents to remain hopeful. I became very protective over them.

Before I left my parents' house that day, I thought to myself, 'What could I do to put a smile on their faces while I'm gone?' It came to me immediately. I grabbed post-it notes and wrote out a lot of them and put them all around the house and in mostly hidden places. For example, when my mom next opened her medicine cabinet in the bathroom, she would find a note that said, 'Hey there good lookin!' When she next opened her nightstand she would see, 'Sleep tight sweet thing'. When they turned a corner they would see, 'Smile! You're on candid camera!' In the knife drawer, there was a note saying, 'Careful! Sharp items! xoxo'.

They so appreciated these heartfelt little surprises and my mission was accomplished. I believe they smiled every single time they found one. I smiled just picturing them finding them.

****

Boarding the Runaway Train

I remember times in my life being moved and inspired. The love and compassion inside me would move me to do good things for people. A friend would be feeling down, and I would mail her a card, or call her to check up on her. I would hear about someone's relative passing away, and I would attend the funeral and call and/or send a card to the family. I would feel for these people and something inside me would compel me to respond in some way.

Realizing the circumstances my parents were in, and empathizing about what they might be feeling, I responded along these lines. However, up until this point in my life, my usual experience was that the love and compassion inside me would idle at a safe distance, traveling side by side in an inactive state until those moments of empathy, at which point the love and compassion would ignite and move me to action.

With my parents, the empathy I felt was overpowering. It was as if the love and compassion inside me suddenly crashed together and catapulted ahead – roaring forward in a straight line. The momentum was unstoppable. The energy running through me was involuntary and palpable.

In the midst of this current family crisis, I had a lot of clarity very early on. I believe this clarity is what kept my actions on target. I also realized that my love and compassion were all encompassing. It was not focused only on my parents. The energy of what was running through me was focused on the whole situation and every soul involved in it. It did not discriminate or hold one person over the next. My mom was the "sick one", and next in line was my dad, however, they were not more important than my siblings, myself, friends or anyone else whose lives were affected by my family's situation. I didn't have time to "use my head" so much during this time when it came to matters of the heart or people's emotional states.

I'm sure the intensity I felt was partially due to the knowledge I had about my mom's illness. While always hopeful, the real and looming possibility was that she was going to die. We did not have the luxury of time. I especially did not ignore this fact.

What was this clarity I had that caused my love and compassion to become free-flowing and uncontained?

How is it possible to have such immediate clarity in life while facing an unknown situation I had no experience in?

How was I able to sustain my outlook and actions for what ended up being 2 ½ years straight?

Why didn't I "fall apart" and disengage?

I only processed these questions after both of my parents died, when I was rolling to a stop after the long, roller coast ride with them. What I've come to realize in answer to all of the above questions is this:

I was in a state of acceptance. I didn't spend time or energy wishing things were different.
> *(This preserved my energy.)*

I did not place judgment on anyone. I was compassionate.
> *(This opened me up to love, the most*
> *powerful source of energy.)*

I had a clear and unwavering vision.
> *(This empowered me.)*

I made a choice to be fully engaged in alignment with my vision.
> *(This inspired me to action.)*

From the very beginning when I first realized the extent of my mom's illness, I had a vision for the situation. It was so clear. I wanted my parents to experience their final days in this life the way they wanted to, and I was going to take the lead to support them in this. I also wanted them to be comfortable at home with excellent care. I had very little experience in caregiving, except for my own small children. I had even less experience with medical needs and hospitals. I had never experienced someone this close to me dying. I had never experienced someone this close to me with a serious illness. I had experienced my dad's disability, however, since I could remember, his disability was very normal to our household.

I didn't know what was ahead for my parents, and it didn't matter. I didn't spend time thinking about what was ahead. My thoughts were focused on how best to handle this situation according to my parents' wishes and keeping their desires in balance with everyone else's involved.

I personally value connecting with people on a deep level. I was focused not only on my parents, but on my desire to connect with them. I knew we didn't have the luxury of time. My actions were consistent in that they were born not only from me wanting to support my parents fully during this time, but also I was willing to do anything it took in order to gain more quality time with them.

My clarity helped tremendously. Any time something would happen that wasn't in line with my vision, I automatically moved in the direction of re-alignment. For example, when my dad's first live-in (after my mom died) got so drunk she wasn't able to help my dad one night when he needed her, my sister and I went right over there at 9pm, packed her things and called her friend to pick her up. The next morning, we made many calls, and got a new live-in. There wasn't any rhetoric or drama. It was just taken care of. Was it easy? No. And that fact didn't matter. We simply acted.

****

Enter Yogi

My mom called me and asked, "Do you think the puppy is still available?"

I responded, "Why? Do you want it?"

She quietly said, "Yes," and started to cry.

"Okay!" I said immediately. "I will call the breeder and find out and call you back."

Prior to my mom's "news", she had picked out a Golden Retriever puppy from a breeder. The first question my mom asked her oncologist at their first meeting was, "Can I still get my puppy?" The doctor strongly discouraged her. My mom contacted the breeder and explained what was happening and gave the disappointing news that she would not be bringing home the puppy.

I called the breeder and the puppy was still there! I told her that we're coming that weekend to pick him up.

I called my mom back, and she was in tears she was so excited. She was so happy the puppy was still available and couldn't wait to bring him home, despite the doctor's opinion that a puppy would be too much for her. I called my brother and sister, and we all agreed we would drive to Aptos that weekend and pick up Yogi.

I never questioned my mom about her desire to take home that adorable little puppy. It didn't matter if I or anyone else thought it wasn't a good idea. What mattered was that it was important to my mom and I knew she could handle it, and even if there came a time when she couldn't, I would help. I wanted her to have what she wanted and enjoyed. I knew the companionship of dogs gave my mom so much.

On our way to the breeder that weekend, we stopped at a local coffee shop in Aptos. It was so pretty there near the ocean. The breeder lived in the mountains and there were a lot of trees around. When we arrived, puppies were running all around. We took pictures. When my mom picked up Yogi for the first time, the puppy licked her on her chin immediately.

My mom told me that day in Aptos was one of the happiest days of her life. It was a beautiful day and all of us kids were with her. My mom took Yogi home and worked with him like all the puppies she's owned in the past. She trained him well. She enjoyed him and loved him.

Four months later, my mom made the difficult decision to find a home for Yogi. She was too sick to care for him any longer. We found the woman who had adopted Yogi's brother and she drove 2 hours to come and pick up Yogi and take him to her home to live with her and her family. She showed us pictures of her huge, grassy yard and her two children and Yogi's brother. She assured us that Yogi would have a great life. I can tell the woman felt sad about taking the puppy, however, my mom let him go without a fuss.

She cried after the woman left and my brother went over to my mom and hugged her. I remember watching my brother – so tall and caring – hugging my mom as she put her head on his chest. After a few minutes, my mom said, "That's all," and stopped crying. She was strong like that. She allowed herself a certain amount of self pity, then it was over.

There is so much more to Yogi than a cute Golden Retriever puppy. It was my mom's liberty of choosing what she wanted – what was important to her. It was about her engaging fully with that puppy for as long as she could and enjoying him every step of the way – even when she was tired of getting up to care for him. She was ready to let him go when she did. It was very emotional. Every day was very emotional. So many changes were happening all the time. I thought about what Yogi represented for my mom:

Golden Boy

Your tiny feet are paws of delicate perfection.
        Through half open eyes you drink in the world.
Your body trembles with gratitude – for me,
        for me.

You see who I am, don't you? Through those sleepy eyes.
You are not alarmed by my touch
        the opposite is true.
        I love that. I love you.
But I don't really know you.
        You don't have a human soul!
                You can't know me…
                        You can't love...

This is when you nuzzle in deeper
        with effortless intention you make me see
        your body melts with adoration – for me,
                for me

On with my day
        one foot in front of the next.
I know what is waiting
        all the work at my desk.
All the people that need something and want it now.
        All the demands I place on myself
                the circles of upset I allow.

And then there is you
      my ultimate demand of the day
      completely dependent on me in every way.
      Never doubting that I'll come through for you
         the one constant in my life I know is true.
I'm starting to remember who I am
      as I eagerly greet your affection
      your squirms of excitement welcome me home.
You draw me into your fun, immersed in the moment of all you do.
      I love that. I love you.
After my third awakening in the middle of the night,
      twice for your needs and once for mine,
         I happily watch you sleep.
I marvel at your breathing – unaffected and pure.
      Are those smiles of enjoyment I see?
      Drinking in the world even in your dreams!
         I want that – for me,
            for me.

Here I am in the dark before dawn, like so many times in the past,
      only now I have my golden boy to join me on my path.

You may not be my savior, in the body of this young pup,
      but the message you send me constantly
      one I clearly forgot and need reminding of
         is that I'm worthy, I'm beautiful,
         I am loved.

    I had no idea when I shared this poem the impact it would have. Using his typing stick, my dad emailed me after he read it:

> *dear lea,*
> *   i never get on the computer this time in the morning, particularly when i'm going to work, but i just read your poem, after wiping my eyes with kleenex every other paragraph.*

this is absolutely the best ever!!!!!!!!!!!!

you incredibly captured mom's emotions (and mine), and more importantly, you showed that you really understand why this little creature is such a big deal for us.

i like mom's response about it not being "a savior" but i am amazed how the Holy Spirit works in all of us, you with this poem, and even through a little creature (Golden Boy).

It also meant so much that you drove mom that day you're taking the time to do us this favor, without hesitation. you're lack of hesitation is what made me cry over the phone. it showed that at that time, we were a priority for you!

i certainly realize that why it can't be that way all the time, with any of you kids, cause you have you're own lives, but i so much love and appreciate all of you (including mom!), regardless of what you do.

(hope this makes sense).

THAT POEM IS A TREASURE.

with much love to all,   dad.

****

Alignment and Insight

The day we found out the most devastating news of my mom's condition – when we learned that the chemo didn't do anything for my mom – was the day before my scheduled 9-day leadership seminar with a group of 100 women on a ranch. It had been several months since the news of my mom's cancer diagnosis. My mom had already been through whole brain radiation treatments which were 'successful' in that her tumors shrunk and she no longer had headaches. My mom did a round of chemo and lost her hair. (My dad shaved his head to support her. My dad had also decided to retire from his job at the VA. Even though he couldn't physically help my mom, he sure was helping her emotionally. He was right there by her side.)

The doctors were willing to do more chemo treatments for my mom if she wanted, however, they did not think it would improve her situation, although it may extend her life. She would also feel very sick (which my mom already experienced with the first round.) My mom decided not to do any more chemo. We all respected her decision. My mom loved to be active in life, and without chemo, she could still be active, even though potentially her life would be shorter.

I remember sitting next to her in the hospital lobby in a sunny atrium, and I had my head on her shoulder. Our whole family was just sitting there absorbing this news. I started crying softly as I leaned against her. I had such high hopes for her treatment and it was very discouraging and disappointing to hear the doctor say there is nothing they could really do for her. My mom was a little out of it. She said a couple of things that didn't make sense. She mumbled something about me being without a mother and then shook her head as if dazed when she said it. I felt so bad for her. What was it like to hear that kind of news? I didn't know. I really had no idea. I just hugged her and we cried together.

That evening I had such a bad headache. The kind of headache where the pain is pinpointed in one place, unrelenting and pounding. These headaches were rare for me, but when they did happen, I was usually down for the count. However, I had to pack for my seminar. I knew I had to go. My head hurt so much my eyes were watering and one of my eyes was closed shut. I began packing. I told myself, 'I don't care about this headache. I'm getting ready. I'm going.' There was nothing I could do for my mom at this moment. She had my dad and plenty of people around her. I knew if I didn't go to this seminar now, it would be a missed opportunity that could very well help me navigate through what was happening with our family crisis.

I continued to pack and was getting nauseous. It didn't matter. I threw up, and then continued packing. Oliver and the kids helped me with getting the tent ready. Thank God I had already practiced setting it up the weekend before. I'm not a camper and had to learn so much for the trip since I knew it included isolated camping of some sort. That part was not something I was looking forward to.

I arrived at the ranch the next morning and stood with the large group, listening to instructions. I began wondering what I was doing there. I wasn't operating at my best. That first night at the ranch, I slept only one hour or so. I was uncomfortable in my tent. It was angled and on rocks. I was happy that I put the tent together properly on my own though. I was also exhausted from the group exercise that lead us to our destination. When we finally arrived and settled in for the night, I was wishing I had packed a rolled up cushion to sleep on.

As the seminar progressed, I learned many things. That week, there were moments that I laughed so hard, tears were rolling down my face. It felt so good to laugh like that. What a pressure release. There were also times I cried just as hard as I laughed. Either way, I released a lot from inside me. I thought this seminar was about leadership – leading others. It was not. It was about 'leadership of self'. I learned the only way to even begin to lead others is to first lead myself. There was a lot of soul searching that happened during this week. There were also physical challenges that I experienced – all of which I overcame and realized just how capable I am.

During my alone-time in my tent, I created my first draft of my personal vision statement for my life. This experience at the ranch was perfect timing and supported me immensely for what laid ahead of me when I returned home. It wasn't only the events I participated in, but it was also the fact that I made the decision to go in the first place. I had every reason not to attend. Oliver and I had our business, and Dom and Sophie needed care, and my parents needed support.

Even with all these facts, I intuitively knew that *I needed support.* I wanted to be a certain way during this family crisis. I knew I had to take care of myself. This time away on this ranch was the first of many choices I made toward self-care – toward re-grouping to assess my own frame of mind and my own needs. I just knew that if I wasn't clear on "what's really going on" in my life, I would forever live in chaos – at the whim of everyone else's needs. I also knew that I couldn't be the woman I know I am if I didn't STOP in life to ask myself questions – to get to know myself, and care for myself in a gentle, loving and forgiving way.

What I'm writing here was only clear at the time intuitively. I also believe that the experience I had through the process of working out my earlier marital issues gave me valuable insight from which to pull from during the crisis with my parents' circumstances. I learned how to observe, surrender, and act from compassion. Now I have gained the added clarity of being able to write what I learned. This is power, because I can duplicate these lessons in a conscious way now. I can also attempt to explain to others what I've learned, although I know it's not so much what I say, it's more about how I live.

My personal vision is what I fall back on in life. It helps me know what to do when I don't know what to do. It's something I recite almost daily. The interesting thing is, even in my failed attempts to live it, I still feel good. I feel good because I know I'm being me. I know I'm making my best efforts in life. That's all I can ever do – is my best effort. Since I first created my vision statement I've molded it more and more. Here's my latest version, which I only slightly modified since I first wrote it in my tent at the ranch:

> *I am a compassionate and courageous woman, committed to engaging with people in an open and playful way, having faith that through God's grace and surrendering to his guidance, the lives I touch with love, integrity, and gratitude, will bring forth the peace and humanity within each of us, creating a ripple effect of kindness and joy.*

What ripple effect do I want to create? Kindness and joy. Will I succeed? It doesn't really matter, because the outcome is out of my control. Why bother with a vision then? My vision is the ideal world I want to live in. I can only control how I'm being and what I do, and that's more than enough to make a difference. I believe that what I do does have the potential to change the world *because of the ripple effect*. This frees me of any pressure because I only need to focus on what I can control – which is me – and the rest will happen on its own.

"I didn't create this universe and I'm not running it."

(Author Unknown)

Who am I?

What is important to me?

How do I want to be?

What can I do?

"The quality of your life depends partly upon the quality of the questions you ask yourself daily."

(Quote by Dr. John Demartini)

I felt like a fish out of water during this family crisis. But I approached it with a "let's do this" mindset. I knew I could figure it out, God willing, and with the right support and resources. The pace was fast and chaotic, and nothing felt secure. I was in it, riding the waves. In the midst of it all, the paradox was, there was more living going on during these short months of my mom's illness compared to the entire 10 years of my life prior.

This small window of time during my mom's illness was real, raw life – rich with meaning and full of love. I was amazed at the power of it all. The intensity, while unwelcome, I decided to embrace. In doing so, ironically, embracing the journey toward death was nothing short of magic – not in a fabulous sense, but in a sense of pure perfection. There is a sense of freedom that comes with the absolute knowing that all is happening exactly as it's supposed to.

Again, these thoughts I write in retrospect. After the crush of grief and the bombardment of *big life questions* that came flooding from inside of me to the outside, to be answered back from within. Even though I speak of the journey with my parents at the end of their lives, it's the journey *after* my parents left this planet that has been most impactful. Why? Because of the absolute realization that I, and every person alive, are all on a journey toward death. So why don't we feel the magic of life? More insights to come.

****

The Mind

My mom was interested in seeing her cousins who live in San Jose. She was particularly fond of her cousin, Chris. She had very good memories of joking around with him, and the days when he would chaperone when my mom and dad first dated. My mom enjoyed the company of men more often than women. She felt comfortable in their presence. She liked the easy conversation and the absence of drama. My mom wanted to see Chris and her other cousins, so I coordinated a trip. My sister and brother-in-law, Norman, came also.

We weren't there for very long and my mom soon wanted to go home. She asked for a cell phone and wanted to call my dad. She had trouble dialing the phone and I could tell her anxiety was rising. I noticed that she was becoming more and more uncomfortable without my dad around. My dad and her dog, Emma, were like her security blankets. My mom was never quite comfortable in larger groups, so even more so now, I think she just couldn't handle it. It also had to do with the fact that she was having trouble following conversations. We found out later that her brain radiation treatments caused a side effect that affected her brain function, particularly her memory. Norman offered to take my mom home. He had just barely arrived and he turned around and graciously left with my mom.

Later that evening, my sister and I had a 3 hour conversation on the phone. We've never talked on the phone for this long. The main theme of the call – my mom. We talked about my mom's erratic behavior. At this point in my mom's illness, my mom could still communicate and take care of herself. She was acting pretty much like normal, although had higher anxiety for sure. My sister sympathized with my mom, however, it's really hard to be around someone who is so anxious and shows it in 'mean' ways – especially toward my dad. My mom often voiced her dissatisfaction in dramatic ways.

I wondered, 'What's the difference between my mom's brain causing her behavior or her personality causing it?' One thought was that if her brain was causing her erratic behavior, then she cannot help it, whereas, if *she* is acting out, she knows better and should be able to control it. I concluded that it's not that simple.

My mom and I were similar in personalities in certain ways. We are both organized, efficient, sharp, strong, reliable, quick-tempered when under stress, have challenges being flexible and asking for support, are dedicated, trustworthy, comfortable with routines, have high expectations of people which often led us to feelings of disappointment, etc. I could really relate to my mom, and I understood her 'poor behavior' was caused by triggers that she just didn't know how to handle. I explained to my sister (who has a different personality type) that I believe very strongly that during those times my mom lashes out reactively, she is in pain – she is hurting the most. (I felt like I knew this because for myself, when I get triggered and lash out, it's the most miserable feeling I have.)

I was trying to give my sister a peek into our world. I've always admired my sister's ability to hold her tongue and keep her cool. I have more of that 'hot-headed Italian' vibe in moments of stress. In one sense I like this about me because I release the stress (although unfortunately my family is the one that usually gets the brunt of it). Ever more, I'm changing this about myself because I realize it's hurtful to people, creates distance with the people I love most, is disempowering for me, and just not how I want to be. I'm learning new ways to handle stress – like taking more time for myself. This quiet time on my own fuels me back up and calms me down. I'm vigilant in carving out this time now because I know how much it benefits, not only me, but everyone around me.

I don't believe it matters what caused my mom's outbursts, or whether she should be able to control it or not. Because the "outbursts" gave her much-needed anxiety relief, I don't believe my mom could control them in the moment. She didn't know how – just like if her brain is causing her behavior – she cannot control that either. This didn't make her reactive outbursts okay. It's just a point I'm making to better understand it from the outside looking in. I still very much believe that when people act out reactively, there is just pain all the way around. My mom was an awesome woman – so much strength, love and character. This reactive subject is one that is close to my heart. I just "get it", so I'm more empathetic when I witness it.

I've learned that I can change any part of me that I want to change. It's not easy, but I can. Years ago I didn't think like this. I just thought, 'It's just the way I am. It's my personality.' Now, I think, 'It's my default way because it's what I'm used to. It's not who I am.' Once I acknowledged this, I discovered there were so many things I could practice to level out my emotions – such as asking myself questions: "What is really going on here?" "What am I feeling?" "What do I really want?" "What are my choices?" "How do I want to be?" Then practice, practice, practice – knowing there is no end, however, there is *progress* and it's the progress that makes all the difference. Each time I'm successful being how I want to be, especially in the midst of triggers or stress, I gain real evidence that change is possible – not only possible, but inevitable.

I'm including one of my poems below because it relates to this issue of reactivity and the suffering it causes. Out of all the poems I've written, I found two of them printed out and sitting in a folder my mom kept in her desk drawer. Below is one of those two poems. I found it after she died. I'll never really know if this poem held some significance

for my mom, or if it was just a coincidence that she kept it in her folder.
I tend to think it struck a chord inside her.

The Torture Dance

I realize what I'm doing is wrong, shortly after I'm doing it.
        This means I'm getting better, right?

It's been almost too late for way too long.
        Is this the day?

He need not say anything anymore.
Sometimes when he walks near me
        I feel him fading right through me.

As I pass by him, I want to hug him
            but I don't.
I realize it's not that I can't
            I just won't.

He doesn't say good morning anymore,
or smile my way, or kiss me goodbye,
or wish me a pleasant goodnight.
        I just realized
                neither do I.

I cry more often than ever before
        and breathe deeply as the tears fall.
I don't interfere as I feel them softly roll
        and rest where they may.
Ahhh – it's kind of nice.
        But not for long.

My past - the memories - they haunt me.
I feel them seep into my body and move about,
        until they finally join the chaos in my head.

Thoughts frantically skipping around in the confines of my skull
    doing their torture dance.

It's then that I notice the luggage by the door
    sitting mischievously.
I swear they're smiling at me.

    This is the day.

My body does not move, yet inside I'm being pulled down,
    slowly and systematically.
I thrash about, screaming insanely within –
    wildly and without inhibition.
My internal wails manifest into a mere tremble
    for my husband to see...
        He has no idea what's going on inside of me.

I actually feel his sadness.
His posture displays clear defeat.

As he gently closes the door behind him,
I think of those times he expressed his fears to me.
    My focus on his faults.
    My hampering on his dreams.
    My frustrations with all the little things.
    My sudden reactive outbursts
        over events so minor
        so meaningless
        so inherently insignificant.

How many times did I vow to change?
    He probably knows the exact number.
Why didn't I stop my hurtful ways?
    This I cannot answer.

So I do what I think, and nothing more.
    I trust the feeling of comfort and its deception of peace.

I hold on to what is familiar - my own destructive stance,
even as my mind starts racing again
and my thoughts begin
their torture dance.

I told my sister about what happened when we came home from our cousins' house that day when my mom was acting so unreasonably. I went to my parents' house after. My mom was very upset. She was yelling at my dad. I remember her angry tone as she was pacing around the house. I was sitting at the kitchen table, very calm. I was leaning back in the chair just watching the scene. After a certain amount of time she stopped ranting. I got up, went to her and gave her a hug. She started crying and sobbing and I just hugged her and told her, "It's all okay." She had no more anger left inside her.

She was in emotional pain. Pure and simple. Does this mean I want to be around that level of upset on a regular basis? No. However, I chose to sit with it at that moment. It was kind of surreal when it was happening. I was actually quite relaxed at the kitchen table, leaning back in the chair. I wasn't enjoying myself by any means, however, I felt a loving energy inside me. I was acutely aware of the emotions in that room – my mom's and my dad's. I had compassion for them and just let my intuition guide me. The truth is:

"People need loving the most when they deserve it the least."

(Quote by Louise Hays)

By the time I left the house that day I definitely felt like I left my parents in peace. I don't feel I did anything nor did I have a false sense of power that I could bring them out of their emotions. What really happened was that I didn't interfere in what I intuitively felt was a natural release of pent-up emotions. I also intuitively felt it was necessary to stay in the room at the time it was happening. Time stood still. At no time did I have a desire for the moment to be any different than it was. I felt like I tasted freedom – to be at peace in the midst of chaos. It was only because of my feelings of peace, which protected my energy, that I was then able to approach my mom with love at the moment my intuition guided me.

****

Gradual Shift

It's interesting, now that I look back, that my dad and my siblings and I took so long to "get" that my mom needed someone at the house much more often, including overnight. She was always the one who took care of things for the family. We were used to looking to her for solutions, so it was simply odd to now have to consider that she was the one in need.

My mom's biggest frustration was not being able to drive. She loved her car, a 1969 SS Chevelle. She had this car since 1970 and it represented freedom to her. She really enjoyed driving her car and the deep hum of the 396 engine. My sister was the keeper of the car keys, and my mom was so angry with her. Even though we explained why she could not drive – she could hurt someone or herself – she wasn't agreeing with us. My poor sister. I remember my mom looking at her in anger and demanding she give her the car keys. My sister slowly shook her head back and forth, looking very uncomfortable, yet standing her ground, as she gently and firmly said, "No."

We called Dr. North, who was willing to be the "bad guy" to explain to my mom why he cannot allow her to drive. After that phone call, my mom did agree. It seemed to make a difference that a doctor told her. She was very sad about her loss of independence. She was experiencing loss after loss. At this point, it was approximately 8 months after her diagnosis.

I witnessed something that gave me more of an understanding of how much my mom was affected by her loss of independence. One day, my dad left through the back door of the house and went down the ramp, heading for his van to go out for a bit. I saw my mom's back as she stood at the door with her hands on her hips staring after him. I walked over to my mom and stood next to her. She looked mad. She said, "Look at him. He can just go and do whatever he wants." I stared at my mom, then I looked into the distance at my dad as he maneuvered his wheelchair onto the lift to get into his van. My mom was jealous of my dad's "freedom"? He needs so much care just to get out of bed, go to the bathroom, bathe, eat, etc. But then, I understood. I stood next to my mom and followed her gaze as she glared at my dad while he struggled to get into his van. Even though he had his disability, he could still get out on his own. My mom was actually more limited than he was in many ways.

On another occasion, I remember my dad casually saying to my mom, "You know, I could go first. Who knows. I could have a heart attack or something." My mom reacted immediately. She said angrily, "Don't you dare! Don't you dare go first!" It was kind of comical in a dark way. I suppose that was her way of expressing that she needed him.

We all dealt with the progression of my mom's disease. The doctor explained that the brain radiation, while it did its job in shrinking the tumors, caused a negative side effect. The lining of her brain was deteriorating, and my mom was experiencing forgetfulness similar to a dementia patient.

My mom called me while I was at work. She was having trouble with her printer and was very upset. She had worked for several hours on a document and then could not print it. I attempted to help her over the phone without success. It was very unusual that my mom called me at work, especially for something like this. By the time I was at her house next, she lost interest in the printing. That was the last project she ever worked on. I remember feeling bummed for her that she wasn't able to complete it herself that day and feel that sense of satisfaction.

When I went to her house a day or so later, she was having trouble with balancing her checkbook. At the time, I didn't think much of it and listened to her questions to help her. I didn't think at first how strange it was that a bookkeeper was having trouble balancing her checkbook. She showed me her statement and started using her calculator to add up numbers. It didn't make sense as I watched her. When she didn't get the number she was looking for, she said, "Well, maybe if I try this…" and I watched as she took the same numbers and started subtracting them instead of adding them. I was very confused. I started realizing she was also sincerely confused. That was the point in which I took over my parents' finances, and she let me. I'm not sure if she realized what was happening, but it wasn't normal for her to relinquish control like that.

Our family all witnessed more and more incidents of my mom's odd behavior. It was obvious she was not able to think straight. She started making coffee constantly throughout the day. She would go to pour a cup of coffee then put her cup in the sink instead and turn the water on full blast into the cup. She would also take a full cup of coffee and pour it into the back of the coffee pot. The coffee pot overflowed many times. Also, the microwave became an issue. She wouldn't remember what she put in there, and would cook things over and over.

We really knew she was having trouble when it came to Emma. I saw her put boiling water in the dog bowl. Also, once she forgot to bring Emma in from outside and Emma was left out all night.

Even with all these examples, and after the doctor told us what he thought was happening, it took our friend, Lori, to point out the obvious. My parents needed someone in their home much more often to help my mom. My dad, with his disability, simply couldn't help her. In fact, he often skipped meals because he couldn't get my mom to help him pull things out of the refrigerator. You would think my dad would have been the first one to recognize the problem. Our family just had a hard time coming to terms with the fact that my mom – the leader – wasn't able to take charge anymore.

****

Special Delivery

After a visit with my parents one day, I said my goodbyes and started walking to the front door. For some reason, I decided to turn around and look back at my parents as they sat in their usual places. The sun had set and the house was quiet. I saw my dad's back as he sat at his desk. I then glanced at my mom as she sat on the couch. All the attention in the past months had been devoted to my mom and her cancer, and the doctors' shocking news of her terminal illness.

I suddenly had so much compassion for my dad. He never complained since my mom's diagnosis. He used his social worker skills and helped as much as possible during this time. What he couldn't do for her physically, was made up for by his presence and what he did for her emotionally. He was amazing, as was my mom. All of us always thought my dad would "go" first – including him. He even had a song picked out that he told me he wanted to play for my mom at his funeral some day: "Come Rain or Come Shine" by Ray Charles.

What must this experience these past months be like for my dad? My dad couldn't converse with my mom anymore. She just couldn't hold a thought for more than a few seconds. What must he be feeling? What would make him feel better? WAS THERE ANYTHING I COULD DO FOR HIM? On my drive home that day, the below poem came out from inside me, and I walked in the front door of my house, found paper, and wrote my thoughts down – in letter form – from my mom to my dad. I had no idea the impact this letter would have.

When I gave this letter to my dad, he sobbed like I never saw him sob before. I started to second guess myself if this was such a good idea. My dad reassured me though, numerous times, how much my poem comforted him, even after my mom died. He said he ALWAYS thought of her when he felt the warmth of the sun. I am so happy I was able to provide some comfort to my dad during his times of grief.

To Dad: A Letter to you from Mom, your Wife
(Some things I believe, if she could, she would write)

Dear Hank,

There's a woman inside me, and she often forgets,
    so please remember
        for her.
    But for me, there is no need for such clarity.

My brain will lose connection time and again,
        but know that I will not.
                I will not.

So when the woman inside me asks you to explain,
        and you struggle to do your best,
                I ask, for her sake,
                to let go of what grips you.
                See me instead of the woman in need.

I may appear anxious.
I may look confused.
I may seem frustrated, angry and uptight.
        At times, the woman inside me is all of these things.
                I, however, am not
                        and can never be.

Thank you for being close by her side
        when she needs you the most.
        Oh, the burden you must bear.
        Will it get easier? For you and the woman in need?
                This remains to be seen.
        Any which way it goes, it's all okay and just as it should be.

Sometimes I wonder if you understand the woman inside me.
        It's okay to wonder.
                It's okay with me.

She favors you, you know. She always will.
        She becomes anxious at those times you choose
                to leave the house,
                        even though your outings are brief.

        Why does she feel this way?
                Why doesn't she acknowledge you
                        for all the loving things you do and say?

It's okay to wonder.
  It's okay with me.

What challenges lie ahead remain to be seen.
  Let's not waste precious energy.
How to best support this woman in need?
  She must feel scared and alone at times.
    After all, she has quite a cross to bear.
  She must feel loved and cherished as well,
    with all her family and friends that care.

Trust that through God's grace
  you will know what to do
    and that is…to simply be you.

This is not your obligation or responsibility.
  Just think of it as your gift to me.

In this time of uncertainty, constant change, blessings and strife,
  isn't it natural to want something on which to rely?
    Cravings for stability.
    Yearnings for security.

I hope you'll find comfort knowing this….

The sun will set this evening,
  and will rise soon enough again,
    repeating this pattern day after day.
  More often than not, her rays will be generous.

Soak in the warmth and think of me –
  not the woman in need.
Think of the love that is all I am and all I can ever be.
  Love me, even when I'm not here to see.

And as you enjoy the sunshine, know one more thing.
The rays that touch you –
they are tender kisses from heaven
being sent special delivery
to you from me.

Love always,
Brenda

****

Children in the Mix

Oliver, Dominic and Sophie were so much a part of this journey with my parents. They were my support system. It felt like I had a new job or a new project that they were backing me up on – but it was much more intense than this because of the element of serious illness, emotional upset, and constant changes. I would bring the kids with me often to my parents' house. They understood "Grandma is sick" and that "Mommy is helping". They would play at my parents' house, like usual. My parents saved the doll house people and little furniture from when I was a child. My sister and I would play for hours with those toys, and now our kids played with them and enjoyed them just as much. The kids were learning and absorbing more than I realized during this time.

One morning, Sophie, then 5 years old, woke me up in my bedroom. "Mommy," she said quietly as she pushed on my arm and shook me awake.

"Good morning, " I said with my eyes half open.

"Mommy, come here, come – I have a gift for you," Sophie said.

"Okay, Sophie," I said as I slowly got up out of bed. As much as I wanted to lie in bed a few more minutes, I couldn't say no to her.

She took my hand and led me to the other side of the bed and was motioning me down to the floor. I got on my knees.

She said, "No, no, go down more."

I said, "You mean sit?" She said yes. I sat down with my legs crisscrossed.

I was really curious what was going on. She went behind me. All of a sudden I felt her tiny fingers massaging my shoulders. She said, "See, Mommy – like you do for Grandma."

It's hard to explain what emotion went through me as I felt her tiny fingers massaging the top of my shoulders. I can just say it was the sweetest, most endearing feeling knowing how much Sophie understood. She must have witnessed how much my mom really enjoyed the massages I would give her. My mom would sit on the floor on the carpet in her family room with her legs straight out in front of her. I would sit on the chair behind her and give her a neck and shoulder massage. I never saw Sophie really paying attention to this. She just fluttered about the house. Obviously she saw more than I realized (as kids usually do).

For me, as a wife and mother and business partner, my time and energy were definitely being shifted during this crisis. I don't recall Oliver ever complaining about my decisions. He truly was my hero during this time. Not only did he take over certain responsibilities I had in the business, he was "Mr. Mom" more often at home. I cannot tell you what a gift this was to me. He made it much easier for me to find the liberty to be with my parents the way I wanted to be. My conscious was much more at peace knowing Dominic and Sophie were in Oliver's care. My friends also helped out a lot during this time. I would call them sometimes during an unexpected emergency with my parents and ask them if they could pick up the kids from school for me, and they would – no questions asked.

I did not hide what was happening from Dominic and Sophie. I remember one time Dominic saying, "You're going over Grandma's again? When will you be done helping her?" I realized that in his mind I wasn't doing a very good job at helping. Another time I remember Sophie sitting next to me on the couch while I was talking to my friend on the phone. Tears were falling down my face and Sophie was watching me. She got close to my face and put her hand on my cheek. I told her, "I'm sad right now. It's okay to be sad." She nodded. As young as she was, she really did seem to understand. I really felt it was important not to hide my emotions. They also got to see me feeling better too, and laughing. I felt it was important that they see me express a wide range of emotions.

I continued with my work in our IT business. The fact is, crisis rarely happens at the most convenient times. I had a lot of responsibility in the business and was in the office 3 days a week and worked from home too. Then, I would pick up the kids from school and help them with homework, Oliver and I would make dinner and I would do chores and laundry, tuck the kids in bed and fall asleep as I was reading them books as they nudged me awake, "Mommy! Keep reading!"

What my siblings and I were doing for my parents during this time was like being in training for a job that required emotional intelligence to succeed. Because my sister and I were self-employed, we had flexibility to respond to the ever-changing crisis, however, the downside was, no one could take our work shifts. Our work waited for us. It was extremely challenging to temporarily hire someone to do my duties because our business was small and my responsibilities involved 'wearing many hats.' Had I known my mom's illness was coming, I could have found the help I needed in the business. I also had no way of anticipating what was going to happen even a day later. Had I known this chaos would last almost 2 and ½ years straight, I probably would have hired some help in the beginning. But that's not how it went.

There were times when I was driving on my way to work and I

would pass up the office and park at the nearby vineyards and sit in my car. I would just sit there. It was a survival instinct. I had never felt more overwhelmed in my entire life. I was in the position when all those balls in the air came down, and it was simply not possible to pick them back up. They were scattered too far and wide. The odd thing was there was a certain peaceful feeling that came with this fact.

The act of surrendering is powerful. It's not like I shrugged my shoulders and thought, "Oh well. It's impossible to keep up. Too bad. So sad." It was more like, "Oh, God. I really cannot keep up. Okay then. I'll keep doing my best. I trust You that all will be okay." For some strange reason, I did feel everything was okay.

At those times when I felt I didn't have the time to take a break, were the exact times that I stopped. I would pull over my car, or sit down wherever I happen to be, and just sit in complete silence for about 10 or 15 minutes. Then I would get up and continue my responsibilities. There was no such thing as 'family leave' from my work like my parents' doctor suggested when I questioned how we could continue to manage my parents' care. I became quite resourceful. My vision was clear.

Part Four

Devotion

In the midst of all the experiences I was having during this journey alongside my parents, the most impactful lesson I received was the realization I had after <u>one comment</u> my dad made to me. I'm sure he had no clue how his comment impacted me.

I stood in front of my parents' front door, ready for my next visit. Whenever I visited them it was as if I was entering a different world. Time stood still there. Things were calm, yet magnified. I enjoyed these visits. Compared to my normal life, it was actually pretty relaxing over there. I could just *be*. Time was a paradox. While I felt like I had all the time in the world, it flew by. Six hours felt like ½ hour, and an hour felt like 10 hours. Time had no relevance.

This particular day, I entered the house like I always did. I opened the door and said cheerfully, "Hi! I'm here!"

I heard my dad's reaction. He sighed and said, *"Lea, whenever you come over it's as if a light just entered the room."*

I was taken off guard. I felt confused for a moment by his statement. You see, during these visits, during the doctor appointments, the caregiver interactions, the managing of the finances, during all the many human interactions I had daily, I wasn't strategizing or thinking very clearly. I just did what had to be done. What was my dad talking about?

Me being "*a light*"? I felt totally inept most of the time, tired and disheveled, as I did my best to work through the chaos. I could sense though by the way he said that statement, and the expression I saw on his face (which I still remember clearly) that he had SO MUCH appreciation for me.

I wanted to know what I was doing that had such a positive effect on him. In that moment my mind was spinning. I was thinking, 'I want to duplicate whatever I did so he can feel this way again'.

I asked him, "Dad, what am I doing that makes you feel that way?"

My dad shook his head and said, "No, no, you don't understand. *It's just who you are*."

I didn't say a word. I stood there feeling totally raw and at the same time totally lovable. In that moment I suddenly understood something – really understood – and my life is forever changed by this knowing. I realized that not only was I enough, but that there was nothing I needed to DO. The awesome reality is that it was ME that my dad appreciated more than anything I was doing for him. Sure, I had skills that I was putting to good use that benefited him and my mom greatly, however, I understood that while I did do things that helped them, what was the most meaningful to my dad, and what carried him, was my *essence*.

Before this moment, I did not view myself as my dad did. I like myself, but did I feel like I was a "*light*" and that my mere presence could have such an impact on another human being? I'm trying my best to explain how I felt that day, and how I still feel – not only about myself, but about everyone around me. I actually see people differently now. Everyone has a light, with different degrees of brightness, ready to illuminate in full force at any moment.

****

The Thing Is

Looking back, I think that part of why my dad's comment was so impactful to me was because he said it – not in response to something I strived to do and executed successfully – but in response to how I was *being*. I was just being *me* – with no "conscious trying". If I had been feeling in that moment "on" and accomplished and that I was being a "star performer", I probably wouldn't have been as affected by his comment that I was like a "light that entered the room". After all, I understand the concept of what it means to be a star in life – to work hard and perform well. I've always had a sense of great satisfaction at these times. It feels good to be a star! However, in that moment, and in many, many moments throughout my parents' journey, I did not feel like a "star performer" – I felt wide-eyed, in shock a lot of the time, acting out of necessity and not when I felt ready, stumbling, messing up and re-correcting, grateful when things went well, and willing, while not necessarily ready, for anything.

The truth is, my dad didn't care what I looked like or how many times I messed up. He probably saw me as a shining angel with a clipped wing. I take that back. He didn't even notice my clipped wing. He just saw my *light* and it was *a gift that I gave to him*, and *his appreciation* was *a gift that he gave to me*. There is no other gift in life that can compare to the gift we give when we allow the essence of who we are to be shown to another, and moreover, when that essence is fully received. This exchange is nothing short of magic. It's like heaven on earth.

It took me a couple of years to make sense of what I learned that day at my parents' house. One day as I was walking to my treadmill for a workout, instead of starting my run, I was inspired to turn around and go into my home office. I leaned over my desk, took a piece of scrap paper and wrote out the below poem.

The Thing Is

The thing is, I've received this gift,
      but it's hard to describe what it is
      in words…this knowing…this gift that came to me.

I once thought words were so meaningful
      and now I know
          their extreme limitations.

This gift I received from the depths of realness
      is not a gift received and taken with our hands.
      They're all good – the gifts that can be grasped.
      Who says these tangible gifts aren't real?
         I, for one, say they are not.

What is real is the stirring that arose inside the soul
to compel the offer from which one can grasp.
      They're all good – the tangible.
         Yet there is something incomparably better.
      This something is the only thing that really matters in life.
      This something – there are no sufficient words for.
      There are no adequate labels that exist in the world
         for the *grandness gifts of all.*

Yet words can help the imagination of it.
Words can help put the thoughts in the mind,
      from which point that thought has a chance to travel on a
      treacherous journey –
         a journey that is not real, yet must be endured
           ready or not.

This journey is filled with risks at every turn – joyful and sorrowful,
      happy and filled with angst.
It's dangerous and exciting and at times extremely passive and flat.

It hurts – a lot.
There is pain that will persist
      right before the floodgates open
allowing the beauty of it all to rush in to meet
      the soft pounds of your heart –
give…..receive….give…..receive…..with each gentle and resilient beat.

The journey is challenging and downright hard, and whether you
      embrace it and step into it,
          or hold yourself back in tight resistance,
    you will move through it,
      because you must.
    Because there is no other way
      because the alternative isn't an option for you
          any longer.

You will thrive or decay, because movement is real
    not stability.
    Nothing real stands still.

Movement, action, being, dancing, shouting, laughing, sobbing,
    scribbling, giving it your all, with all you have to give,
      from where you have to give it –
    All these wonderful words that cannot do justice
      to the gifts I speak of.
    The craziness of it all, yet the goodness of it all –
      simply what is.

    And it is good.
    And what is good?
    You can feel it
      and *you can feel when it's real.*

Action is happening whether you're physically moving or not.

Your greatest pursuits are born from the confines of your stillness
    in the intentional pursuits of your mind
       from which place you take action…
          bursts of effortless moments upon moments ….
          adding up to your dreams.

Then marvel at the actual ease of it all.

Our journey is about hellos and goodbyes.
    It's about you and me.
It's about showing up in all our glory
    and being humbled by all our flaws.
It's about all the little happenings
    in between the low and high extremes
       and how we choose to be.

    It's about seeing the goodness in it all -
    the grandness and richness of it all
       no matter how wonderful or how tragic.
    It's about having the courage to be <u>you</u>
       in every possible moment you can.
    It's about allowing the gift of yourself
       to shine in the world.

This gift I speak of, that cannot be described in words –
    the only thing real in this world –
       is that which is good in you…and me….
         and every other human being –
    All that is good
       in action.

    But it's not what you can see or figure out.

It is not what you can see or figure out.
    So stop.
    Stop trying.

What's real is the stirring in our soul
  connecting with the souls of others
    inspired by the simplicity of
    authenticity and compassion.
There is no right way. So there is no pressure.
There is no "should" or "have to".
There is nothing to do because it's always been there
  and can never leave.

There is a goodness in all of us,
  the gift of which can only be felt
  when we allow ourselves to embrace our nature –
    our unique and loving nature
  and then move in the world from this place.

  Move in the world from this place.

No matter what – we are human –
  so we can expect to start and fail –
  and start we must
  and trust the abundance of retakes in the waiting.

  Start again and again
    being who you are
    wherever you are
    whatever you're doing
    however you're feeling

  Enjoy the simplicity and celebrate.

From here the gifts abound –
  flowing out and in and back again…
    the gifts that cannot be grasped.

The grandness gifts of all are circling around
within our reach
coming to us
as we give .... and receive....
with each gentle and resilient beat.

****

Love

Expressions. They speak many, many words in one instantaneous moment. It's really incredible when I think about this. For me, seeing my dad in helpless situations was common. He had a serious disability. He was used to needing help, and learned to graciously receive it. My mom on the other hand, was not used to needing help, or receiving it. The day with my parents at a coffee shop was a moment I will never forget. It was the last time my mom was out in public.

My dad and I encouraged my mom to get out a bit and come with us to the coffee shop. We knew she enjoyed coffee shops, as she would often go after her runs or with her bike club. She and my dad would meet at the local coffee shop just about every morning before they went to work. It was almost like a neighborhood bar, only they served coffee instead of alcohol.

My mom hesitated to go because she wasn't feeling well, but agreed. This is the day it really hit me how sick she was – seeing her out in public. She leaned on me as I helped her to the door of the coffee shop. She was only able to shuffle her feet. It took a while to get from the handicapped parking space to the door, and then I helped her sit down at the first table available.

We weren't there long. We had just ordered, and my mom said she had to go to the bathroom, and she started getting panicky. I immediately helped her stand, and then looked around and realized how far the bathroom was. It was no great distance for the average customer, however, with my mom not being able to move well, I knew it would take at least 5 minutes to get to the far end of the restaurant. We started our journey – my mom shuffling and me holding her up, guiding her. We entered the bathroom stall and I was thankful we were by ourselves in that bathroom. I realized quickly that my mom needed more help than just walking.

I could tell by my mom's expression that she was embarrassed and uncomfortable. She had a nervous smile and averted her eyes. She surrendered all resistance as I helped her with ease and cheerfulness, like what was happening was no big deal. I felt her gratitude. She had had an "accident". I did my best with what I had, and helped her stand back up. Even in her weak state, I could see the great effort she made to assist, and I told her how helpful she was. Then I said, "Let's go home now." She nodded in relief.

My dad felt so helpless in these situations, however, he too always did as much as he could. Back home, I got my mom in the bathtub and she felt so much better after. I realized that she really did need more help for basic things like bathing and brushing her teeth. She attempted, but she got more and more confused.

My parents had so many friends from the church and the school where my mom worked. So many people offered to volunteer their time. I learned so much from interacting with all the people who were helping. I saw them go through so many different emotions. I remember meeting with a group of my parents' friends at a local diner to talk about a care schedule. I asked a lot of questions as far as who was comfortable doing what.

One of my mom's friends almost started to cry. I think she felt bad admitting that she wasn't comfortable helping with the intimate care. I reassured her and everyone that ALL help is so appreciated and to please choose to help in a way that they truly desired and were comfortable with. I said that it simply wasn't necessary to help with something just because they thought it would be more helpful than something else would be. We had so many people that we could coordinate the care quite well to cover all of my mom's needs.

That's exactly what happened. My mom was so well taken care of. I will forever remember all the people who helped our family during my mom's illness. It was truly a time of crisis and even the smallest of efforts had such a huge impact.

For all those who may wonder or feel conflicted about how to help someone during their family crisis, I thought about our particular situation and what was most helpful to us. First, I would say to reach out again and again. Offer a certain day in the week at a certain time that you know will work for your schedule to either come over to reprieve a caregiver, or to go to the store to pick up food or clothing or supplies, or offer to walk the dog, or babysit a child, or to use one of your talents to help with day-to-day things. Perhaps offer to organize paperwork, or do a deep cleaning of a room of the house (it may be overwhelming for the person who is sick to have a team of cleaners in the house, however, to offer to come over 4 different days over the span of a couple of weeks, for instance, and deep clean one room at a time, is one idea).

Yes, it's important to ask questions to see what help is needed, however, often, during a time of crisis such as this, people don't always know what would be helpful. Often giving specific suggestions so people can say "yes" or "no", or come up with their own variation is helpful. The point is, at certain regular intervals – put it on your calendar – reach out. If you really want to help, and have the time to help, and can help without building up resentment, then do it. Martyr types are not really helpful. I find that the martyr mindset comes with drama, and drama adds confusion to an already naturally dramatic situation.

It's easy to think "they have so much help", however, don't assume it. What appears to be rarely is how it is. There is a delicate balance between being imposing and being available. Be a good listener, yet use your instincts as well, and don't take anything personally. The people that I found to be most helpful during our family crisis were those that understood that balance of listening to what may be needed and figuring out through what was said and unsaid what would be truly helpful in a given situation. These people checked in regularly and made it known and clear on more than one occasion that they were ready and willing to step in, and they were specific in their offers of help, and they followed through. Seeing these people walk in gave us feelings of pure relief. It's as if they were saying as they strolled in confidently, "Reinforcements have arrived." Ahhhh, I thank God for them. Their common traits were compassionate, attentive, respectful and kind. They were our earth angels.

****

Hospice

I'm really glad we sought out hospice early on in my mom's illness. A neighbor of mine who lost her mother when she was a teenager mentioned that hospice was a great help to her family. She also mentioned that hospice can be called in if a doctor determines an illness is terminal with 6 months or less time to live. "Really?" I asked. "I always thought hospice was there at the very end, like 2 weeks before." She said no, and suggested that I give them a call.

I did some research and called around and ended up going with a hospice organization that my parents' insurance worked with. Hospice is a free service, which I was very happy to hear. It sounded like it would be so helpful. Nurses would start coming to the house which would make getting my mom out to appointments unnecessary. Nurses also can bring prescription re-fills and give guidance on medical equipment needs, oxygen assistance, etc. Hospice also can arrange to have a chaplain come by to talk, or a social worker. We can call at any hour with questions. They also have pamphlets of information about the end of life experience, etc.

I talked to my sister and she agreed that we should definitely arrange for someone from hospice to come over and meet with us and dad. Now, the challenge was getting my dad to agree. I thought to myself, 'What words can I possibly use to tell dad that I would like to contact hospice?' I felt like whatever I said would be relaying the underlying message to him, 'Mom is going to die soon.' I know he didn't want to think about that.

I remember sitting in front of my dad while he sat at his desk, and I mustered up the courage to bring up the hospice subject. I told him about my neighbor and that she felt hospice was very helpful, and that I talked to Julie already and she agrees that it would be helpful. My dad kicked into "know it all" mode and slammed the idea immediately. He spoke about his experience at the VA hospital, and how it wasn't necessary right now. It was amazing how clear-headed he sounded as he explained all his knowledge to me. I recall shaking as he talked because I knew I wasn't going to just say, 'Okay' and let the matter drop. I was nervous at the thought of challenging him.

I don't recall a time where I felt the desire to disagree with my dad and articulate my own opinion to sway him to change his mind about something. In this case, he was making himself very clear. No hospice. I looked him straight in the eye as my stomach knotted up and my eyes started to tear up and I said with all sincerity, "Dad, Julie and I need help. We don't know if Hospice is the answer. We just want to give it a try. If it doesn't work out and you don't want them here anymore, then we can talk about cancelling it."

My dad looked at me and after a brief pause said, "Okay. If it will help you and Julie, okay." I started crying and said thank you. I think he must have understood where we were coming from. Yet another positive trait about my dad, he was a reasonable man. In fact, so is my entire family.

This reminds me of times when we would have family meetings when care needs changed. Even though the conversations were never comfortable, we would end up with an agreement.

Below is an example of notes I typed up after one of our family meetings. It was during a time when my parents were having challenges keeping caregivers long-term for my dad. Also, my dad could be obsessive about his care and my brother and sister and I, being his children and wanting to help him, actually didn't want to help him with personal care, even though we did in emergency situations. Since those situations were coming more frequently, it was becoming a problem because we wanted to be my dad's kids, not his caregivers. (I always imagine my mom's feelings. She didn't want to be my dad's caregiver either. Hiring caregivers were particularly helpful for her, although because she was with my dad the most, she was put in the position of helping him often for intimate care because of the realities of my dad's condition.)

My dad would always say that the worst part about being a quad-riplegic was not the fact he couldn't walk or move his body below his chest, or that he couldn't move his fingers or hands – it was the bowel and bladder issues he experienced. They were unpredictable, uncomfortable, and completely disruptive.

There was so much stress during the time when my parents were having trouble keeping caregivers for my dad.

I had the idea to hire back-up caregivers instead of relying on just one. I was looking at the results of their current situation. As much as they wished they could keep a caregiver forever, and as much as they wanted a caregiver to be available to come over at a moment's notice – it was just not plausible. The idea of hiring multiple caregivers – one main one, then others to be on call – wasn't received well by my parents at first. They agreed to a family meeting. *I'm so glad my siblings and I started assisting my parents with my dad's needs prior to my mom's illness.* We learned more about their day-to-day life which put us in a better position later to step in more when they needed even more help.

After discussions on important matters, I usually make notes and type them up for future reference. I've found this to be a valuable asset in my life. It's human nature to forget details from a discussion or meeting, especially an emotional one. My typed notes help me reclaim clarity after time passes, as well as help remind others as to what was agreed to. One other benefit is that I've found it really lowers emotional drama because everyone can more easily get on the same page when they refer to something they agreed to in the past.

Proactive Plan for Dad's Care

Reason for proactive plan:

1. Family members can no longer do dad's intimate care, i.e. condom and bowel care.

2. To do everything we possibly can to avoid

the "crisis mode" our family finds itself in whenever a personal care attendant is unavailable or quits.

        3.   This plan will help preserve the closeness of our family unit and secure as much as possible the emotional and physical well-being of each individual family member, while at the same time giving dad the care he needs.

    Note: Julie has personally met and spoken with a social worker and has gained more knowledge about dad's disability, including health risks, daily care necessities, surgical procedures, care options, the inadequate hospital care for quadriplegics, etc. She has shared this knowledge in detail with Lea. This plan has been created taking into account dad's special medical needs due to his disability.

Goal:

    1. Eliminate the need for family to be involved in dad's intimate care.

    2. To continue with in-home personal care attendants for dad, with a continually updated list of at least 4 back-up attendants, including continually updated enrollment with a nursing agency.

    3. Have a plan to follow so that dad and family know what steps will be taken when attendants are unavailable for whatever reason, or quit, or if dad finds himself in a medical emergency situation.

Dad's Responsibilities:

    1. Continue the mindset that looking for personal care attendants to assist in your care, including all aspects of your intimate care (i.e. condom and bowel care), is a process that must be gone through on a regular basis, i.e. every 3 to 12 months – in other words, expect and accept the fact that a change in attendants is inevitable and could very well be a frequent occurrence.

    2. Continue to advertise for and interview people for a

back-up personal care attendant position, or solicit agree-ments with co-workers/friends/previous attendants, until you have at least 4 willing people available to be called if your regular attendant is not available. The back-up list of names and phone numbers must be kept updated and made available to family members.

3. Call a nursing agency for an assessment as often as necessary to retain the ability to use a nursing agency if need-ed.

4. Do not ask family members to assist with intimate care, i.e. condom changes or bowel care.

5. To facilitate any necessary doctor visits in the future, take the following steps:

A.   Establish a primary care physician, and give family members his or her name and phone number, and your medical number.

B.   Explain to the physician all aspects of your condition and the health risks that are specific to you. Make sure these details are recorded in your medical chart for easy reference by other medical personnel.

C.   Obtain a letter from your physician ex-plaining your condition and the health risks that are specific to you (i.e. dysreflexia), and give a copy of this letter to fami-ly members.

D.   Keep the relationship with your primary care physician going by meeting with him or her at least once a year. If necessary, ask the doctor each year to update the letter (explaining your condition).

Dad's Plan of Action for the following scenarios:

If your primary personal care attendant is unavailable, and all back-up attendants (including co-workers/friends/ previous attendants) are unavailable, and the nursing agency cannot assist you in the following scenarios, outlined below is the plan of action for each situation:

A. *Scheduled Condom Change:* *wait until an attendant, co-worker, friend, previous attendant, or nursing agency is available. If necessary, ask a family member to help you until someone arrives, i.e. turn you if you are in bed, or help you in or out of bed.*

B. *Condom Leak:* *immediately call an attendant, co-worker, friend, previous attendant or nursing agency, then ask a family member to keep you clean and dry until someone arrives, and help you into bed if needed.*

C. *Scheduled Bowel Care:* *if an attendant, co-worker, friend, previous attendant, or nursing agency cannot arrive in time to avoid a possible health risk, call a family member or co-worker to go with you or meet you at the hospital emergency room to act as your advocate while your bowel care is performed there. (Bring along the letter from your doctor explaining your condition and dysreflexia - this will expedite the process.)*

Family Member's Responsibilities:

1. *Each member of the family is ready and willing to help as outlined above.*

2. *If dad needs to have a medical procedure or needs to go to the hospital for any reason, the family agrees and knows the importance of an advocate being with him at all times during his stay - whether it be an hour, a day or longer. Lea and Julie primarily will make sure that either a family member or a friend of dad's is with him as often as needed around the clock, and will schedule shifts and make sure dad has everything he needs for his health and emotional well-being until his discharge.*

3. *Lea and Julie primarily will assist dad in writing ads for personal care attendants, posting the ads, and using all available resources to assist dad in finding personal care attendants.*

****

Care

My mom was a member of a bicycling club and would do long rides often. She really, <u>really</u> missed bike riding. I remember once being at the house and helping her get her bike out. She was feeling good and she got on the bike and rode a block or so. She looked so happy to be on her bike. I watched her smiling as she coasted down the block toward us. That was the last time she ever rode her bike.

It was close to Christmas in 2008. I was at my parents' house hanging out. Nothing eventful was happening. All of a sudden we hear singing outside. I peeked out the window and saw a bunch of people on bicycles. It was my mom's bike club! I helped my mom outside and we stood there and listened to them sing. We were both tearing up. It was such a great sight and such a sweet idea for my mom. My mom's mood definitely lifted and stayed that way for the rest of the evening. This reminds me of what surprises like that do for people. Good memories truly do comfort. Experiences that bring joy are such wonderful and lasting gifts.

Below is what a typical care schedule looked like with our volunteers. Because of all of these volunteers, my mom was able to stay at home for the duration of her life. She was most comfortable at home, so this was a huge gift to her. Margarita was someone we hired to help when we realized we were maxing out the volunteers' time. I appreciated the honesty of our friends as far as what they were able and willing to do. Believe it or not, we had very little drama during this time. When I think about why this is, when I've heard so many horrible stories from others in similar situations, I'm not really sure. Perhaps I was the one not feeling the drama. Perhaps there was some and I was just too focused to get involved. I am so thankful that my experience with all our help was very positive and nurturing.

I included the below list because it may be helpful for someone in a similar situation – someone who is organizing the care for someone else.

The below saved me and my sister a lot of extra phone calls because we let the volunteers know that this list was posted so they would know who is next in line to come in. They could then call each other directly.

Also, by writing out basic things that needed to be done around the house, and basic ideas around caregiving specifics, ensured that things actually got done more often than not, and without a lot of repetitive asking, which can be draining. Whatever I could think of to do to make things more efficient, I did!

Caregiving Schedule

Margarita, phone:
Shirlee, phone:
Rosanne, phone:
Ana, phone:
Julie, phone:
Lea, phone:
Dino, phone:

MONDAY

6:30a.m.	*coffee/breakfast (Shirlee)*
12:00 p.m. – 6:00 p.m.	*lunch/dinner/household/ caregiving (Margarita)*
Overnight (by 7:00 p.m.)	*Shirlee*

TUESDAY

6:30 a.m.	*coffee/breakfast (Shirlee)*
8:30 a.m. – 12:15 p.m.	*lunch (Julie)*
1:00 p.m. – 5:30 p.m.	*dinner/household/ caregiving (Margarita)*
Overnight (by 10pm)	*Julie*

WEDNESDAY

6:30 a.m. – 12:00 p.m.	*coffee/breakfast/lunch/ household/caregiving (Margarita)*
6:00 p.m. – overnight	*dinner (Lea) *REMEMBER TO TAKE OUT GARBAGE FOR PICKUP!*

THURSDAY

6:30 a.m. – 11:45 a.m.	*coffee/breakfast (Lea)*
12:30 p.m. – 5:30 p.m.	*lunch/dinner/household/ caregiving (Margarita)*
Overnight (by 8:00pm)	*Ana*

FRIDAY

6:30 a.m.	*coffee/breakfast (Shirlee)*
12:30 p.m. – 5:30 p.m.	*lunch/dinner/household/ caregiving (Margarita)*
Overnight (by 7:00pm)	*Lea*

SATURDAY

6:30 a.m. – 12:30 p.m.	*coffee/breakfast/lunch (Lea)*
12:00 p.m. – 6:00 p.m.	*lunch/dinner/household/ caregiving (Margarita)*
Overnight (by 9:00pm)	*Julie*

SUNDAY

Morning shower	*(Shirlee)*

Morning thru lunch	coffee/breakfast/lunch (Julie)
5:00 p.m. – bedtime dinner	(Dino) *pick up dog mess in yard
Overnight (by 9:00pm)	Julie

*<u>Bedtime– please confirm</u>: -coffee maker, stove, oven is off
-heater temperature is at 68 degrees
-lights, TV's, radios off in all rooms
-all windows and doors are locked

Household Duties

<u>Cleaning:</u>
Dishes (daily)
Kitchen (daily)
Bathrooms (once a week, or more frequent as needed)
Dusting (once a week)
Sweeping floors (twice a week, or more frequent as needed)
Mopping floors (once or twice a week, as needed)
Vacuuming (twice a week, or more frequent as needed)

<u>Laundry:</u>
Wash/dry/fold/put away (once a week, or more frequent as needed)
Bed linens (change beds once a week)

<u>Water plants</u> (once a week)

<u>*Grocery shopping/errands*</u> *(as needed)*

<u>*Meals:*</u>
Prepare/cook/serve
Bake (if time allows)

<u>*Mail:*</u> *Bring in mail from mailbox and put on dad's desk. (Lea is in charge of paying bills and handling incoming mail.)*

<u>*Trash Cans:*</u> *take out Wed. night for Thurs. morning pickup (Lea will take out Wed. night; Margarita will bring in Thurs. morning)*

<u>*Dog (Emma):*</u>
Feeding Schedule: 2 scoops in morning, and 2 scoops around 5:00 p.m.
Fresh water in bowls in kitchen and garage (daily)

Caregiving

Please read materials we will provide on "caregiving guide for dementia", and interact with mom following these guidelines.

Keep informed of mom's medications and assist dad with administering if needed.

Keep informed of hospice status and interaction with hospice staff along with family.

Encourage music instead of TV when dad is out.

Encourage mom to ride stationary bike (with music on), or take walks with mom.

Encourage mom to take a bath or shower and wash her hair (twice a week). (*Make sure there is soap, shampoo and conditioner available to her.) (Note: Hospice can assist if needed.)

Encourage mom to brush her teeth (once in morning and once in evening). (Note: Hospice can assist if needed.)
Brush her hair/head massage (daily)
Neck/shoulder massages (daily)
Offer to play Dominos or Cards, when time allows
Daily prayer, if receptive

****

Normal Chaos

The below email that I wrote to my sister is a great example of what it was like during visits at my parents' house when my mom was dealing with her illness. Some people probably thought, 'It must be awful to be in the Gambina family's situation'. Just like many things in life, unless you've experienced it, you can never really know. For me, the experience was real, raw life, which was invigorating at times – if that makes any sense. It was awful, with a mix of sweetness, love and delight. As an example, the motto my dad came up with that he and my mom would blurt out at times was, "This is a f....ing nightmare." Then they would laugh. Then sigh. Then smile as they looked at each other lovingly – their expression one of wistfulness and vulnerability. Real. Raw. Life.

What could you do? It was what it was. We had so much appreciation for the smallest things. I remember being over there, before my mom had challenges functioning, and she plopped down an omelet for my dad's breakfast. My dad thanked her, like he always did, but the appreciation was more palpable than your usual, "Thanks for this delicious omelet". There was so much energy surging through their home during this time. It was intense, yet subtle at the same time. It was as if not one second of time was wasted over there. Nothing had to be said – it's just how it felt. It was like the difference between viewing a normal TV transmission to one that was HD – bright, clear colors that were so beautiful, regardless of the image being viewed. It was appreciated for exactly what it was.

Hi Julie. It's 9:40pm and I finished all the paperwork for the week. Dad called me twice to help adjust his leg because the nails of his other foot were hurting him. I'll check in on him before I go to bed.

Mom was grouchy when I first got here. She did get up and eat with me at the bar (dad had already eaten). After dinner, dad gave the Dixie cup with the pill, but mom refused to take it. When I asked her why she doesn't want to take it, she said, "Because it doesn't seem right." Basically, she's having a hard time trusting. I asked if she trusted us, and she said, "Who, you?" and I said, yes, and she said that I haven't been there and Julie does the pills. She inferred that she trusts you. I just said that the reason for the night-time pill is that it helps her sleep all night – differentiate from night and day – so she doesn't get up at night, which gives her a good night sleep and us too. Then she asked questions about what she does at night, and we gave some examples. She still didn't take it, but later had a headache and I offered her Tylenol and she took that right away. I gave her a neck massage and we were all talking and she laughed a couple of times. I asked her later if her headache was gone and she said yes.

I also asked her about the "ouch, ouch" that I kept hearing her say, and asked if she's hurting, and she massaged her right upper leg and said it hurts. (Let's keep an eye on this.) Dad was getting in bed at this point. I asked mom how she was doing "with this whole process", and she said that "it's not going to get better, and that's what makes it hard." I said that the doctors don't seem to know 100% what's going to happen, and no one really knows. I said she'll still have good days, and she said, "Yes." After this point, we just got a bit "punchy" and I swear we both started cracking up at the dumbest things and we were both laughing so hard we were crying – we laughed over me remembering to let the dog back in and putting a dog toy on my bed to remind me; we laughed when she sat down on the family room floor and I said, "I thought we were going to your room?" and she said "We are" and just looked up at me in silence and I said, "I'm sorry, your current body position told me otherwise"; we laughed when she peaked in dad's room leaning over his empty chair to say goodnight and I said it would be funny if she tripped over his footplates and it's like "gosh I was just saying good night"; we laughed when she started to say to dad, "Lea told me I need too...." Then she started to trail off, and I said, "Mom, stop telling stories!" and she laughed and started to talk again, and I cut her off then said, "excuse me, go ahead" and we went back and forth and were just cracking up. We laughed when I was setting her up for a massage in her bed and it was a big commotion and I said, "you're probably thinking just give me a f...ing massage already!"...... hard to explain....it was really dumb stuff but it was so funny.

She had no problem with me helping her into pajamas. I stayed in the bathroom with her and brushed my teeth while she went to the bathroom. She said she didn't have to put new Depends on, so I'll wait until morning to have her change them. (She seems to like them.) She had fresh pajamas on, and I gave her a nice massage while she laid in bed and tucked her in. We'll see how she sleeps because she didn't take that pill! She slept all night last night, but Shirlee said she took the pill and didn't have any problem with it (probably because it was with her dinner – so we should remember that.)

Good night! Wish me luck with a full night sleep!

Lea

Below is another email I found that I wrote to my friend, Lori (who is also a social worker and my dad's co-worker and dear friend). The email was written a month and a half before my mom died. I'm still amazed at my mom's physical agility. I usually hear about cancer patients being so thin and sick looking. I think because my mom stopped the chemo, was physically in such good shape and her body was so strong, and she had the drive to keep moving and eating – her body just wasn't weakening that easily.

Hi Lori. Thanks for checking in! Things are going well. I'll be seeing my parents a lot this week because my sister is going out of town. It's getting tiring driving back and forth so much, but it's necessary and I do want to see them. When I'm there, I can't imagine being anywhere else, but it's hard when the kids tell me not to go. I'm going to bring Sophie with me this weekend. She said she wants to help!

My dad is doing well. I'm sure it helps that my mom isn't giving him as much trouble over leaving the house, so he's been able to enjoy it more. He was really sick a couple of weeks ago – he said it was a bladder infection, although he never went to the doctor, but he was able to get antibiotics over the phone. He's really enjoying this nice weather. What a difference when it's sunny out as far as his spirits.

My mom is doing okay, although she's having a really hard time walking now. Last time I took her out for a walk, she got as far as the driveway and said, "This is so hard." I told her she doesn't have to walk to enjoy being outside. She wanted to "join in" and is disappointed that she's having trouble getting around. We're concerned for her safety because she's been bumping into walls and falling down, but we don't want to restrict her either. It's a tough balance. My sister is doing a good job with overseeing her medications and working with hospice. She's constantly adjusting the medications so my mom is not "zoned out" like she would be if she were in a nursing home (they have so many people to care for, apparently they don't have the time to adjust medications all the time.) Hospice is coming twice a week now. My mom's body is so strong! It's really pushing through this illness. Most people would not have survived this long.

Oliver and I have a good friend, Pat, who passed away suddenly last week. I just talked to her just before Christmas! I tried calling her too on the day she died, without knowing. I found out Saturday night, just in time to make her memorial service Sunday. I'm still shocked that she is gone. She had stage 3 breast cancer 9 years ago, and apparently it came back, and she did not tell anyone. She confided in a good friend who helped her get her affairs in order – this was back in May! She kept her prognosis a secret from her family and friends – even her kids. You would never have known she was living with a terminal illness! She was full of energy, positive and fun. Whenever we talked, she'd ask how my mom is doing and gave me advice and support. She also gave great advice about kids, marriage, etc. She was in her mid-fifties and went through all the "kid stages" and she was so witty and caring. I'll miss her so much. I've learned a lot from her, and I respect her decision to keep her illness a secret. I remember her telling me when she first got cancer that people treated her differently and had a certain "look" that she couldn't stand – pity I guess. I think she just wanted people to live their lives, and she wanted to live hers – on her own terms. She was very close to her kids and her sisters. I feel good about our last visit and I don't have any regrets. It really taught me not to take people for granted – you never know when you'll see someone again. She wrote a poem and asked her daughter a few years back to read it at her funeral. She did. It said something like "When all I am is love, and you need me, turn to whomever is next to you and hug them – give them the love that you need from me." She was an awesome lady.

Anyway, that's the update on my life. Do you regret you asked? I better get to work…...I miss you! I wish we lived closer to each other.

Love,
Lea

****

Getting Ready to Go

It's seems natural to think about someone's last words before they leave this earth. The last words I heard from my mom were over breakfast one morning at her house. That particular morning, I helped her into her seat at the kitchen table. She usually sat at the kitchen bar in her usual spot, but the barstools were too high and she could no longer get up on them. I put a bowl of oatmeal in front of her on the table and sat down with a bowl also. My mom rarely spoke anymore and I expected that we would eat in silence like usual.

She surprised me when all of sudden she said, "I have to stop thinking so much." I sat up straight and was on full alert. She rarely spoke – let alone sentences! With her short-term memory issue, I scrambled to think of what to say quickly before she forgot her train of thought. I asked her, "What are you thinking about?" She was looking down at her bowl and stirring her oatmeal. Then she said wistfully, "Oatmeal."

A moment later she surprised me again and asked, "What are you thinking about, Lea?" She was looking straight into my eyes as I looked back into hers. I paused for a moment. I had no words, and no time to think. I simply said, "Oatmeal" as we continued to look at each other. She smiled at me with genuine amusement and then her eyes lost focus and she stared off into the distance.

That was our last conversation. I found myself agonizing a bit over it. I replayed it in my mind and thought I should have said something other than "oatmeal". Then I reassured myself. There really was nothing left unsaid. I loved her. She loved me. And we both knew it.

I have few regrets when it comes to my parents. That fact is a gift I'll appreciate the rest of my life. If anything, I wish I had asked my parents more questions about their lives. I didn't realize how interested I am in hearing more of what they had to say. Actually, I realize how interested I am in hearing more of what many people have to say. To me, what people think and feel is important. How can I understand people if I don't know what they are thinking and if I don't listen to what they are saying? I'm much more curious about people and their lives – their "story".

We can learn so much by hearing people's stories. More importantly, by hearing their stories, we are more likely to empathize with them more and create a closer connection. There is simply no other feeling as a soul-to-soul connection. It's often vulnerable and uncomfortable, which is also what makes it's so meaningful when people are able to cross that invisible border and really connect.

> *"People will forget what you said. People will forget what you did. But people will never forget how you made them feel."*
>
> *(Quote by Maya Angelo)*

I believe my brother, Dino, was the one who heard my mom's very last words. He had so much patience. There were times when he came over and would sit with my mom for hours and hold her hand. It was during one of these times that my mom said to my brother, "It's okay, Dino." I think this is such a great gift for my brother – my mom's last words being directed at him.

****

Lullaby

In the midnight hours of February 28, 2009, I was alone with my mom on a cot next to her hospital bed in the family room. My dad was in his bedroom in bed for the night. He had his own challenges, and I was just hoping he was able to sleep through until morning.

I had a moment of feeling overwhelmed and scared. I was 40 years old, in my childhood home with my parents, yet they could not comfort me. They were no longer capable. I was awake all night caring for my mom, trying to make her comfortable, giving her the morphine in the exact intervals per Hospice. I called Hospice at least a half a dozen times that night. I would put the phone to my mom's mouth so they could hear her breathing. I could tell my mom was uncomfortable, but I had no experience caring for someone in this state. At times she would move her body slowly and her facial expression seemed like she needed something. She was grimacing. Was she in pain? Was it okay to give her more morphine? I called Hospice so many times during the night and the nurse was so patient and helpful.

The nurse reassured me that all was normal. Apparently, the different sounds of my mom's breathing was as it should be. At the time I was there experiencing it, I wasn't thinking "my mom is dying". I'm so glad my mind wasn't thinking like that because I think I would have freaked out being there all by myself. I didn't know that by that very afternoon she would be gone. I was so focused on making sure she was comfortable.

I did try to sleep some. I had a cot next to my mom's bed. It was very uncomfortable. I didn't really sleep because I kept hearing her and every time I heard a different type of sound coming from her, I would get up to look at her and touch her. I ended up just sitting in the chair next to her leaning on the edge of her hospital bed. She was more peaceful now after the last morphine dose and I could sense this and it helped me too. I was so worried about giving her too much and killing her. This sounds so awful to say, but it's true. Drugs always freaked me out and I knew this was strong stuff. I'm happy for these medications though because they absolutely helped keep her comfortable.

From people who knew other people with cancer, we kept hearing how my mom was having an "easier time with it". I'm not sure if this is really true. I know my mom. She is strong, never complains and can handle pain. I just think she was handling it resolutely.

I read in the Hospice materials that hearing was the last of the senses to go. I was holding her hand, watching her. I knew she couldn't see me and I didn't know what to say. I just sat there with her quietly. Then I just started to hum lullabies, softly. My head was next to hers, and I kept humming. It felt right in the moment – as if we were just hanging out together relaxing. Maybe she could hear the lullabies I was humming and maybe not. It didn't really matter to me. I do believe she could feel my affection.

Looking back now and knowing that this was her last night on earth, I am very grateful that we had this time together. It just happened that way, and I suppose it was meant to be. I took very good care of her that night.

The sun began rising and the day began. My dad's caregiver came over and got him dressed and up. My brother came over and I got some sleep in the spare room for a couple of hours. I was so grateful I was able to sleep at the drop of a hat, and was able to get back to sleep right away after being woken up. I hung out all day at the house. We watched "Little House on the Prairie" in the living room where my mom slept. This was a very popular show when I was a child and brought back nice memories for the whole family to have that show on.

I mentioned that my mom was sleeping. Actually, I'm not sure I would call it that. Her breathing was not normal. We were turning her in regular intervals. She did have a fever and thank goodness my brother was able to handle the suppositories. This kept her fever down and made her more comfortable. She wasn't able to take anything by mouth anymore. She just wasn't awake anymore. I guess this is what dying is like. Again, I wasn't thinking about that at the time. I was just "in it". Her breaths were fewer and farther in between.

We had a comfortable set-up for her. I'm glad we decided to put the hospital bed in the living room because it was big enough and there was a lot of natural light. The room was open to the kitchen and we were always around her. She wasn't closed off in a room by herself. We had put her favorite posters and pictures around her. I felt happy that she was in the comfort of her home.

Later in the afternoon, my sister came over. I remember her asking me how I could handle being there for so many hours. My dad was pretty emotional. I didn't know how to answer her. It wasn't so bad for me. I just figured all the emotions were normal for the situation. Shirlee came over too (our friend who made herself available on a moment's notice whenever we called). It was my dad, me, my brother, sister and Shirlee there.

When my mom's breathing started to stop, and seconds would go by then she would breath again, we knew the end was near. The Hospice nurses educated us, and I was appreciative to have some knowledge of what was happening. We all gathered around my mom and Shirlee stayed back. I was so glad she was there because she was true support. I knew she would spring to action for anything we may have needed. I was so grateful.

I remember looking at my mom's face and thinking how cute she was. She looked so small and peaceful. Her skin was so smooth. She really was taken care of very well. Because she had an appetite until the last week, she never lost a lot of weight. Her last Sunshine Sausage Croissant was a week prior. I remember she ate half of it. She was having trouble getting it up to her mouth. I started to assist her and she weakly pushed my hand away and put the food down. It was at this point I believe she decided she had enough. She appeared frustrated not being able to put the food in her own mouth. She didn't eat after this day.

Around 5pm my mom took her last breath. My dad was sobbing. I kissed her on her forehead, then stood up looking down on her. I gently touched her face with my left hand. She looked so cute. I can still picture her. She looked so peaceful. I started walking away and didn't look at her again. I don't remember much about what anyone else did or said. I just remember my mom's dog, Emma running around the house in every room looking up. It was as if she was following my mom's spirit. Emma, who never left my mom's side, never went back to my mom's body. She somehow knew my mom wasn't there anymore.

Business was being taken care of – the mortuary had to be called so they could pick up my mom's body. I wasn't involved in this and I don't know who took care of this. I remember feeling grateful that my brother offered to stay with my mom's body. I really didn't want to be with her body. I felt comforted that he would make sure they were gentle with her when they wrapped her up and took her body away. I also was glad we decided on a closed casket. I liked the thought that her body would be left alone. The topic of organ donation wasn't an issue because of her cancer, so I thought the next best thing is for her body to be treated gently, and while I don't know what happened once they took her body, I like to picture that's what happened.

I walked outside in my parents' backyard and just sat there on a bench on their deck and looked up in the sky. I just sat for a while and no one came to me. I was grateful. I didn't know what to think. I didn't know how I felt. I just sat there looking up in the sky.

My brother and sister and I spent the night at my parents' house that night. The next morning, we went to I-Hop for breakfast. We were all so wiped out. My brother and dad went back to the house and my sister suggested that she and I go to yoga. She had been going to a studio that was only a couple of blocks from my parents' house. I really liked this idea. My mom would have loved the thought that Julie and I did yoga together at this time. She would have been there with us – and she most likely was. I was very glad we did this.

****

Onward Auto Pilot

There were so many decisions to be made. My sister and I spared my dad from going to the appointment at the mortuary, which I was so glad we did. I felt like we were at a timeshare presentation. A man in a suit lead us into an office room and had us sit down. He pulled out a binder and started flipping pages explaining all the options for caskets and linings and hardware and prayer cards and crosses, etc. My sister and I would look at each other, our impatience with this process was building. He then led us to a room where they had partial caskets displayed up and down walls so we could see the different materials and all the parts of the caskets to choose from. Both my sister and I were just amazed at all this. Did people really care about the materials and different handles, etc.? Apparently so.

We wanted to "get to it". We stopped the presentation and I remember asking, "Please show us the least expensive casket." He showed us this navy blue casket with silver hardware. My sister and I thought it looked really nice. "We'll take it." Then I asked, "Show me the prayer cards, please." He led us to a corner. We picked up a few and read the prayers. We found a card that had a nice picture of the back of a woman hugging Jesus in the clouds. We both liked it. We also liked the prayer:

Miss Me – But Let Me Go

When I come to the end of the road
and the sun has set for me.
I want no rites in a gloom filled room.
Why cry for a soul set free?
Miss me a little, but not too long.
And not with your head bowed low.
Remember the days that we once shared.
Miss me, but let me go.
For this is a journey that we all must take.
And each must go alone.
It is all part of the Master's plan.
A step on the road to home.
When you are lonely and sick at heart,
Go to a friend that we know.
And follow Him in doing good deeds.
Miss me, but let me go.

"We'll take it," I said. Apparently these cards come in a package with a cross, so we chose a nice cross. We refused all other offerings and went back into the office to sign papers. My mom worked for the Diocese of Oakland for many years and we were able to get a discount because of that. I noticed this wasn't on the papers, so I asked for the discount and after him going in and out of the room – just like they do when you're buying a car or a timeshare – we got our discount. My sister and I were not emotional. We wanted to get this "business" done, and we placed no meaning on our decisions. It was about what made sense.

I chose the flowers. I wanted simplicity because my mom liked simplicity. My mom was never into flowers too much. I went to the florist there on-site at the mortuary and chose a nice large bouquet of flowers that could be laid onto the casket. It was the type of bouquet that a woman could cradle in her arms. It was perfect.

Planning a funeral is like planning a party when you're recovering from the flu and cannot think straight. We persevered. My dad, brother, sister and I made our best efforts to consider what my mom would have liked. She was so into her music and I remember the bulk of our discussions were surrounding this subject. The most eerie thing happened. I was at my house getting ready to drive over to meet my sister who was at my parents' house. My sister was there already with my dad. We were talking over our cell phones about different CD options to play at the service. I scanned some at my house and read some off, and my sister was doing the same at my dad's house.

At this point, I had to get in my car to head over there. When I got in my car, my sister was reading out names of some CD's my mom had. There was a CD on the floor of my car. I don't normally have CD's loose on the floor because I'm always concerned that someone will step on them. I went to pick it up and noticed it was the movie soundtrack of "Notting Hill". Just as I read the words in my mind *"Notting Hill"* I heard my sister's voice say *"Notting Hill"*. She had picked up the same CD at my parents' house at the <u>exact moment</u> that my eyes scanned the title. I was incredulous. It was as if my mom was sending us a message to play that CD at her ceremony. I take that back – she was definitely sending us a message to play that CD. That's exactly what we did.

Our plan was to have my mom's service at the Catholic Church that she worked at for almost 30 years, however, we ran into an issue. The pastor would not allow any outside music to be played in the church. We could only use specifically approved church songs. I made a quick and easy decision to change the venue. I wasn't willing to compromise on the music. It the most important thing for my mom's service because my mom loved her music. She always had music playing in her house as she puttered around, and worked long and hard updating her I-Pod with her favorite music to listen to during her runs and bicycle rides. We found a nice venue in a beautiful and smaller chapel. This change also allowed us to create the service any way we wanted.

****

Simple Elegance

I remember thinking how nice the service was. The casket was simple and the flowers draped over it beautifully and there was a pretty picture of my mom on top of the casket – she was looking pensively off into the distance in the picture. It was a candid and beautiful shot. My dad always loved this picture of my mom.

None of us had any intention of speaking at the service. It was all a whirlwind really. My sister and I did end up speaking. At a certain point I just recall deciding to stand up and go to the podium. I wasn't used to speaking in front of large audiences. I just felt compelled to pay tribute to my mom. I don't recall what I said exactly. I do remember feeling like the service was for all the people in the audience – not for us – not for me, my dad, my brother or sister. This was for everyone else. It was for the people who lost my mom and wasn't privileged to spend the same time that we all got to spend with her in her last year of life.

I remember speaking about the Sunshine Sausage Croissants that my mom just loved to eat and that I would get for her every time I visited at the local fast food place. Every time I would buy them I thought how unappetizing they were to me, however, she enjoyed them and that's all that mattered. I realized when I talked about those croissants, the audience was very silent. I looked at a couple of people in the crowd and saw the extreme sadness in their faces and the tears. Some people were just staring at their laps. There was such a silence. I started to say, "You know, it wasn't all awful this past year". I began to think authentically about how it was. I told a couple of stories.

One story was when I was over my parents' house and I asked my mom if she was ready to go to bed. She was sitting on the floor and said yes, so I got up and started walking toward her room and was almost to the hallway when I realized my mom wasn't behind me. I turned back and remember her still sitting on the floor with her legs straight out and Emma next to her and she was just looking up at me, not moving. I said, "Are you ready?" And she said, "Yes, but I can't get up." "Oh!" I said. I walked over to her and took both her arms and said, "One, two, three" and pulled her up. It took a couple of tries and we started laughing and the dog started to get all excited because we were laughing. This was a sad moment in a sense because my mom was deteriorating and this marked the beginning of the increasing physical help she would be needing, however, this wasn't in our minds at that moment. We were having fun together.

There were so many clumsy and awkward moments – moments that could have led to disappointment and tears, however, I was pretty resolute. I made light of almost everything. This lightness really, REALLY helped. I cannot think of one situation where when I put a spin of humor on it, it did not make it better. I learned how important it is to "go with the flow" and not take things so seriously. We certainly were experiencing a serious situation – my mom was terminally ill. There is nothing funny about this. However, it is and was possible to make something of each moment – something more tolerable – even enjoyable.

For example, when my mom would be puking, I could either be tense and stressed and clean the mess up with stoic efficiency, or I could say, "Mom! You know, if you wanted me to stay longer, you could have just asked." She would smile as I helped move her to a better location so she wasn't on the carpet anymore and I'd have an easier time cleaning up. I was constantly distracting her and saying the unexpected. I could tell she appreciated this. I would just think, 'What was it like for her?' And then I'd follow my instincts. It seemed to work well – meaning, she was comfortable with my help.

One time when I was over my parents' house my mom asked me to listen to a phone message she got. She had one of those old cassette phone recorders that had a blinking light when there was a message. She pressed play and I heard a garbled voice. I couldn't make out what the man was saying. He wasn't really talking, it was as if he was moaning something. I said to my mom, "Is he okay? Does he need help?" My mom started laughing so hard she had tears in her eyes. She said, "No! It's your father! He's singing that song 'I Just Called to Say I Love You'!" Oh my gosh! I listened to it again and could make out the song. It was the one by Lionel Richie. I started laughing too. He sounded so bad, like he was in pain. My mom couldn't wait until my dad got home to tell him what I said.

I came over to my parents' house one morning and my mom was sleeping. I happened to be right there when she first opened her eyes that morning, and I received such an incredible gift from her. She opened her eyes and slowly recognized it was me. She moved her body up a little and said with relief, "I love it when you are here in the morning." I could feel how comforted she was that I was there. It felt really good to me to know what my presence did for her.

At my mom's funeral, I also talked about how real and raw the past year was – it was real life – and how grateful I was that I was able to care for my mom like she cared for me. I was "all in" during the experience. It was fantastic and awful, a sweet nightmare, a peaceful, raw concoction of all the beauty and pain life has to offer. I am grateful for the gift I was given – the gift of caring for my mom. One imperfect person caring for another imperfect person. Me giving 100% and her giving 100%. There were so many moments in that last year that I truly felt "all is well", even in the midst of all that wasn't.

My mom's funeral was cool. That's probably weird to say, but I remember thinking it was just perfect for her. She would have loved it. I'm sure she was smiling down from heaven. The coolest part of my mom's funeral was when my sister drove my mom's Chevelle. I sat in the passenger seat and we made our way from the chapel up to the burial site. We were following my mom's bicycling group. It was such a clear, beautiful day. There was a winding path we had to travel to reach the burial site. My mom was buried near a statue of St. Francis of Assisi.

My dad was involved in choosing the site and the gravestone. At first, he didn't want a flat stone. He said he never liked them, however, when it came down to it, he preferred to spend money on the location of the gravesite versus on a bigger headstone. The site was next to a concrete path that was also near one of the driving paths. He could easily park his van and get to her site in his wheelchair without having to maneuver through grass. The gravestone was simple and nice. We all agreed this was best. We included my mom's name, her picture, the year of her birth and death (1945 – 2009), and the words "I hope you dance." This was inspired by one of my mom's favorite songs. She loved to dance, and when she did, she was happy.

The gravestone had a space for my dad. It was really weird to see it on the ground, and I always wondered how my dad felt looking at it knowing that some day, his picture and dates would be also be on that stone.

Part Five

Yearning

After my mom's funeral, my sister and brother and I thought we could finally breathe now and have more down time in our lives after the whirlwind of the year we had. I was preoccupied a bit with thoughts of my dad. I could see the sadness in his eyes and body language, even though he didn't speak of my mom or his feelings. For me, my mom's passing hadn't sunk in yet.

My sister called me one day and said that she picked up the phone to call my mom and then realized her mistake. She had forgotten for a split second that my mom was gone. From our brief conversation, it was obvious my sister was missing my mom. I was inspired by our phone call and wrote the following poem. The little girl is my sister.

This is What It Feels Like

I was a little girl once...
      yes, I'm remembering...
      bouncing up and down with my mother nearby.
She always said I was one step ahead of her.
      She was sharp, but somehow I challenged her...
         little ol' me.....being me.

She and I would lock eyes – we both knew….
           the gears in my head
                      moved just a bit faster than hers.

Did you know that when I was little,
        I liked to stand on my head to watch TV?
I don't know why….I just do different things like that.
        I like that about me.

As a teenager I liked to wear thigh high leather boots.
           Well… I just really liked them…
                 so I used what little money I had to buy them.

Did you know I would take a taxi to school
        when I was running late?
I could always find a way… I was one step ahead…
        and she was always there…just a phone call away.
             In fact, I picked up the phone today…and…

Did you know I'll be 40? On my next birthday…

I'm busy with my family and career…things are going well…
        I'm moving fast and lean.
Pilates – that's my thing…my voice is calmer after.
        Why is my voice so high and frantic sometimes?
           I don't really want to know….

This house is quiet.
My family is away for the day.
My tasks half undone but further along.
        Yes, this is good…this time I have…
           to catch up, ya know?
      to get further – to get some things done.
      Yes…I'm sure of it. Yes…here I am….

The house is quiet.

I want to pick up the phone…
  that's what I want…just to say hi.
    "Hey, mom, let's go to lunch."
  I'm going to cry…
    yes….I bounce up. I'm off…
  only a few hours left until my family is home.

I have things to do…important, pressing things to do.
Yes, I must do them…because if I don't…
well, if I don't…then, well, time is wasted
and things wouldn't get done…yes, and then….well,
if they don't get done…then….then…
  what was I just doing?
  oh…yes…I was going to cry.
  yes…I was going to cry…but if I do…well, if I do then…
  maybe I won't stop.
  Of course I will, eventually…but I know…I know…
  I won't feel like it. Yes, I'm sure of it…
  I won't feel like stopping… and then…well then…
  I will start gasping.
  Yes, I'll cry hard and the lump in my throat…it'll…well…
    what will it feel like if that lump is gone?
  and my stomach…the nervousness in my stomach…
    that I notice when it's quiet…
    like now…no one is home…just me…here sobbing.
    Just me…and I was right…I knew…
    I don't want to stop…yes, I always knew
    I was sharp too…
      and one step ahead…

Mom, I'm sad…I'm sobbing and I'm sad…
  and that lump…it's still there and…
  why is that? Do you know, mom? Why is it still there?
  I want to ask you this…I want to know…lots of things.
  And what if I want to ask you?
    That lump is there when I want to ask you…
    that's it, isn't it, mom?

that lump is there when I want to talk to you...
I miss you...and then I want to cry...
I feel like a scared little girl. I'm scared because...
do you know why, mom?
I want to ask you this...I want to know...

I'm a scared mommy that's crying in her quiet house.
I'm...a scared... mommy...
that's crying...in her... quiet...house...

I'm breathing...fresh out of tears...
breathing and sitting on the floor
looking at my feet...casually...
and then up and out the window beyond.
I'm just lookin'...for you, mom, in the sky...
it's blue today with cozy clouds...
and you're out there in them...I'm sure of it...
watching your little girl...sweet
and wonderfully out of control
sitting here on the floor...

I smile....a hesitant smile....soft and true... feeling my love for you.
So, mom...this is what it feels like...this is what it feels like
to really be missing you.

****

Wishful Thinking

My dad was healthy, and Jessica, his long-time caregiver, was still taking care of his most complex needs. We just needed to find someone to come to the house during the day here and there (or so we thought). After all, my dad was very independent and once he was up in the morning he could leave the house on his own. Emma was trained to close the door behind him, and my dad could use the garage remote to close the garage and secure the house. He could drive places, and come home and let himself in all by himself.

Each member of our family believed that my dad was able to function independently. Even my dad was agreeing to our ideas. We all figured that he'd been commuting to work for almost 30 years. What none of us put together was that while he was at work, there were always many people around to help if he needed something. We totally underestimated my dad's needs.

Here is the first ad we put out to find help for my dad:

FREE RENT + COMPENSATION FOR RIGHT FIT

We are looking for a responsible "roommate" for our dad, Hank, to share his 3 bedroom/2 bath house in Newark. The "roommate" would receive free rent and utilities, a private bedroom, private bathroom and private living room (decorate as you wish, and bring in all your own furniture for your private areas), plus you will receive additional compensation – all in exchange for making sure Hank is cared for.

Hank is a quadriplegic who is relatively independent considering his disability (i.e. he can get in and out of the house by himself, and he can drive in a specially equipped van). He is a resourceful, independent individual, with many interests and regular activities. He already has personal care attendants who handle getting him in and out of bed, getting him dressed, bathing, and other personal care needs, etc.

Our goal is to work with the natural lifestyle of the roommate/caregiver and provide as much flexibility as possible, without conflicting with having consistent and reliable care for our dad. A 2nd room can be negotiated if you are a single parent with a child.

If you view this opportunity as a "job", perhaps this is not the right fit for you. In fact, this living situation could very well work around your current job depending on your hours/location. Our ideal candidate will have a real interest in taking care of another person, and will view the living arrange-

ment as a "win-win": He or she will appreciate the benefits of free living plus additional compensation, and in the course of maintaining the household and living their normal lifestyle, will willingly take responsibility for caring for, and coordinating care for someone in need. Although Hank is independent while in his wheelchair, he does need certain assistance due to the limitations of his disability – however, since he has personal care attendants, the type of assistance is more of regular household chores and meals – something that if you live there, you would be doing for yourself anyway.

Hank would need his roommate/caregiver around daily (time frames very flexible; Hank is out and about a lot) to help him with miscellaneous tasks around the house, laundry, cleaning, grocery shopping, etc., and preparing and serving most meals (the most critical ones being breakfast at approx. 6:30 a.m., and dinner at approx. 5:30 p.m.), and to be there overnight, every night, with reasonable exceptions (which can be negotiated prior to moving in, however, weekend coverage is needed on a consistent basis – again, with reasonable exceptions).

Once Hank's personal care attendant helps him into bed at night around 7:45 p.m., Hank should not be left alone in the house for more than a couple of hours – and not on a regular basis. Sometimes Hank would need assistance in the middle of the night, so it is important that you are comfortable with getting up once in the middle of the night briefly, perhaps a few nights in a week – sometimes more, sometimes less.

An important responsibility of Hank's roommate/caregiver will be to coordinate care for Hank if they will be out of town, or away for an evening, etc. (a list of people to contact will be provided for this purpose).

We should note that Hank has a beautiful, docile Golden Retriever named Emma. Emma is an indoor dog and loves being around people. The only responsibility the roommate would have for the dog is to give her fresh food and water dai-

ly. (Hank's daughter, Julie, takes care of all her other needs.) Emma is considered part of our family. Hank's 3 children live locally and play an active role in his care. He has a strong support system.

We're advertising for a "roommate" because that's what he needs – someone that lives with him, and is willing to co-ordinate their time for his basic care – someone who views the overall benefits of this living arrangement as a true opportunity.

Well, during the time period of calling people who responded and interviewing them, we quickly realized my dad needed much more than what we were looking for. It didn't take much for my dad to find himself in a tough situation. For example, he got stuck in his chair for 6 hours sitting in the house and could not call anyone because he was stuck in one place. He literally had to just wait until someone came over. Also, he wasn't able to open any blinds or the back door if he wanted to go out on the deck. He also couldn't get food, or when he tried, often he would drop things, then he couldn't pick it up to eat it.

Fortunately, Jessica, my dad's long-time caregiver, agreed to move in my dad's house with her family, which was such an awesome thing – the best of all possible situations for my dad being without my mom. My sister and I cleared out the house in one weekend to make room for Jessica and her family. There was no time to be sentimental packing up my mom's clothes and other items around the house. We had to get it done quickly. It was like pulling a Band-Aid off fast.

****

Losing a Limb

My dad's grief was overwhelming for him at times. He told me that he felt like he lost a limb. He also said that every time he prayed, he would see my mom. He seemed concerned that I would think he was crazy. I assured him that I did not.

171

My dad rarely talked about my mom. When her birthday came around, I asked him if he wanted all of us to go to the gravesite, or get together and acknowledge her birthday in some way. He said he didn't think he could get through that. I let the idea go.

My dad never connected with anything that would be considered group therapy. He felt that because he was a therapist himself, that he would naturally begin to lead the group. I didn't quite believe this was a good reason not to try group therapy. I felt he could really benefit from the experience of hearing other people's stories of loss and perhaps he would not feel so alone. I could not convince him. What I was successful at encouraging him to do was to start writing in a journal. To get over his perfectionist tendencies, I told him not to think. I suggested that he write freely.

My mom's funeral was March 5, 2009. My dad started his journal on March 17th, and entitled it Ramblings. He stuck with it consistently for a little over 3 weeks. Here are his last written words:

> *3/17/09:*
>
> *Lea, my eldest daughter, started all this. She <u>gently</u> prodded me on a few occasions of late, to write. I'm not sure where I'll go with this. Lea told me that my experiences and relating them would be helpful to others, and that I have something to offer.*
>
> *It's very hard to write about this, but my loving wife of 43+ years of marriage, died 2 ½ weeks ago. I purposely used the word "died" rather than "passed on" for my benefit. Brenda was a very direct person, and kept me "tough" and somehow it feels more direct, but harder to say. I miss her <u>so much</u>. It hurts a lot – and I'm stopping now.*
>
> *3/18/09:*
>
> *My mind is spinning right now. It's so much like being carried by a wave and being submerged in water when I get sad, and raising up out of the water when I feel somewhat better, up and down – sometimes going deep.*

Emma was lying in front of Brenda's closed bedroom door this morning, I think waiting for Brenda to come out. Last night she barked by her open door when she saw a different bed (Jessica & Ryan's) inside Brenda's room.

I'm starting to pray and meditate again, more regularly I hope.

Since Brenda's death I have been focusing more on my mortality. I'm trying to be real, in that I'll be 70 in Oct. I've been so fortunate in <u>so many</u> ways. Dino, Lea, and Julie, Brenda's friends who cared for her and who I have been drawn closer to. My health all these years. Way too much to list right now. What is most clear in my life right now, and for a while, is a deep <u>sense of gratitude</u>. It's a feeling, but much more, probably the closest I can get in words in experiencing God's grace.

I've been thinking a lot about my own death, and a lot about the after life. Been reading a lot about different views on what happens. I find it scary, but when I pray I feel consolation. I give up control to a point.

Then I think of Brenda, and how close I feel to her, even when my love Brenda is not bodily present. In my room there is a heart by Brenda's picture saying "I said a prayer for you today." Every time I go by, I say a prayer.

I just thought of something somewhat humorous. When Brenda was here and I either went to the bathroom often or stayed a long time in there, she would comment. I find it ironic now, in a funny loving way.

So many things remind me of her. There's got to be a heaven. I'm praying that I use my remaining time on this earth doing God's will. I forget to ask for the Holy Spirit's guidance or just stop and breathe in God's presence so many times during the day.

3/18/09 p.m.
I received a poem/prayer from the cancer support group

that is the best I've seen to fit the grieving process. I have it right next to Brenda's pictures on the bookcase where she is at the finish line running a race. Toward the end it seems to speak to me that "there's something left for me to do." Again, I pray it is in line with God's will.

Above all else, I hope I leave my children with a legacy of prayer and meditation. I'm beginning to be convinced in the latter part of my life that it's crucial. So much time I feel was wasted, but I believe God loves me anyway.

We get so distracted in our lives with every day matters, because we constantly forget throughout the course of the day that we can turn these "every day matters" into prayers, then compassionate action.

I pray that I can show some of the compassion that my children give to me. It's particularly ironic that they're the ones that are teaching their dad in my "wisdom years."

With all the reading I've been doing, mainly about spiritual matters, the same core themes have come up repeatedly. Compassion, present-moment living, prayer and meditation, forgiveness, and the fact that we are all one.

My children and close friends that cared for Brenda are beautiful examples. I love them so much. And here's the big revelation for me: They have all had the good fortune (God given) to have been touched by the grace of Brenda while she was with us on earth, and now from heaven.

3/21/09:

I have been spending time with Lea, coffee at Starbucks, her visiting me at home, calling every day. I love her so much. When she visits, I feel she really wants to see me and talk to me. I love Dino and Julie very much too. I'm so proud of all of them.

Lea and I have the same (or close) to the same outlook on spirituality and life. She has so much <u>depth</u>. May seem like a strange word to use, but it fits for me.

Having Jessica's family live here is real good so far. It's only been a week. Lea and Julie helped me decide when they talked about their roommates over the years – and Lea did a lot of research on other options and helped me decide. She was so supportive. Not trying to convince me on anything but presenting me with the facts.

I'm so proud and thankful how the kids supported Brenda and I, particularly as things grew more serious for Brenda, but all through the process for over a year.

I miss Brenda so much. Everything reminds me of her.

Dino is coming to visit sometimes with me and play Dominos. We both love to play and I really look forward to his visits. Julie's too.

3/25/09:

On my desk, as I write this, there are three cards Lea sent me this past year. She wrote a little something (BIG SOMETHING) in each card. One says, "I am so proud of you. You are a strong man." Another says, "I think about you all the time. I love you." And in the third she wrote to both Brenda and I "I'm happy to be able to care for you both right now. It is the most natural thing, and know that I will make sure that you are always well cared for – so you never have to worry about your future. God is on our side. Love, your daughter, Lea."

These are not just words. They are sincere messages from the heart!

The third one was a Valentine card that said in the front, "There are some things the heart never forgets...like how it feels to be loved."

This morning I was sitting by the back sliding glass door, with the sun shining on me. "Brenda was warming me", as Lea referred to in a priceless letter that she wrote from Brenda to me, when Brenda was unable to express herself in words.

The letter was a miracle in itself, as I now can feel Brenda's warmth through the rays of the sun. No I'm not flipping out. God's creation and grace expresses itself in many ways, we just stop long enough and be still enough to appreciate it.

While I was at the glass door, I was trying to pray and meditate. I was "all over the place" and asked the Holy Spirit to guide me. Then the phone rang and I debated answering it. I decided to answer it, and it was Lea. When I got off the phone, I thought, should I go back to praying or get on with the day? I then thought, I asked the Holy Spirit's guidance, so why not go start the day on that note, and get out of the house. I was going to go to Starbucks and then grocery shopping.

Then a thought came into my head, the agency, "Second Chance" where I first started volunteering after my accident in the early 70's is right down the street on Thornton Avenue, less than ¼ mile away. I went down Thornton, pulled in the parking lot, and got out. I talked to the coordinator there, who happened to be the son of the Mayor way back at that time. I told him some of my background and he said he'd have the executive director call me. I also left a message when I got home. I just wanted to check the place out, and wouldn't it be ironic if I wound up volunteering at the same place I started 30+ years ago!

I felt so exhilarated and energized when I left that place, not so much that there might be a spot for me, but much more importantly, I felt the Holy Spirit's guidance. Some may say I just needed a psychological lift, but wouldn't it be a great way to live out the remainder of the life God gives me remembering each day that the Holy Spirit will guide me if I just allow myself to be directed.

When I was talking about my history of the agency with Mayor's son, he mentioned a woman who was a counselor at the agency where I worked part-time while attending Cal State Hayward for my Masters in counseling. This agency was

Community Counseling and Education Center, and is still in Fremont and the woman is now the Executive Director!

I remember she called me several years ago and suggested we go to lunch one day. I forgot what happened from there, but we never got together. I vaguely remember seeing her at the agency's open house when they moved. Anyway, I left a message for her as well.

Again, it does not matter to me if anything materializes from either agency, what really matters is that I felt guided and directed, and in a new (or old?) direction, and had the positive energy (grace?) to take a step.

I'm certain God has something He/She wants me to do for whatever is left of my life on this earth.

I just had a thought, Brenda might just be directing me as well.

MAYBE I SHOULD SPEND MORE TIME IN THE SUN!

3/28/09:

It's Saturday afternoon and I'm home alone. As much as I like some quiet, it gets lonely after a while. I miss Brenda. We had our disagreements, like any married couple, but we really loved each other and that I'm sure of. I still love Brenda, and she's immersed in love without limit.

It's nice to know that Jessica and family will be home later. That helps a lot.

I was thinking, I have missed so many opportunities in life, and still do. All these missed moments are those when I forget God is right with me and all I have to do is ask the Holy Spirit to guide me. Father Jim reminds me of that "leap of faith", as our minds and intellect are so limited. I know I have doubts, but that's when I must make that "leap". The alternative is not to believe the hype, and that is depressing and shows a lack of trust in God. In the spiritual group at St. Edward's this morning, Father Jim talked about all our reading,

*analyzing, rules, laws, formulas, etc. when it's really so sim-
ple. You come from that place in your heart.*

3/29/09:

*I just returned from a great visit to Lea and Oliver's
house. We had a deep conversation about spirituality and I
really appreciated Oliver sharing a very moving experience
of his and becoming vulnerable. Lea too, sharing how her
pain experience has helped her to help others who are suffering. I would like to talk to Oliver again, as I feel he is really searching.*

4/5/09:

*I'm home alone on a beautiful Saturday afternoon.
"Brenda's rays" are warming me, and I've had a nice morning. After mass I went to breakfast with Father Jim. It was
nice. After breakfast he said, "Hank, you're a shot in the arm
for me." What a compliment!! We share so much of the same
spirituality.*

*I've been thinking. All this reading and "searching" I
love it when I come across a great book. One of late, "50
Spiritual Classics" has been great. I've felt somewhat guilty
reading so much and "practicing" so little, but I remember
Father Jim said to enjoy it, don't spoil it, and most importantly he said, "It feeds you."*

*In many ways I feel I already know what to do. Most
all the spiritual masters, as I said before, repeat some core
virtues: compassion, forgiveness, present-moment living, We
Are All One on this Earth, and a lot more, but really if I practice those, I'm sure I'd be doing God's Will.*

But not without prayer and meditation.

*I'm stopping now, and my prayer is: "Holy Spirit please
help me remember that you are present to me, and in remembering your presence I surrender to and follow your guidance."*

4/7/09:

I miss Brenda! So many things remind me of her. I received a survivor's insurance check in the mail yesterday for $8,000. I DON'T WANT IT. <u>I WANT BRENDA</u>.

4/8/09:

Pretty depressed today. That word "survivor" on the check made Brenda's death real all over again, if that makes any sense, but it's the way I feel. I shared this over the phone with Lea and she was ready to change her plans and come and sleep over. That was so supportive, more than she will ever know. I look forward to seeing her tomorrow and assured her that staying the night wouldn't help. I've got to go through this a lot by myself – WITH THE HELP OF GOD.

****

Physical Response

My dad wasn't at his best. He would call Jessica many times in the middle of the night. He was compulsive about his care. He was frantic a lot. I could empathize with my dad. After all, he had just lost my mom. He'd never lived in that house without her. He'd never dealt with his disability without her. He'd never lived with anyone else his entire adult life. He was used to her presence. I'm sure he was just occupying himself as much as possible in a way most comfortable for him – focusing on his physical condition. Also, what was it like for my dad to get up in the morning and not have work to go to? To not have my mom to help and nurture?

One evening, Jessica called me and said, "Lea, I'm really concerned about your dad's leg. In a few hours, the redness has spread from his foot to his upper thigh. I think he should go to the hospital, but he doesn't want to. I think you're the only person he will listen to."

My dad had an infection in his foot. Shortly after my mom died, he had hurt it and didn't mention it to me for weeks. He was in his van in the driving position and he spasmed and his foot bounced up and when it came down, it hit a metal piece that was sticking up on his wheelchair foot plate. It punctured the bottom of his foot creating a small little hole. Being a quadriplegic, infection is always a concern because his body doesn't heal the same as others with his poor circulation and paralysis. He had told Jessica about it, and she had been treating it, however, there was a crust, like a callous, surrounding it that had come off, and underneath you could see it was infected. It kept getting worse and worse. The redness surrounding the area was spreading each day.

My dad was very afraid of hospitalizations. He had such unpleasant memories from his accident, and he also witnessed patients every day through his work at the VA hospital and saw what these spinal chord injury patients went through. The only other hospitalization he had in his life since his accident was a planned bladder surgery when he was in his 30's. I knew the reason my dad didn't tell me about his infection was his wishful thinking that it would all just go away. He didn't want to face it.

That night when Jessica called me, my dad had another nurse friend over that lived nearby examining him. She also agreed he should go to the hospital. He refused. I asked Jessica to let me talk to him. I said, "Dad, what I'm hearing from Jessica is that in a few short hours, your infection has spread from your foot to your upper thigh. If this is true, then I'm going to ask Jessica to call an ambulance to get you to the hospital so they can take care of this infection." I expected an argument, but surprisingly my dad said, "Okay."

This first hospital stay involved a learning curve for all of us. We always knew if my dad ever needed to be in a hospital that he would need 24x7 care there, and my sister and I arranged that for him. When my dad was released, I took detailed notes of how to care for his infection and we had a home health nurse assigned to visit and check on him. Once home, we noticed my dad was weaker. The fact that he was in a hospital bed lying down for a week was very hard on his system – especially his respiratory system.

****

Choices

"Dominic, I have something to tell you," I said, as I motioned to Dominic to sit next to me on the couch. "I won't be able to drive and go to your field trip tomorrow." Both Dominic and I had been looking forward to going to his 2nd grade field trip to the beach. He was excited that I was driving, and that I could take him and his friends in our car. He started crying when I told him the news. He asked me why. I explained that grandpa is in the hospital and I would be there helping him. He asked, "Why can't Auntie Julie help him?" I said, "Auntie Julie is helping him too." Dominic was upset and disappointed, as was I!

I decided to draw him a picture. I took out a big plain white sheet of paper. I drew a figure lying down on a bed (grandpa), and I put an ambulance there and a doctor and nurses. I put a tear in grandpa's eye, and said he is feeling scared and alone at the hospital because he just got there and he is still getting used to it. Then on the other side of the paper, I put all the people in our family, and in another corner all the people in my sister's family. I explained to him that with grandpa's illness, it does interfere with a lot of plans, for a lot of people. I explained that sometimes in life we have to make hard choices – like my choice to help grandpa instead of going on his field trip which I was looking forward to.

I drew some more. I drew his school and the beach. I drew both him and I with cloud thought bubbles above our heads, dreaming and looking forward to our fun beach field trip day. Then I drew us again, with tears, and I said we're both disappointed that our plans that we were so looking forward to had changed.

Then I drew the last picture. I drew a picture of me and Dominic during our "mommy and Dominic make-up day". We were smiling and happy. I told him that we will go out, just the two of us, to make up for this disappointment. Dominic was feeling better now, although still a bit sad. He seemed to understand.

We did have our "mommy and Dominic day" a few days later. We went to Dominic's favorite book store together. We got ice cream and hung out. We had a lot of fun– just him and me. Dominic told me all about his field trip and how much fun he had, despite the fact that I didn't go.

Looking back, I realize how during this time in my life, I was doing exactly what I wanted to do in the big picture of life, even though the details of what I was doing weren't always exactly what I wanted to be spending time on. However, I was fully engaged in life. What was there for me to complain about? My mind was simply not looking there. I was too consumed doing what mattered most, and what was most fulfilling to me – using my strengths toward a vision that was bigger than myself, and one that I was so connected to, it inspired me to act without hesitation, confusion or upset. I was feeling lots of love.

****

Drama

The living situation with Jessica and her family was not going well. I remember talking to my dad and he would seem very reasonable and seemed to understand what I was explaining about his behavior, however, it was as if he couldn't help it. Jessica gave the news that they would be moving out, however, she was so good about it and gave us notice. She wanted to wait until we found someone else, and I knew we had to find someone quick. I didn't want to take advantage of her loyalty to my dad. I was just so thankful that she was still willing to take care of him like she used to – just not living there. My sister and I started working right away on other options. It's not that easy to find live-in care for a quadriplegic, but we knew we would find someone.

My sister was connected with a woman from her church who I'll call Lucy. We had reservations about her because Lucy had a pre-teenage son, however, my dad liked the idea of helping out a single mom by giving her a nice living situation. My dad interviewed her and met her son and really liked them. We also met her and she seemed nice and caring. My sister received reassurance from the person at the church who recommended her that if anything went wrong, we could call him and he would intervene. We decided to give Lucy a try.

Lucy was great at caring for my dad, and we still had Jessica coming for all the complex needs of my dad involving bowel and bladder care, bathing, etc. Lucy cooked and cleaned and doted on my dad. She made some great meals, which was a huge benefit. Her son seemed to have some issues with lying, which was our first sign of trouble. Then we caught Lucy in lies too regarding missing medications from my dad, for example. We also found empty alcohol bottles and her son expressed that he was worried because he didn't want his mom to ruin their new living situation. Well, long story short, it turns out Lucy was an alcoholic. Things got pretty dramatic.

In July that summer, we went to a hall in Fremont to celebrate my sister's husband, Norman's birthday. (We didn't know it at the time, but this day would be the last time my dad drove his van). My dad left the party while it was still light out and went home. My sister and I left and got back to my sister's house around 9:00pm. The phone rang at my sister's house. It was my dad and he was completely frantic. He said that Lucy was passed out on the floor of his bedroom. Thank God my dad was able to call us! (He had a special phone next to his bed that he just needed to hit with his hand and depending on how many times he hit it, it would automatically call specific people. One hit was my sister's phone number.) My sister and I rushed over to his house together.

We arrived and quickly went into my dad's bedroom and saw Lucy on the floor. We got her up and helped her as she stumbled to the other room and we maneuvered her to lie down on the couch where she promptly passed out again. My sister called the man she knew at the church and told him to come get Lucy <u>now</u>. He agreed. The next problem we had was that her son wasn't home. He often was out roaming around. With Lucy out of the house, we then waited until her son showed up the next morning. While my sister handled getting Lucy's son taken care of, I was on the phone figuring out how to get new care for my dad. These were the most stressful of times when the caregivers wouldn't be working out because my dad really needed the care. Both my sister and I had young kids, husbands and were self-employed. It was impossible for us to do the care ourselves without major consequences to our own lives. It was hard enough what we had been doing the last couple of years with managing both of our parents' care needs and finances, and basically their lives.

My sister went above and beyond and listened to Lucy's son's wishes about contacting a family friend that lived in another state. Lucy called us and expressed how sorry she was, and that she was worried about losing custody of her son. Her son wanted to stay with his mom, but wanted to be close by the family friend in another state. My sister was able to contact this family friend. We bought both Lucy and her son one-way train tickets, and my sister dropped them off at the station and waited until she saw them board the train. We were glad to see them leave, and also felt good that we helped facilitate a safe situation for them.

Meanwhile, I was on the phone and it turned out that Jessica's sister, Christina, and her fiancée, Chris, were interested in moving into my dad's house and taking care of him. They came over that very afternoon and agreed to a trial run. We were ecstatic! It was so nice to have the connection with Jessica, which made us very comfortable. Christina and Chris were great, and it ended up that the trial run went well and they stayed and were dedicated to my dad and our family during many challenging situations to come.

Following is the live-in agreement we used to align expectations. The agreement was not reviewed to determine legality. It is just something I wrote up and we decided to use in our situation for the clarity of all involved.

Living Arrangement Expectations and Agreement

Expectations and agreement for living arrangement with Hank Gambina, and [NAMES] (Roommate/caregiver), in Hank's home in Newark, California:

PG&E, garbage, water, internet access, cable TV: Hank will cover, with the understanding that roommate/caregiver will be respectful and aware of utility usage, i.e. turn off lights when not in use, turn off heater and A/C in house when no one is home, etc.

Food, groceries, household supplies: Hank and roommate/caregiver will cover their own food and grocery expenses. Hank will cover the cost of household supplies. Roommate/caregiver is responsible for shopping when necessary.

Meals: Roommate/caregiver is responsible for preparing and serving all meals – including for Hank.

House cleaning: Roommate/caregiver is responsible for all house cleaning, i.e. sweeping, mopping, dusting, windows, blinds, kitchen, bathrooms, bedrooms, etc. – including Hank's bedroom and bathroom.

Laundry: Roommate/caregiver is responsible for all laundry – including Hank's, i.e. washing, folding, changing bed linens, etc.

Yard: Hank will keep gardener for lawn cutting and edging.

Storage: The house has minimal storage space. It is expected that caregiver will figure out another location to store any belongings that will not fit in available closets and storage places in the house.

Dog, Emma:
Roommate/caregiver is responsible for feeding Emma

twice a day, and giving her fresh water daily. No other food should be given to Emma other than dog food.

Emma should always have someone with her when out front. She should stay on the lawn area.

Emma enjoys being around people, and should be indoors most of the time (generally she goes outside alone only to go to the bathroom; she should never be left out in front yard alone).

<u>Sharing House:</u>

Bedrooms: Each bedroom is a private area for the person whose room it is, and can be decorated however they wish. There is a twin bed in the extra bedroom that should remain, however, Roommate/caregiver can use the room as a multi-purpose room, such as an office, etc., as long as a guest of Hank can sleep there when necessary.

Bathrooms: Back bathroom is Hank's private bathroom; middle bathroom is Roommate/caregiver's private bathroom.

Kitchen: Kitchen is shared.

Family Room with Picture Window: This is Hank's private area, and the accordion door can be closed for those moments when he or Roommate/caregiver wishes to have some privacy.

Living Room with Sliding Glass Door: This room is shared, and will be considered Roommate/caregiver's "living area". (Hank enjoys sitting in the sun by the sliding glass door.)

Backyard: Backyard is shared.

<u>Lifestyle Expectations:</u>

No smoking in the home by anyone.

No drug usage or excess alcohol usage by anyone.

Roommate/caregiver may have guests visit if pre-arranged and agreed to by Hank.

Expectations for Hank's Care: (Note: *Either* [NAMES] can provide the below care, and they can coordinate amongst themselves who will be available when so that Hank is not alone in the house for more than an hour):

Day-to-Day Assistance: Due to Hank's disability (he is a quadriplegic, and his vision is impaired), it is expected that Roommate/caregiver will assist Hank with all day-to-day aspects of life, i.e. cooking and serving meals, making and pouring drinks, assisting with medications, cleaning, laundry, picking up things he drops, helping him with sorting or organizing items or papers, straightening his desk or other areas for him; basically helping him with anything he is unable to do for himself because of his disabilities.

Note on Meals: Preparation and serving breakfast (around 6:30am), lunch (around noon), and dinner (around 5:30pm) for Hank is expected daily.

Note on Medications: Julie, Hank's daughter, is in charge of keeping record and tracking all medications that Hank takes. She fills his pill box on a weekly basis. No changes to medications should be made without first consulting Julie by phone. Hank has been known to make adjustments to his own medications based on what he personally feels and thinks, versus what the doctor prescribed. Hank has agreed to consult with Julie prior to making any change to either a dosage of a medication (frequency), or before stopping a medication, or starting a new one, however, he doesn't always remember to do this. *Please call Julie if you are asked by Hank to do ANYTHING with his medications (including vitamins or supplements) other than simply assisting him with taking what Julie has already put in his pill box. [PHONE NO.].*

Doctor appointments: It is expected that Roommate/ caregiver accompany Hank to occasional doctor appointments and take notes at the appointments to share with his daughters.

Spending the Night: It is expected that Roommate/ caregiver spend the night every night at the house. Note: Once Hank is out of his wheelchair and in bed for the evening (approximately 8:00 p.m.), it is important that the Roommate/ caregiver be in the house.

Middle of the Night Assistance: There are times when Hank will need assistance in the middle of the night due to his disability (quadriplegia), i.e. straightening his legs, etc. This can occur approximately once a night – sometimes more often.

Cell Phone: Roommate/caregiver should be reachable by cell phone when he or she is not at home.

Clarification of Acceptable Time Away:
One day per week from 12pm-9pm (as requested), plus miscellaneous hours as described below.

One weekend (Fri. evening to Sun. evening) every other month (or equivalent).

Vacation: One week a year vacation is acceptable after 9 months of living in Hank's home.

NOTE: It is imperative that all time away is pre-arranged and that a replacement for Hank's care is arranged for prior to leaving. A list of contact names will be provided for those people that are available to cover certain hours of the day, and/or overnights. As much notice as possible is needed, otherwise, there may not be available coverage, i.e. a week or 2 notice for miscellaneous hours, and a month's notice for overnight coverage.

50 hours per month allowed to be coordinated to cover #1 above (the 9 hours a week plus other miscellaneous hours) when there are no planned weekends away or vacation in that month.

40 hours per month allowed when there is a planned weekend or vacation away in that month.

NOTE: The 50 or 40 hours is a guideline to help control costs, and provide flexibility; the hours are not meant to carry over month-to-month and should be viewed as "maximum" numbers. We realize that this number will be exceeded for those months that Roommate/caregiver takes a weekend off or vacation, and that is okay. Roommate/caregiver is responsible for coordinating coverage for all time taken away.

No "Employee/Employer" Relationship: Roommate/caregiver understands that this agreement is to provide clarity for a mutually desired living arrangement, and understands that he or she is not an "employee" of Hank's for any purpose.

Insurance: Roommate/caregiver understands that he and she is responsible for his and her own medical insurance, renter insurance, or any other insurance, and that Hank is not responsible to provide any financial or other support to Roommate/caregiver, or initiate any insurance claims, in the case of injury, or lost or stolen items, or other unforeseen circumstances that may befall on Roommate/caregiver. The same is true in reverse, and Roommate/caregiver is likewise not responsible for Hank.

Term of Living Arrangement: After the 2 week trial period beginning [DATE], Hank, Roommate/caregiver, and one of Hank's daughters, will meet and talk about continuing the living arrangement. If it is agreed that the living arrangement will continue, there will be no set time period for this living arrangement, however, at least 30 days notice in writing to the other would be appreciated if either Hank or Roommate/ caregiver wishes to end the living arrangement.

Communication: It is important that Hank and Roommate/caregiver get together on a monthly basis to "check in" with each other to see how the living arrangement is working for each person, and to openly and respectfully discuss any concerns or desires.

Goals: The 1st goal of this live-in arrangement is to provide consistent, reliable care for Hank, with the Roommate/ caregiver being responsible for the coordination of care when he or she is away – keeping in mind that the people on the contact list should not be over-utilized, which is why guidelines are given above.

The 2ⁿᵈ goal is to work with the natural lifestyle of the Roommate/caregiver and provide as much flexibility as possible, without conflicting with the 1ˢᵗ goal. Once Hank is in his wheelchair, he is relatively independent considering his disabilities, however, he needs someone on a daily and overnight basis as outlined above so he is well cared for.

The dates and signatures below of Hank and Roommate/ caregiver show agreement with and understanding of the terms of the living arrangement outlined above.

****

Writing Escape

In the summer of 2009, I took the opportunity to ask my dad questions and jot down his answers. Unfortunately, I only have notes, as my dad wasn't able to participate much after his physical ailments overtook him. Fortunately, I have some insight from him, and I'm very grateful I had the presence of mind to bring my laptop over and write on subjects that were most important to him. My dad enjoyed talking about "deep" subjects like spirituality.

I asked my dad for his explanation of the meaning of "compassion". I took notes then wrote-up this description based on what my dad said. I remember reading it back to him and him grinning from ear to ear, saying, "You got it! How do you *do* that?" I'm glad I got it right for him. (It's great fun for me to talk with someone, get a sense of what they're trying to say, and then write it down in summary. Then, my favorite part of all, is when the person reads it and says exactly what my dad did, "*You got it!*")

"Compassion is the action word for God. I believe in God because I see goodness. I see people who are compassionate with no strings attached – a natural outpouring. God is a term. We cannot see God. The closest you can come is a little child – innocence, natural authenticity. It's not about observing "good people". With any human, we fall short from experiencing God because of our humanity. Compassion is the complete opposite of egocentricity. Compassion is beyond thinking about "helping others" – it is a natural state of being. Compassion is not about keeping track to "score points" or to achieve a feeling of goodness or personal fulfillment. It goes beyond due to its natural state – devoid of ego. Doing good works is concrete – tasks that truly help others, i.e. building homes for tornado victims, giving food to the hungry at Thanksgiving – and givers truly gain. Going even beyond these important good works is where compassion comes in. Authenticity without reciprocity or expectation – and beyond conscious awareness of personal satisfaction. How can this compassion – this natural goodness – come from humanity alone? How can one explain the experience of compas-

sion? I can only say that humans show compassion – glimpses of compassion – without presence of thought – they act with altruism – an authenticity that touches another's soul."

These writing sessions with my dad were so precious. I could see that my dad was able to escape from his grief and worries when talking about his favorite subjects, and I was the perfect audience. I am very interested in the topics that he wanted to discuss:

-Spirituality
-Meaning of Life
-Fear vs. Love instead of Evil vs. Good
-Gratitude
-Acceptance
-Ecumenism (unity among faiths)
-Compassion
-Stillness
-Joy
-Belief

I discovered something quite interesting during one of our writing sessions. I said to my dad, "We could write a book!" I was shocked by my dad's response. He said, "Who am I to write a book?" I stared at him with my mouth open. I thought, 'Wow. He really doesn't know how awesome he is.'

I told him, "Dad, first of all, the fact that with your disability you've managed to…."

He cut me off and said, "I wouldn't want to stand on my disability." My dad always deflected when it came to focusing on his disability. He made great efforts to be treated like everyone else, and he didn't like the idea of "special treatment" because of his disability, and did not want to glorify it.

I explained to my dad, "But, dad, do you realize who you could reach with your story?" I got his attention. I said, "Dad, your story is a story of hope. You've persevered against all odds. You've also done much more in your life apart from overcoming your physical challenges."

My dad started giving my mom all the credit, like he usually did. I validated my mom and all her efforts and told him that I understand that without mom, he wouldn't have had as much opportunity to live the life he did. Then I said, "Dad, please don't invalidate your own efforts. You and mom worked as a team. You also did your part to get where you are."

I went on to say, "All the books you enjoy reading – they are written by human beings. They are no different than you or me. They have something to say, and they wrote it down for all to read as an offering. You have something to say too – something that could greatly support many people."

He did not argue with me. However, he did say that his main love is the process of us writing together, and that if it didn't become a book, that would be okay with him. It was okay with me too because I felt exactly the same way. At this point in his life, the process of him speaking and me writing and reading back to him what I summarized, was such an enjoyable process for us both. Talk about "clicking" and feeling completely understood.

I wish I had more time with my dad (and my mom) to sit and listen to them talk to their heart's content about all the subjects that they loved. What an incredible legacy that would have been. That shortfall is partially what inspired me to write this book. I want to preserve as much as possible of my parents' memory. I am so grateful for them. However, writing a book seemed like a daunting task. I've never done it before. Also, I had thoughts of, "Would it really be that interesting?" Then I would remember that little lecture I gave my dad about how all books are written by human beings no different than him or me. I would have a similar conversation with myself when I'd slow down on my writing. I would tell myself. *"I have something to say…and someone will appreciate hearing it."*

I do believe that *everyone* has something to say that, if said, has a huge percentage chance to be impactful for many, many people. Why?

Because we are all so unique as individual human beings, and different people can "speak to" certain people. Meaning, my style and personality may fall on deaf ears to certain personalities, however, to another person, the way I'm expressing myself can be heard crystal clear and because of this, that person will be touched and find value in what I'm writing. I believe it's this way for *anyone* that decides to write a book – some people will "get it", appreciate it, and as a result, will experience a positive impact from the words, and others will not.

The point is, if there is even *one person* impacted by the words of another, it makes the effort worthwhile – not to mention the personal therapeutic effect and gain that comes with the process of writing. The fact is, if *one person* is impacted, there is a certain percentage beyond that one person that will be impacted as well. And the really exciting part is that each one of the people impacted has their own circle of influence, and there is no telling whose life will be touched by someone's words. *It's all about the ripple effect.* And when words are written down, *they last forever.*

This understanding I have is also what motivates me to work with "life vision". It's the same premise – if I (one person) move about in the world authentically, being who I am, I will have a positive impact on at least one other person– most likely more. This vision is inspiring to me, and makes my personal, and seemingly isolated, efforts as one human being worthwhile to me. Those efforts that I make – even when I am alone and I am tempted to skip – matter. I think of the impact that I'm sure to make, and I am inspired to take action.

I'm not saying I act at all times even when I don't feel like it. Sometimes I drag my feet, eat a cookie or take a nap. What I'm saying, though, is that because I have a vision, I act much more often and more consistently than I would have otherwise. This is because I'm clear on *why* I'm taking a certain step. I'm able to see past the moment of challenge to the bigger reason, which is what helps me move.

It's not easy, but it's easier taking action with a vision, than it is using "push and prod" tactics. When I use sheer will and push myself with thoughts of punishment or shame when I don't live up to my own expectations, I also bring results, however, in a much less pleasant and much more inconsistent way. I believe the use of willpower cannot give lasting results if the "big why" is missing. It just becomes an uphill battle, and at this point in my life, I'm interested in flowing in alignment with what's most important in life – to me – in context with my connection to all others.

We're all in this thing called life together. Might as well join forces. I find life to be much more fun and interesting this way. Who made up life's rules and deadlines anyway?

****

Project

One project I proposed to my dad that he took me up on was to write a list of his favorite books. He had so much fun doing this. He took it very seriously and also marked the ones that were his all-time favorites. My dad has read many, many books in his lifetime. I remember him saying that when he was in his Masters program for his MFT degree, the students were only required to read 2 out of 10 suggested books, and my dad read all 10. He said he would have been a full-time student if he could have made a living out of it.

Below is my dad's list. This list is priceless. I'm so glad I thought to ask him to write it. His opinion holds a lot of weight. This list comes from a man who was 70 years old, lived life fully, despite a severe disability that most people would have died from many years earlier, or developed addictions to cope with. My dad learned something in this life, and even though we don't have a book written by Hank Gambina, at least we have words from those my dad learned from and greatly assisted him throughout his journey on this planet.

Hank Gambina's Favorite Books on Spirituality

(List complied in 2009)

Author	Title
Abernathy & Bole	The Life of Meaning
Bailey, J.K.	Already on Holy Ground
Chittister, Joan	Welcome to the Wisdom of the World
Chopra, Deepak	The Third Jesus
DeMello, Anthony	Awareness
*Dowd, Michael	Thank God for Evolution
Dyer, Wayne	Your Erroneous Zones
Dyer, Wayne	Wisdom of the Ages
*Dyer, Wayne	Change Your Thoughts Change Your Life
Kennedy, Robert E.	Zen Spirit Christian Spirit
*Kornfield, Jack	The Wise Heart
*Lesser, Elizabeth	The Seekers Guide
McCleod, Melvin	Mindful Politics
*Moore, Thomas	The Soul's Religion
Moses, Jeffrey	Oneness
Robinson, Jonathan	The Complete Idiot's Guide to Awakening Your Spirituality
*Rohr, Richard	Simplicity
*Rohr, Richard	Everything Belongs
Rohr, Richard	Things Hidden
Thich Nhat Hanh	Going Home
Thich Nhat Hanh	Living Buddha Living Christ
*Tolle, Ekhardt	The Power of Now
Wallis, Jim	God's Politics

Wallis, Jim	*The Great Awakening*
*Walsh, Roger	*Essential Spirituality*
Zubko, Andy	*Treasury of Spiritual*
	Wisdom

*= the best of the best

It was so fun watching my dad work on the above project. It's quite interesting to see how he narrowed his favorites down. I printed copies of this list for him and he enjoyed handing them out to people who visited him. I'm so grateful for this list. I've read 3 of the books so far, and I'm interested in reading more, if not all. There is so much more for me to learn, and I feel like I'll be connecting with my dad as I read and learn from the books he was so inspired by.

"Change the way you look at things and the things you look at change."

(Quote by Dr. Wayne Dyer)

****

Curveball

"Hi, dad, how are you?" I asked him on my cell phone as I was halfway to his house. It was a Wednesday, and I was on my way after work for my weekly visit and overnight stay at his house.

Surprisingly, my dad answered, "Great! I just got home, and I've been out since 7:30 this morning."

He went on to tell me that he went to the bookstore and had his coffee. Then he went to the mall and bought a picture. He said it reminded him of one I had. It was a picture of Venice, Italy, and he was very excited because he negotiated a good price. By the time I hung up the phone,

I was thinking how nice it was to be going for a visit when my dad was in a good mood and things seemed to be falling into place a bit.

Barely 10 minutes later, I got a call on my cell phone from Shirlee. She said, "Okay. I'm on my way with your dad to the hospital."

I said, "What? What happened? I just talked to him!" She said that he lost his sight. She said he was at his desk, guzzled a sport drink, then all of a sudden his vision went black.

I calmly said, "I'll see you at the hospital." Then I made a turn and headed over there instead of to my dad's house. It was surreal how calm I was.

I arrived at the hospital and found my dad. He was in a total panic. He was saying, "Lea, what am I going to do not being able to see? How will I get around in my chair? What will I do?!!"

I said, very calmly, as I put my hand gently on his shoulder, "Dad, why don't we do this. Why don't we wait to see what the doctor has to say and go from there?" I started massaging his shoulders. He started calming down and saying, "You're right, you're right. Okay, we'll wait."

By the time my dad left the hospital that evening, he had regained some vision. He could see shapes of people, however, could not see detail enough to recognize who they were. He was actually very relieved though because he just kept saying, "At least I can maneuver my wheelchair!"

He saw a specialist the next day. Turns out, he had a ruptured blood vessel and blood was filling up in his eye which blurred his vision. There was a new medication that helped clear this up that he began taking. He was one of the fortunate ones that experienced some improvement in his vision, however, he was considered legally blind, and could no longer drive. He also couldn't see well enough to read.

He was still thankful that he had some improvement because the thought of being in darkness really, really upset him. (I can imagine.) I was surprised at how happy he was because his vision was still very poor, and two things were just taken away from him – driving (his independence), and reading (his #1 enjoyment). One thing about my dad, he tended to focus on the positive.

****

Social Release

During this period of crisis with my parents, I hadn't been socializing as much. Priorities shifted, and I was okay with that – to a point. I decided to have my old high school friends over for a get-together. I seem to recall it was Christmas time. I've kept in touch with friends I've met throughout my life pretty well, and I'm close with many of them still. I remember in the days before the party I thought about some high school episodes and I smiled. Memories can do that. They can make me smile and they can make me cry. I wanted to smile. I had way too much intensity and sadness, and I just wanted to hang out with friends.

I was inspired to write the below poem. The stories in it are all true. (I've changed the names to protect the innocent!)

The Egg in My Purse

Memories of high school – a time when life was nice and light.
Laughing so hard at the simplest things –
    like someone having the hiccups,
        or seeing soda shooting out of someone's nose.

A time when the big drama talk of the day was about slipping
    on french fries in the cafeteria and falling flat on your face
        at the feet of the boy you had a major crush on.

I miss the laughter!

I should be belly laughing every damn day.
    After all, aren't little kids hilarious?
I suppose they have their moments, but sadly, no,
    I don't belly laugh EVERY DAY
        like I did back in the day!

When my kids fart, it's not funny. Well, actually it is funny,
unless they're the wet gassy ones that I have to leave the room for,
      but belly laugh?
      It's just not the same.
      It's not like the "egg in my purse" incident.
           You had to be there.
           (Let's just say, if there is ever a smell around you –
             blame the egg.)

I have more memories from high school that still make me laugh:

      Like the time a bird crapped on Lisa
           when she stepped off the school bus.
      The funny part was how mortified she was.

      Or when my sister was following me and my friends
           in the hall and slipped on the stairs and went
           down the whole flight on her butt as her books
           flew up all around her –
      It was all so dramatic, poor thing.

      Or when I threw up in the garbage can in front of
      my homeroom class as I sweated and waited for my
      teacher to write me a permission slip to go to
           the nurse's office.

      Or when all day long, Stacy said she had something
      to tell me, but couldn't remember, then at the end
      of the day, she excitedly said,
           "I remember what I was going to tell you!"
           "My dog died!"
      (It was really funny the way she said it! Or
      maybe I just have a morbid sense of humor.)

I remember laughing loud and hard in high school
      – <u>every</u> <u>single</u> <u>day</u>.

Okay, friends! It's been 24 years since high school.
    It's time to create those moments again!
        We're long overdue for belly laughs!
    As adults we can be soooooo serious!
    How about being a little unreasonable for a change?
        That's it! Be responsible, but be *unreasonable*.

Why can't we juggle oranges in the grocery store?
    Okay, well, if you can't juggle, then forget that one.
        Wouldn't want to bruise the fruit.

Don't forget the opportunities in those elevators!
    What's wrong with shaking hands with everyone in there
        to introduce yourself?
    Or passing out your leftover Valentine's Day stickers?
    Better yet, stick them on their shirts to spread the joy.

When you're driving - pull over, blast the stereo,
    and dance on the sidewalk!
Don't let the weather stop you either.
    So what if it's pouring rain!
    Keep a slicker in the front seat for just these occasions.

Imagine how it would feel to drive to the top of Mount Diablo,
look out over the view, and scream,
    "Woo hoo!!" as loud as you possible can?
    With your arms straight up in the air!
        Then jump around and wiggle your butt.
            Why the hell not? And who really cares?

If we think about it….if our kids were with us,
    and they did any one of these things,
        most people would think they were delightful
        (or unruly, but let's stay focused on the positive).

As adults doing these things, we would get a mixture
    of nervous smiles and some frowns.

Basically, most people would think we're a little bit silly,
        but no doubt entertaining –
                a little bit "off", but harmless.

I say, "Let's get off!" Wait – that would be crossing the line
        (although it is *unreasonable* to get off in public...)

Anyway, I say, "Let's get crazy!" Throw people off!
        Mix some spice into an otherwise normal day.

Smile at people that frown. (Yes, I stole this line
        – but it's a good one!)
Tell jokes in grocery store lines.
Ask strangers if they know who invented pants.
        or ask if they believe in Santa Claus,
                and if not, why.
Do whatever pops in your mind that's not unkind!

And, if all these public displays are just too hard at first,
        at the very least, start carrying an egg in your purse!

Part Six

Enduring

For the 2009 holiday season, Oliver and I decided to go to Italy to visit his father and his half sisters. We had been talking about doing this for years. Oliver's Italian side had never met Dominic and Sophie, and his father was 70 years old. Even though he was healthy, we just didn't know how many years he would have left.

I was visiting my dad one afternoon and we left the house to go to a nearby café for lunch, as we often did. I asked him how he felt about me going to Italy for 5 weeks over Christmas. I knew it was the first Christmas without my mom, and I also knew how the first holidays prior to this one were. My dad was essentially silent and wishing the day away. He had no interest in celebrating. Holidays were a drag at this time because care needs fell mainly on my sister and me. Caregivers of course wanted time off to be with their families, as did the on-call caregivers. My dad had no interest in going to my sister's house 5 minutes away, so my sister and I decided to rotate holidays – meaning we would "babysit" my dad during the holiday so the other could celebrate it elsewhere. My sister agreed to handle Christmas so I could go to Italy, and I would handle Thanksgiving before I left.

My dad was very supportive about Italy. He had a lot of guilt about all the time that us kids were spending caring for him, and also the time and energy we spent for my mom. He had a stable living situation at this time with Christina and Chris and he was doing okay for the most part. His attitude made it so much easier on me to go to Italy without feeling bad about it, however, I knew it was the right thing to do either way. I knew he had the care, so it was a bonus in my mind that he was supportive of me taking this trip.

During our conversation, I also asked him if he ever thought about or wanted to live with Julie or me in our homes. I was just curious because friends of his had made comments after my mom died pretty much assuming that my dad would move in with one of us. My dad immediately refused that idea. He said he didn't think it would be a good thing for either my sister or me. He knew how much care he required and he also knew how hard it was on my mom and he didn't want to be more of a burden than he already felt he was. He said it sounded nice to him in one sense, however, he knew it was not a good idea. He also liked being in his home.

This attitude of his was another bonus. I also did not believe it would be a good choice for him to live with either my sister or me. We had played with the idea of my brother living with him at the house, however, my brother wasn't too excited about the idea because he knew my dad's intense care needs, so this idea was quickly dismissed.

****

What a Way to Go

During the same visit when my dad and I had the Italy discussion, we were strolling around the streets of Newark on our way to a café. We actually went the opposite direction than usual to go to a different place. This other direction required crossing the railroad tracks near my parents' house. My dad was used to riding his wheelchair in the middle of the street to get over the tracks because of the asphalt that was lifted on either side. He couldn't get over the tracks any other way.

We arrived at the tracks and I watched my dad move his electric wheelchair out into the middle of the street. I got very concerned about how slow he was going. I realized pretty quickly that he wasn't realizing his impairment. I've seen him do this before, several years earlier. He used to go much quicker and was much more alert. This time, because of his eyesight and his more feeble state, he was going too slow. Traffic was stopping all around him, and I couldn't push his electric chair. We finally made it across, but not before people stopped in the middle of the street and got out thinking we needed assistance.

Because the sidewalks weren't as wheelchair friendly on this side, I suggested to my dad that we turn around and go back. We arrived back at those train tracks and we were waiting near a piece of cement next to the automated arm that comes down to stop traffic. A train started coming and that arm started coming down right next to my dad. It clipped his wheelchair foot plate and it got wedged underneath. I struggled to get him loose. We were way too close to those tracks and the train was coming fast! Both my dad and I were so focused and we moved out of the way as the train passed.

We had to go across through the middle of the street again – this time my dad was much sharper – I'm sure from adrenaline. We got to the other side and I said, "That would have been an interesting way to go!" My dad started laughing and we were joking about it all the way back home. That was probably the most excitement my dad had in a long time.

I convinced my dad to promise me that he would not venture out that way again – even if he was with other people. He argued with me at first. I explained that the street by the tracks is even worse than it was years ago, and his eyesight is worse, and he's slower in general, and that it's just not necessary to go that way when there was plenty of shopping and a café the other direction on sidewalks that are flat with the safety of traffic lights. He did finally agree and saw the logic. I was surprised he was initially against my suggestion being as he was almost hit by a train, however, I understood that it was yet another limitation placed on him. He always had the freedom to go in whatever direction he wanted in the neighborhood. I'm sure it was just hard for him to accept even more loss of independence.

****

Up and Away

Our Italy trip was approaching. It wasn't so easy making this 5-week trip happen. After all, we had a small business, and had never been gone longer than a week or so. Six months prior to our trip, after we purchased the tickets and committed to making it happen, we paid attention to our day-to-day in a different way than ever before. Each thing that happened in the business, and in general, we asked ourselves this one question: "How could this be handled if we were not here?" Then we would figure out the best solution. By the time our trip came, we had solutions for our home, mail, bills, business, dad's care needs – which was a combination of us working remotely through the internet, and people helping out back home.

We made no plans for our time in Italy, other than hanging out with the Italians and being open to whatever transpired.

Oliver's family was very excited about our arrival. They live in the Southern Region of Italy (down in the "boot") in a region called Calabria. They live in a house that had been in their family for generations. As is common in the area, the home was divided into apartments. There were four 2-bedroom apartments in the home. Oliver's sister, Valeria, had recently gotten married and she and her husband, Piero, remodeled the ground floor apartment. Her parents lived in the apartment directly above them, and the other two apartments were closed and reserved for Oliver's uncle and his family.

We had no idea where we would be sleeping when we arrived at their home because we knew the apartments were small and we had a family of four. I pictured us on couches or blow-up mattresses. I remember visiting Oliver's father and his family in Germany before Oliver and I were married, and they were living in a one bedroom apartment – his sisters in the bedroom, and his father and his wife, Fabiola, on a pullout couch in the front room. (They had to move the dining table out of the way each night to pull out the couch).

Our trip to Italy took 24 hours door-to-door. We had a plane transfer in Atlanta, then again in Rome, where we got on a smaller Italian plane to get closer to where they lived. We were exhausted when we arrived. Both the Atlanta and Rome airports were very big and we literally had to run to reach our connecting flights on time. We were hot and sweaty by the time we reached our final destination. It was very exciting though. We could see the Italians jumping up and down in the distance as we walked through the gates at the small airport. So many family members came to greet us. They didn't speak any English – only Italian and German – so we relied on Oliver to translate for us. We got hugs and kisses non-stop. It was such a wonderful greeting.

Their house was only a half hour away. I remember thinking how glad I was that we decided to take that 3rd flight instead of renting a car in Rome and driving 7 hours. We all could not keep our eyes open during that short drive to their house. When we arrived, we carried the kids inside and put them on the couch in Valeria's apartment downstairs since they were sound asleep. Valeria gave us a tour of her and Piero's apartment. It was beautiful. It was so modern with upscale fixtures, nice flooring, a new kitchen, etc. It had a beautiful Christmas tree that was all decorated. Then I noticed a framed wedding picture on the wall of Oliver and me, and a few other pictures framed and hung on the walls that we've sent them over the years.

Valeria then showed us the bedrooms and explained that we would be staying in their apartment while they stayed upstairs with her parents. What a surprise! They were so happy to have us stay there and wouldn't hear any opposition to it. They even painted and decorated their 2nd bedroom "kid friendly" with bright orange and yellow colors and put 2 twin beds in there for Dominic and Sophie. They had stuffed animals they bought them and little slippers for them too. Their hospitality was incredible. They even bought slippers for Oliver and me.

We went upstairs and saw the apartment where Oliver's father, Amerigo, and his wife, Fabiola, lived. It was nice and bright and had a huge balcony with a beautiful view of the lush green ridges of Southern Italy. Both apartments were small by American standards, however, they had everything anyone would ever need – and then some. They grew their own vegetables, and had olive trees where they picked the olives and would go to a local place to have them pressed and made into olive oil. They also made their own wine. They had espresso available all day in a metal canister on the table. They had fruit trees so they could eat fresh fruit, and they got their drinking water by driving 20 minutes up a mountain to an actual spout that came out of the side of the mountain. It was the best water we'd ever tasted.

After the greetings tapered, we decided to rest a bit downstairs where the kids were sleeping. Oliver and I fell asleep instantly. I was woken up by Sophie (then 6 years old). She said, "Mommy, where's Dominic?"

I said, "He must be in here somewhere."

She said, "No, mommy, I can't find him."

Well, I figured I'd find him immediately in the small apartment because I knew Dominic (who was 8 years old) would not venture out the front door. He was a child that was cautious by nature and took a little time warming up to places and new people. We barely arrived, and we were in a foreign country – and it felt foreign too.

But I could not find Dominic anywhere.

I woke up Oliver to tell him, and we all went out the front door. We didn't see him outside, but thought to first check upstairs in the other apartment. I just couldn't picture Dominic getting up by himself while we were all sleeping, walking out the big front door, going up a long flight of marble steps to the apartment above, then walking in there. Well…that's exactly what he did! We found him upstairs laughing as the Italians were tickling him and playing with him. He had gone up there all by himself.

I was really amazed, and then as I watched them interacting, I realized what was so compelling. The Italians were so warm, loving and enthusiastic, and we all felt so incredibly comfortable in their presence. They were all about making us feel welcome and serving us with whatever we wanted or needed. This truly brought them joy. Dominic felt their loving energy.

I so needed this trip!

I called my dad every day from Italy, thanks to technology. We had a local phone number that could be used through our laptop to make calls. The expense was minimal. My dad truly enjoyed the stories I was telling him about our experiences. He was living vicariously through me. He was such a trooper too. I knew he preferred me being home and closer to him, however, he didn't complain. I really appreciated this. I knew he had some concern about the fact that my sister had a trip coming up that would overlap my trip, however, I reassured him. I had no reason to believe at this point that both of us being gone would be an issue. My dad was doing okay with his health and had excellent care – 24x7. Little did I know how this trip would end up, however, at the moment, I was having such a nice time.

I needed this pampering. Since having kids, I didn't have the luxury to put on my running shoes and go for a jog without a lot of arranging to make sure the kids were taken care of. Here, the Italians were always around. It was absolutely wonderful to be able to jog on the ridges of Italy all by myself. (Until Oliver's dad grew concerned about me. He said that most Italians are good people, but there are also some Italians that aren't. Makes sense. Oliver went along with me after his dad told him this. It was still awesome to be able to run there, even with my bodyguard.)

The weather wasn't that great – lots of rain, so we didn't do many trips and stayed within the local area. Oliver and I were perfectly fine with this. We were so drained from all the chaos back home. Hanging out with the Italians and being served every meal was such a great gift for us. Oliver had a lot of work every day, and my work I was able to handle 1 or 2 days a week, so I was on my own a lot with the kids. I really didn't mind.

The kids were enjoying the service from the family too. Every morning, they would leave our apartment and walk upstairs to hot chocolate and breakfast. If they wanted more hot chocolate they would get it. If they wanted another piece of cake, they would get it. Another slice? No problem. Fabiola baked every single day. It was so good. She exemplified what I always pictured an Italian housewife to be – with her white apron and all. I could also tell that she thoroughly enjoyed her role within the family.

****

Unraveling

During the last week of our trip in Italy, on the same day of my sister's planned flight out of town, my dad landed in the hospital again. Murphy's Law. My sister was so looking forward to her trip, and did everything in her power to set my dad up prior to her weekend away. I think my dad just couldn't bear the thought of both my sister and I being gone. We just couldn't believe the timing. It may sound like I'm saying the timing was planned by my dad. That's not what I mean. I don't think he consciously did anything at all. Quite the opposite. My dad was so afraid of hospitals and did everything he could to avoid them.

My sister was frantic because she really felt the need to get out of town and was counting on this trip. We hadn't yet worked out the scenario of, "What if dad landed in the hospital when both of us were out of the area?" After initially being quite skeptical, I ended up encouraging my sister to go on her trip, even though this put a strain on my dad's caregivers because they were essentially left "holding the bag". However, my sister was my main source of support and I was thinking of her needs too. Even though she was quite adamant about going on her trip, I could sense she was also seeking my blessing to leave, so I gave it to her.

That last week in Italy was extremely challenging. I was on the phone with doctors and caregivers and emailing care schedules, etc. At one point, after speaking to a doctor, I just starting freaking out and literally started screaming and crying in the basement apartment in Italy. The kids were upstairs with the family and Oliver was with me. Basically, I was taking notes from the doctor, who was listing off one ailment after another that my dad had. It was the first I had heard about these medical conditions.

I made a dreaded call to my sister interrupting her on her trip. I really thought my dad would not make it out of the hospital after what the doctor told me. She got right on a plane and headed back to be with my dad. She could get there faster than I could. At least she had a small break.

Here is an email I sent to some close friends while I was in Italy. It gives a picture of what was happening:

> *I'm still in Italy and for the last week have been heavily involved in communications and coordination along with my sister about my dad's medical concerns. He was taken to emergency on Mon. afternoon for breathing difficulties. I was hoping it was a panic attack because he's been filled with anxiety. We really thought it would be more of the same until we received test results. I'm out of my mind. Essentially, my dad has hypothyroid (least of concerns), congestive heart failure (appears to be earlier stages; need more info); urine retention which requires permanent catheter or drainage through abdomen (need more info); and most concerning, an aneurism in his aorta – they are doing a CAT scan to confirm location and size, but the doctor said he will most likely need a major operation, or it will burst at some point and he will die. I'm very afraid that he won't survive a major heart operation! I'm trying to stay positive.... We're getting more info....please pray for all of us....I can't wait to get back home to see him... he is so scared and has so much anxiety.... me too....Lea*

The same day we arrived home from Italy, I drove to the hospital to relieve my sister. The CAT scan showed yet another problem: Degeneration of the spine, which the doctor believed was caused either by an infection, or a tumor. The doctors couldn't believe that my dad wasn't in more pain with the mass in his lower spine. (I suppose that's one positive thing about being paralyzed.) It's anyone's guess how long that mass had been growing. All these things the doctors found were probably there for quite some time and we just weren't aware.

I was jet-lagged and running on adrenaline. I spent 3 days at the hospital with my dad, coordinating care, making notes, etc. (I really wanted my brother and sister to get a break. I so appreciated them taking charge while I was away in Italy.) Even though I just got back, Italy seemed like it happened a long time ago. I was right back "in it" – this chaotic situation. I was losing steam by the 3rd day back.

Here's an email I sent my brother and sister. It shows exactly what was going on during this time. Arranging 24x7 care was always very challenging, but we managed it.

> *It's 8pm and I'm finally leaving dad's. I've done literally 10 hour shifts Sat. Sun. & today, and that's on jet lag after a 24 hour travel. I'm not thinking very clearly. My big stress right now is coverage for Saturday. Need 1pm-9pm; Dino can come 1pm-3pm; I was thinking of calling Shirlee tomorrow when I'm more clear-headed to see if she has time Saturday to help. I asked Jessica, Margarita, Tina and Stephanie – and they all have plans. Thi Thi also wanted Wed. evening off, but then said Sat. is the more important one.*
>
> *With this new true 24x7 schedule, it's going to be much harder when people want time off. The agency may be the answer, however, I'm really concerned about different strangers here, and how do we just have someone come for a long period that dad has never met and they haven't been trained in his specific care? Also, the rates are really high, but if it's reasonable usage, it may be okay.*
>
> *All the time I spent after getting dad home talking with Jess, Thi Thi and Chris, got us only through Friday with coverage. Because we have to "wait and see", it's really hard to pin down a schedule. I'm waiting for Chris' school schedule too. With them both in school now, it's harder. At least they are willing to go with it and try it out.*
>
> *Dad is motivated to get in his chair and now Jessica will be training Chris and Thi Thi how to transfer him in and out of bed, which is great. This is something I got accomplished*

tonight. We're not under as much pressure now for training on the Hoyer lift, although I still think we should have training for future.

I still haven't typed up my 4 pages of notes from the last 3 days coordination with doctors, next steps, etc. How will we get dad to his eye injection appt. next week?? Pay that gurney service again?? And would that be times 2 to take him there and back?? I better stop now…

Please get the chair going tomorrow and pills all set and instructions given to Thi Thi and something she can check off. (By the way, I taped up papers in dad's room to track urine output, and turning schedule.) Also, please let me know if they delivered the hospital bed and lift. It's after 8pm and they're still not here. After calling earlier, I confirmed they had the order and are coming…

I just thought of all my work tomorrow now…shit…just remembered Dominic's and Sophie's homework packet needs to be turned in tomorrow…

Lea

My dad was discharged from the hospital. All his health issues were chronic. We would continue to manage his care from home.

****

To Pay or Not to Pay

After the initial chaos settled getting my dad discharged from the hospital and back home again, my sister called me with a valid concern. She had incurred expenses to fly back and be with dad. She asked if it would be okay to reimburse her from mom and dad's money (which I was put in charge of, even though we both had full access to their accounts).

I knew how my sister was feeling. Sometimes I would think about the gas expenses I was incurring since I lived 45 minutes away and was traveling sometimes 3 times a week. I had this strong intuitive feeling that starting to reimburse expenses from mom and dad's money wouldn't be a good idea.

What I expressed to my sister was the concept that 'Mom and dad cannot afford us.' Meaning, all the many things we had been doing for them – the skills we have been utilizing for their benefit, the connections to resources we had, the time we are spending – if mom and dad were expected to pay for our "services", they couldn't do it, because we would simply be too expensive.

I really felt that if we started down this road – of tracking our "expenses" and seeking reimbursement – that it could develop into problems. We would probably start questioning each other about the necessity of the expenses. For example, the airfare reimbursement that my sister mentioned, I could say, "Well, why didn't you get travel insurance?" And with the gas I was incurring, she could say, "Well, you're the one that decided to live further way."

I suggested that instead of reimbursements, let's learn from each new thing that happens, then discuss how we want to handle it next time. For example, it is foreseeable that we may both be on a trip at the same time again in the future. In that case, we could give someone we trust a Power of Attorney to sign dad into the hospital if it became necessary when we're both out of town. I also said that we've seen how things change on almost a daily basis. Because of this, we cannot possibly predict or prevent all situations that are less than optimal. I really felt it was best to act in each individual situation and use mom and dad's money for 3rd party resources instead of reimbursements to us kids. My sister agreed wholeheartedly. I am so grateful to have such a reasonable sister. I'm also grateful that my parents were responsible with there money during their lives. I don't even want to imagine the added stress if they didn't have money that we could use for their care. Obviously, the 3 of us kids would have had to negotiate and agree on how to pull together our resources. This never became necessary.

****

Home Sweet Home

I wrote a poem when I was younger about an old man's experience in a nursing facility. It was one of my dad's favorite poems. I'm guessing it's because I captured his imagination of what it must be like to live in a nursing facility – something my dad never wanted to do. (Who would?)

A Better Place

He sips through the straw
     as the water is held up to his lips.
He then clears his throat and makes a request,
     "I would like to speak with my brother please, if I may."
The nurse responds with slight disdain,
     "Now, Mr. Marsh, your brother passed away.
     He died 20 years ago, remember?"
He tilts his head, "Ah-yes. Of course. Of course."

He watches her leave the room,
     then his eyes search for more movement.

The thin drapes gently sway.
He studies them, recognizing every threaded design.

Daily he desires to see beyond.
     Today the decision is made.

He pushes the sheet from his body
     and slides down the side of the bed
     directly to the floor
        where he lay to gather strength.

He looks up toward the window, appreciating the new angle
      despite the pain in his arm.
The cool tile soothes the left side of his face.

An hour passes in which time he is able to kneel
      with his elbows on the chair beneath his beloved window.
The drapes are still swaying,
      but now they're behind his head
      and his smiling face welcomes the breeze.

"Mr. Marsh!"
The nurse rushes to help him back in bed,
      scolding all the while.
Within seconds, the mattress is beneath him once again.
"You could have broken your other hip – or worse,
your neck, then where would you be?"
With expertise she begins tucking the sheets securely around
      his body – his soul.
He grabs her wrist, with much less force than he intends.
Their eyes meet as he puts her hand to his chest.
      His heart is thumping beneath her palm.
      "Where would I be if I broke my neck?"
         His intense gaze holds her motionless.
      "Perhaps in a better place, my dear.
      A much better place than this."

    My dad loved being in his home. He always said, "I'm going down with the ship." My dad's prayers about staying home were answered.
    I may have been naïve, but I didn't put much thought into placing my dad in a facility. After the challenges of my dad's hospitals stays, we did some research on live-in facilities to see if it would even be an option for someone with my dad's level of injury. Turns out, my dad would have needed a private nurse even in a facility. Given the fact that my dad was terrified of a facility, and there wasn't a good option for one anyway, all my energy went toward 'how can we make it work to keep dad at home?'

I had worked with a financial advisor and went over in detail my parents' entire financial situation. My parents worked full-time most of their adult lives, right up until their illnesses. This steady stream of income certainly benefited them, as well as having good saving and budget habits, and jobs that included full medical and retirement benefits.

The advisor went over my dad's retirement, savings, and home equity, and told me that even with my dad's excessive care expenses, my dad's assets would last him 13 years. When I told my dad this, he seemed completely relieved. I didn't realize how much he was worrying about money. After hearing what I told him, I think my dad figured he wouldn't be around in 13 years, so he didn't have to worry about money as much. He also trusted me and my brother and sister, and before us, my mom had handled everything. He was happy that someone he trusted was handling his finances for him.

In my attempt to give my dad the 24x7 care he needed, in addition to creating a schedule with 4 hour blocks, I wrote the below so whomever we had at my dad's side at the hospital, knew what to do. I felt this was the best chance to give him consistent, quality care, without expending a lot of my personal time. I realize not everyone reads things through, however, just the act of me writing everything out, gave me more clarity, so it was easier to field questions from the caregivers. By having the below paper, my sister and I also had something to refer to, as well as refer the caregivers to.

DAD'S HOSPITALIZATIONS
(Notes to refer to when dad has to go to emergency or is admitted in hospital)

*CAREGIVERS: We will all work as a team to achieve the below. The one who first accompanies dad to hospital should have this list with them; EACH CAREGIVER SHOULD REVIEW LIST AT BEGINNING OF THEIR CAREGIVING SHIFT AT HOSPITAL.

FROM HOME:

CALL 911: When decision is made to call 911 for ambulance, do so, then immediately give dad his prescribed anti-anxiety medication.

PILL CHART: Take along current pill chart from refrigerator, grab tape, and tape up in hospital room for easy reference. (Nurses always ask about medications, and hospital computer is never accurate because they do not know how and when we disburse pills at home).

EYE DROPS: Take along all of dad's eye drops to hospital (no need to take pills because they will not let us use our own from home anyway).

NOTEBOOK: grab notebook from home and pen to bring along to hospital so all caregivers can jot down notes of things that happened during their shift.

BOWEL CARE: Tues. evenings & Sat. mornings; make sure all supplies are taken from home to hospital. Contact caregivers to have them go to hospital instead of home for bowel care.

ADMISSION INTO HOSPITAL:

Lea or Julie must sign dad in, or other authorized person (would need signed authorization).

AIR MATTRESS FOR DAD: Upon dad's arrival at hospital in ambulance, instruct hospital staff IMMEDIATELY that an air mattress must be ordered; dad is a quadriplegic and it is critical for his skin that he be on an air mattress (the type used for people with wounds; used to relieve pressure on the body).

THROUGHOUT HOSPITAL STAY:

ANTI-ANXIETY MEDICINE: Hospital will not give this regularly; dad or we have to ask nurse to give it; usually dad is too anxious to even ask; ask nurse to have doctor prescribe "hospital dosage", so when we do ask nurse to give him one, we know he will have enough milligrams (last hospital stay we didn't realize until the last day he was there that they only gave him .25 dosages when we requested, and dad was much more anxious than he could have been, had we caught the fact that such a light dose was being given – they just went by whatever current prescription they had in computer)

DAD'S CATHETER: Inform staff that dad has a catheter and what type, i.e. foley, size, etc. Any questions you cannot answer, call Lea or Julie.

DAD'S SKIN: Each new nurse or caregiver should be educated or reminded about the care of dad's skin. When moving him around, it must be done gently and carefully. Dad cannot have any scratches or cuts on his skin, or stay in one place more than 2 hours if he's not on a special air mattress. Pressure sores or bed sores happen quickly with quadriplegics, which lead to infection and increased hospitalization time – all of which we can avoid easily by paying extra attention whenever someone touches or moves dad.

DAD'S POSITIONING: Explain about dad's quadriplegia, his spasms, limited movement, and that he needs help with even the slightest positioning. Remind again about his skin! His feet shouldn't be touching; he should only have pillows behind his back when he's on his side and between his knees, and NOT behind his butt. Any chuck underneath him should be smooth and straight and not bunched up under his skin.

HOSPITAL BED ELEVATION: Since dad is a quadriplegic, the way his bed is elevated and time intervals in certain positions are extremely important. He should be elevated 30 degrees for about 15 min. each hour, or 30 min. every 2 hours, then lowered back down flat on his back. (Last time he was in hospital, we forgot about this, and he was on his back way too much and it caused respiratory problems; however, it's important that he not be elevated for too long at one time because of pressure on his bottom and skin, so it's a balance we need to be aware of, and TRACK DOWN ON A PAPER POSTED AT HOSPITAL, so all caregivers remember to track!)

DAD'S PERSONAL-CARE CAREGIVERS: During any hospital stay, please do extra checks of the skin all over dad's body to confirm there is no redness developing anywhere, or no scratches or cuts, and if there are, we need clear communication on how to best take care of it, i.e. cream application, new positioning, etc.

TESTS ON DAD IN HOSPITAL: A caregiver must be with dad at all times during any test given in the hospital. If the staff protests, stop the procedure and call Lea or Julie to help advocate. Because of dad's special needs, it is imperative that we have someone familiar with his body and care with him during any test.

SLEEPING PILL: Make sure there is an order for this in computer (last time, there wasn't, and we didn't realize dad wasn't getting a sleeping pill at night until the 3rd night! He's in so much anxiety at hospital, he should be given a sleeping pill, even if he hasn't been taking them at home.)

PILL DISPENSION AT HOSPITAL: Like anti-anxiety medicine example above, nurses will not give any prescription regularly to dad that says "as needed" on prescription, even though we may do so at home; HAVE DISCUSSION WITH NURSE ABOUT WHAT WILL BE GIVEN TO DAD WHILE HE'S IN THE HOSPITAL, AND AT WHAT INTERVALS – be sure to have home pill chart in front of you when you have this discussion.

LEA/JULIE: Print extra copies of pill chart to carry in purse so we can answer questions over phone about medications.

LEA/JULIE: Print extra copies of "Contact List for Hank's Backup Care" for purse so we have all phone nos. for all caregivers.

WHEN DOCTORS SEE DAD IN HOSPITAL/WHEN TO CONTACT LEA OR JULIE: Call Lea or Julie so they can speak to the doctor and hear what's going on. *ASK NURS- ES WHEN THE APPROXIMATE TIME IS THAT A DOCTOR WILL BE THERE, AND EXPLAIN THAT HANK'S DAUGH- TER MUST BE CALLED TO SPEAK WITH THE DOCTOR WITH DAD. IF DOCTOR COMES IN, EXPLAIN THIS AS WELL AND HAVE HIM WAIT A FEW MINUTES UNTIL WE ARE REACHED. (A lot of time in the hospital is waiting time; the time when Julie or Lea should be involved is whenever a doctor is there, or when decisions needs to be made, or help is needed to advocate for dad's needs, i.e. dad is trying to ex- press himself, and the caregiver is helping communicate what dad is saying, and it doesn't appear that the hospital staff is listening; any time you encounter a challenge or concern at the hospital, call Lea or Julie for guidance.)*

LEA/JULIE: CALL NURSING AGENCY: Call coordi- nator at nursing agency to give them heads-up that dad is going in hospital, and we need to find someone who can do overnight coverage at hospital. (NOTE: We will first ask dad's caregivers about overnight shift coverage, then use agency to help, since we do not want to have the same person have to do 2 overnights in a row since how much sleep the person will get is unpredictable.)

HOSPITAL COVERAGE: Dad needs one of his caregiv- ers with him 24x7 at hospital – except overnight if he's in ICU, however, if he's NOT in ICU, he definitely needs a caregiver overnight in a regular hospital room. Start making calls to put together coverage at hospital, then print and email list to caregivers so it's all clear.

BEDTIME/OVERNIGHT HOSPITAL COVERAGE: We want to keep the same routine as at home at the hospital; i.e. approx. "bed time" at 9:00pm or so; MUST EXPLAIN TO NURSE THAT WE WANT NO INTERRUPTIONS DUR- ING THE NIGHT, UNLESS ABSOLUTELY NECESSARY, i.e. please ask if they can plan their "checks" at one time in- stead of coming in and out of the room multiple times. DAD'S

SLEEP IS SO IMPORTANT TO HIS STRENGTH & WELL-BEING!

BEDTIME ROUTINE: help dad on his side; give him prescribed medications); ask dad if he wants to be woken up at 3:00am like he is at home, or does he want us to let him sleep. (He can always call out if he wakes up). If dad wants to be woken up, instruct whomever will be with dad that night and the nurse that at 3:00am, dad is to be moved to his back.

LEA/JULIE: Discuss our personal schedules and determine which days during the hospital stay each can be the primary contact, so the other can concentrate on their work and other responsibilities on their day "off".

DAD'S WHEELCHAIR: Make sure wheelchair is getting charged at home. Consider transporting wheelchair to hospital at some point (if he is strong enough to get into it, it's important to get him up in his chair as soon as possible); can call wheelchair Taxi service to transport, or Julie can take in dad's van; ONLY JULIE OR LEA SHOULD TRANSPORT THE WHEELCHAIR.

DISCHARGE: As soon as dad is admitted, we always want to know approximately when the doctor thinks he can go home, so we can plan accordingly. Lea or Julie must be present at the time of discharge. It's a lengthy, complicated process to ensure we have a clear understanding of any medication changes and care needs at home, follow up procedures, etc.

GURNEY SERVICE TO TRANSPORT DAD HOME: If dad has to go home lying down, have the Patient Care Coordinator at time of discharge contact the gurney service.

****

Attachment

I've heard time and again from my dad's caregivers how much he looked forward to visits from my brother and sister and me. I've also heard that he talks about how well he and I get along and see "eye to eye" on things. It was apparent that my dad did listen to me and relied heavily on me. This fact was hard on me because I knew I couldn't "save him". I knew I didn't have all the answers, but I was doing my absolute best. I knew intuitively that I had to stay grounded in order to make the best possible suggestions and decisions.

What grounded meant to me was that I wanted to keep my emotional state balanced, otherwise, I couldn't contribute to the circumstances effectively. This was all intuition, but it was enough to inspire me to make sure I got good sleep every night; to make sure I exercised regularly, even though it was less frequent than normal; to make sure I had some quiet time to myself. In order to have all this, I asked for help and arranged for others to step in to care for Dominic and Sophie, and asked Oliver to take on more tasks in the business to free up more of my time.

The first few months after my mom died, my brother and sister and I jumped right in, similar to when my mom got sick, to help my dad. However, we had just come off of a solid year of chaos and illness with my mom's journey before my dad's issues started, so we had minimal steam when we began jumping in.

The fact that my dad relied on me the most, started to wear on me. He never overtly gave me a guilt trip, however, I knew and felt how much I meant to him and I truly wanted to help him. The problem was, as much as I wanted to, it was clear to me that to continue at such a high level of intensity with managing caregiving needs, etc., for an unknown amount of time ahead, would lead to burnout and illness. I had gained some weight – mostly felt bloated and swollen and gained weight around my middle, which I learned later was from stress hormones (cortisol) being in high gear. I had developed stress lines between my brows that I'd never had before and skin problems, headaches, stomachaches, diarrhea, etc. – all off and on since my mom's diagnosis. I also had started grinding my teeth at night while I was asleep. My dentist noticed and I got fitted for a mouth guard.

Ten months after my mom died, I made a decision. I thought about my siblings' and family's emotional states and stress, who were also my support system. I also considered my own physical and emotional state. I thought about the fact that we all were doing our very best. I also acknowledged the fact that my dad was physically being very well cared for in his own home. I faced the reality that my dad was struggling mentally. He was grief-stricken, had a poor outlook for his future, had many medical problems, and was spending much energy trying to prevent any more change in his life. After assessing all of "what is", I was resolute with my assessment that – while I couldn't understand it – the truth was, "*This is his journey.*"

I shifted my focus to my own wellbeing as I continued to help my dad and love him, even though I knew I couldn't be with him as much as he would like, or for that matter, as much as I would like. A part of me wanted to move in with him and soak up as much time with him as possible. However, I had my own family that I also wanted to be with and that I had responsibilities to. I truly believed, "He'll be okay." This decision to back off a bit helped me tremendously. My dad was living his life, and so was I. An adjustment was necessary as far as energy and focus.

Not long after this newfound decision of mine, I remember my dad had his caregiver repeatedly call me one Sunday morning. I happened to be at a First Communion Service at church for my friend's daughter. I saw the missed calls after my one hour of unavailability. I remember going to my friend's house after the service where she was having a gathering and I went into her bedroom at the back of the house to return the missed calls. I was talking to my dad and realized he was in a full-blown panic attack. What I found out was that, not only was his caregiver with him at that moment, his entire spiritual group was at the house!

As I listened to my dad speaking in a panic, I realized I couldn't help him. Perhaps he would be comforted if I was physically with him, however, I knew it would be a temporary fix. After the call, I engaged with the party going on and stayed until I was ready to leave. I did not leave the party to go to my dad's.

The next day, I pulled together resources for my dad to help him deal with his panic attacks, and even went with him to an appointment later in the week. I did what I could with an even fuller understanding at this point that *this was his journey* and although I didn't understand why he had to suffer so much, everything was exactly as it was supposed to be.

I had such compassion for my dad. I hadn't had much time to grieve or feel the loss of my mom while my dad was alive, however, I was well aware how much my dad was impacted by her being gone. He still couldn't talk about her. He was so obsessed with his physical ailments, and there were plenty for him to focus on. He didn't have his career and couldn't read or drive anymore. On the positive side, he was living at home, and had his children nearby and people who loved him.

Up until the month before he died, I still had such high hopes that he would "pull himself up" and start living again. He always had such a positive attitude. Looking back, a realization that I just couldn't see at the time was this: He didn't really want to live. He didn't have a vision for his life that didn't include my mom. His vision – which he did tell me more than once and I just couldn't hear it – was of God, and my mom sitting next to God. He said he could see them so clearly in his mind. I realize now that the reason my dad, who was perfectly healthy other than his disability, deteriorated so quickly in a year's time, was that he wanted to be with God and my mom more than he wanted to be here on this earth. And I think my mom was waiting for him too. If I had this level of understanding at the time, I probably would have made a different choice for what was to soon come. But I didn't, and there are always positives that can be found with every choice, which I did find. I have no regrets.

****

The Gift

The last "project" that I know of that my dad fully engaged in was my birthday present in April, 2010, two months before he passed away. I arrived at his house one day and there was a very large present on the kitchen bar. My dad was excited to have me open it.

My dad always was a gift giver. Usually small trinkets like little statues made of ceramic or crystal (like Precious Moments), funny stuffed animals, and he especially liked music boxes. He liked giving cards too, and he was even particular about the wrapping of gifts. I've wrapped many, many gifts for him over the years that he gave to people.

I remember him asking me some questions a few weeks before my birthday, so I had a feeling he was thinking about a gift. I think he wanted to make sure that I wanted what he wanted to give me. I told him I would like anything he chose to get for me and encouraged him to get what he felt was best.

Back to the big wrapped box. I went to the bar and started to open it. I found a smaller box inside, then a smaller box inside that one, and then at least one more, until finally I got to a very small box. I opened it up and there inside was a delicate gold chain necklace with a small cross attached. It was very dainty. My dad started describing all that went into choosing this gift.

First, he had his caregiver accompany him to the nearby local jeweler which was within walking distance from the house. He mulled over all the many styles of crosses, and particularly had trouble narrowing down whether he wanted straight edges or more curved ones. He decided on the curved ones and asked me if I thought he made the right decision. Of course I assured him that he had. He also decided to put a raised heart in the center of the cross. I love hearts, so this was perfect as well. Lastly, and the best thing about it, was that he had engraved on the back of the cross, "love dad".

I gave him a big hug and showed him my appreciation and told him how much I loved the necklace. I could tell he was very happy with my reaction to the gift that he so painstakingly chose for me. His satisfaction was palpable and completely adorable. My dad was such a sweetheart. I'm so thankful I have this gift that connects me with my dad. I think about him whenever I wear the necklace and especially when I hold the little cross between my fingers.

****

The Last Mile

My dad was admitted into the hospital again due to very low blood pressure, among other things. I went to the hospital to visit my dad. Jessica was there too, and she was happy to see me because she could go to the cafeteria for a bit. It doesn't seem like there would be much to do hanging out in a hospital room with someone, however, there was always something to attend to.

My dad seemed very frantic. His eyes were dark and he was constantly looking around in a panic. He said that he didn't feel well and he wanted to see a psychiatrist right away. He started yelling, "I want to see a psychiatrist, stat! I want to see a psychiatrist, stat!" I said, "Okay, dad! I'll be right back!"

I quickly went to the nurse's station and asked when a psychiatrist could come to see my dad. I said it was urgent. She said she would contact one, but could not tell me when one would arrive. I said, "In the meantime, is there something you can give my dad? He's obviously suffering and in a panic." She basically said that they don't want to give him medications because they are trying to get them out of his system. I pressed further because I believed that in a hospital, patients are supposed to be made comfortable. The nurse said that their #1 objective is to keep the person's body functioning. This didn't make total sense to me, however, I felt I was gone too long, so I ran back to my dad's room.

The psychiatrist never came, however, my dad was calming down and was in and out of lucidity. I was thinking it must be his body getting used to being off medication. He hadn't been eating much at all, and was taking quite a few prescription medications. Jessica had been back for a while, but I didn't want to leave him until I felt he was doing better. When I was able to have a conversation with him, I felt comfortable leaving, and headed home. He was in good hands with Jessica.

I had just arrived home after the usual 45 minute drive. I got a call on my cell phone from Jessica who was panicking. She said my dad started choking, then he stopped breathing and the code alarm went off. She said doctors and nurses rushed in and the doctor was asking her questions and she didn't know what to say. She gave the phone to a doctor who spoke very fast and asked me if they could put a breathing tube in for my dad. I hesitated, and he yelled at me, "There are people manually pushing on your dad's chest to keep him alive!" I knew I had to give him an answer or my dad would die.

I had no one to consult with. Normally with a question like this I would talk to my brother and sister and we would decide together. I felt very inadequate at that moment to make a proper decision! I knew my dad didn't want any artificial means keeping him alive, however, he also said that he was willing to do what it takes if it meant he would improve and be able to go home. I knew I didn't fully understand what was happening with his body and there was simply no time to ask questions to figure that out.

I asked the doctor, "If you put the tube in, can you later take it out?" He yelled, "Yes!" I said, "Okay, do it," and he immediately hung up on me.

I jumped back into my car and headed back to the hospital. My dad was transferred to ICU. Apparently what happened is the food he was being fed wasn't going down and he started aspirating – the food was choking him. I felt somewhat guilty because I remember feeding him earlier. He seemed fine though. I remember expressing my concern to the nurse and doctor about my dad's disinterest in food. The nurse wasn't too concerned. The doctor said that he was more concerned about why my dad isn't eating, not just that he wasn't eating. The doctor also was concerned that his "levels" weren't improving even with his time in the hospital.

My dad was in the Intensive Care Unit with a breathing tube. He looked a lot better, however, there were tubes everywhere with a whole list of different medications going into him. He couldn't talk because of the tube, and I could tell he really wanted to say something. I reassured him that the doctor said the tube can come out. (What I didn't know was that in order for the tube to come out, he had to be cleared by a doctor to breath on his own. What I didn't really understand at the time is that my dad probably knew exactly what was happening. After all, he worked at the VA hospital for so many years with spinal chord injury patients. He absolutely knew all the challenges he faced, and at that moment, he could not speak.) He was extremely agitated.

One positive thing about ICU is that there is one nurse per two patients, and my dad was the nurse's only patient for the evening. Her station is literally outside his curtain, and he was being monitoring constantly. I felt comfortable that he didn't need someone there 24x7, however, I still scheduled people to come the next day to be with him for moral support.

I went to my sister's house after the hospital. I told her everything that happened. When I got to the part about my dad yelling, "I need a psychiatrist, stat!", I noticed my sister was pretty edgy. She hadn't had the same break from this situation like I've had by living further away and going away on trips here and there. She lives 5 minutes from my dad's house, and just as close to the hospital my dad was in. She was always the first person in line to be called because of her proximity.

She started rambling, "Well, I need a psychiatrist! Stat! This can't go on! I'm going to end up losing it and I won't be able to be there for my kids! For my family!" I was watching her ranting and she was pacing and I was standing with my arms open following her side to side as she paced. I was jockeying in front of her waiting for my moment to jump in and say something – anything to help calm her down.

She was saying things like, "Dino's going to get sick next, or you, and what will I doooo!" She was screeching and completely losing it. I remember looking at her in that animated state, and responding in a similar hyper state, trying to find the words to calm her.

I said, "Julie! Julie! Don't worry! I promise – I'll go really quick!" I snapped my fingers. I was motioning my arms in a sweeping parallel motion, and even stomped my foot as I yelled, "I'm going to just drop! Bam! Flat on the ground – dead. Real quick! You won't have to do anything! Don't worry! I promise!"

At this point I hadn't noticed that she had stopped pacing and was just standing there staring at me in stunned silence. I noticed the quiet which stopped me. We just both looked at each other for a moment. Then she burst out laughing, and I started laughing, then we started crying, and we were laughing and crying at the same time. It was so awful, but such a stress relief to laugh and cry. If anyone witnessed this, I'm sure we both looked completely nuts – and we actually were. Sleep deprived and carayzeee!

This is one of many moments that my sister and I have shared that will bond us forever. We just knew – without ever having to speak – that we both "got it". We really, really understood each other. This was bliss – the feeling of being totally understood.

****

Keeping Everyone in the Loop

It was time to update our friends and family about my dad's condition.

> *Hi everyone. I wanted to let you know that my dad is in ICU. Over the last several weeks, my dad's health, including his food and fluid intake has been declining. We almost took him to the hospital several times over the last 2 weeks due to low blood pressure, concern about dehydration, and some cognitive issues. He did not want to go to the hospital.*
>
> *On Tues. this week, he was even more sluggish and his thinking ability was even more impaired, and he was trying hard just to move his chair. (It became obvious he just wasn't getting stronger over the course of the past week). I asked him*

if he wanted to go the hospital for a "tune up" so to speak, i.e. blood transfusion, and fluids, and he may feel better. He didn't want to go. He just wanted Jessica to help him drink and eat. I told him he did not have to go, but I wanted to make sure that he understood the possible consequences.

I gently explained my perspective of how he's been doing the last week (and Jessica agreed with my assessment), and that he does not seem to be getting better on his own with all our efforts to help him at home. His blood pressure was so low at this point that Jessica could not read it. I gently asked, "Dad, you do not have to go to the hospital, but I want to make sure you understand that it is possible that your blood pressure will get lower and lower, and that means that you may no longer be with us. You could pass away at home. Is that okay?" He was silent for a moment and clearly said, "No, I'm not", and agreed that we can call the ambulance. After that Jessica said he was more energetic and was focused on getting the ambulance there. He told Jessica, "I'm not ready to die."

A lot has happened at the hospital since then, and those details I will not go into too much. For those who are interested in some medical details, he was anemic (which we knew), and had dangerously low sodium levels (which he's had before, but not this low). With a blood transfusion Tues. night, and antibiotic IV, he wasn't any better the next day, and the doctor said there is something else going on. An infectious disease specialist is involved – same as last hospital stay. We are waiting for test results of a scan of his spine, and a culture. He has other medical problems as well, i.e. bed sores developing, a lot of fluid in his lungs, not eating, etc.

My dad has had challenges this past year with anxiety, and the last month, it has become increasingly worse. Being in the hospital has increased his anxiety, and it's so difficult to see, and we are trying every angle to keep him as comfortable as possible.

He went into "code" last night, and he ultimately ended up in ICU on a respirator. He was alert last night, but cannot talk because of the tubes in his throat. My sister was with him, and she tried her best to understand him. She asked a lot of yes and no questions, and he was able to nod or shake his head no, however, it was not possible to really understand what he was trying to express. We asked that he be sedated for the night.

They're putting in a central line to his heart. He is not yet "stable". He's conscious and able to respond and knows who everyone is. This is his current status as I write this.

I did talk to my dad after his last hospital stay about what life saving measures he wanted. At that time, he clearly said he is willing to try a respirator, and even a tracheotomy, if there was a possibility that he could improve and it could be removed. We also know that my dad absolutely wants to live at home, and does not want to be bedridden, other than a certain amount of time when he can eventually be back up in his chair and mobile. Of course we will do our best to base our decisions on how we understand his wishes to be.

I believe strongly in the power of prayer, and collective minds being able to touch a person by stopping and thinking about the person and sending them love and positive thoughts. My dad will feel this, even if you are not physically there with him. Please pray for him during this time that he can feel peace, and pray for my brother, sister and I that we can keep our emotions at a level that we can see past his medical problems and connect with him in a way that he can feel our love when we're with him in the days ahead. We just want to continue to do our very best for our dad.

Love,
Lea

****

Dad's Ready

It was June 30, 2010, only a day or two after the breathing tube was removed from my dad's throat. My sister was at the movie theater with her kids and another parent. She had this strong urge to check on my dad. She asked the parent to please stay with the kids while she went to the hospital. It was a short 5 minute drive.

As Julie explained to me, she arrived at the hospital and went to see my dad in ICU. She said my dad told her, "You came just in time. I'm so tired." My sister immediately called me, very upset, and said that she really didn't think he was going to make it much longer. I was in the middle of working (as always trying to fit in my responsibilities in the midst of the chaos). I abandoned my work, and started the 45 minute drive to the hospital. My sister was very worried that she would be by herself with my dad when he died. She was not comfortable with this. She called Shirlee (our "angel in charge" during my parents' journey) and she came right over.

As I was driving to the hospital I told myself, "If I don't make it in time, it was meant to be." I thought perhaps it was supposed to be my sister with my dad. I really wanted to be there, however, I had 45 minutes to drive and that was a fact. There was nothing I could do to get there faster and I actually was very calm on the drive. I just knew all was going to happen as it should.

A day or two prior, my brother and sister and I met in the meditation room there at the hospital with the palliative care nurse. I wish I knew about palliative care nurses sooner. Palliative care is all about making the patient comfortable. This usually means that the patient will die sooner than later because minimal intervention in terms of medicine and medical technology is used to prolong life. A palliative care nurse has experience with patients and families and knowledge about what's happening physically and psychologically with patients who are dying.

The meeting with the palliative care nurse helped my brother, sister and I understand more about what was happening with my dad's mind and body. She listened to what we were feeling. She answered our questions patiently and fully. She gave us her insight. She offered to also be with us in the hospital room with my dad, which we gratefully accepted.

This one nurse gave us more perspective than all the doctors put together that were assigned to my parents' care. I have no complaints about any doctor, however, the reality is, the doctors have tight schedules and they simply do not have the time to spend with families like the nurses do – especially the palliative care nurses.

When I arrived at the hospital that day my sister called, Shirlee was with my dad, and my sister was in the meditation room. I'm glad she took that time for herself. The room was very quiet with soft lighting and helped provide a sense of calm. Shirlee said the nurses called the palliative care nurse and that my dad was "near the end". I went to my dad and put my face close to his and hugged him and said I was there. Tears started falling from my eyes just like that day I first heard about my mom's tumors. It was like a broken, gentle faucet of tears I had no control over.

I whispered to my dad that I was there and that I loved him, and I said, "Now you get to see mom." He was still conscious although wasn't talking. I could tell he was trying to say something. I put my ear close to his mouth – my ear was actually touching his mouth slightly. I heard him say his last words – I felt them against my ear from his breaths as his voice was barely audible. He said, "I love you." I was crying and I told him, "I know." I said, "I will be okay. You know that, right? I will be okay." Even without his words, I felt like <u>he</u> was reassuring <u>me</u>.

I think he really was ready to leave this world.

The palliative nurse showed up, and so did my dad's friend, Maura, that he used to work with at the VA many years ago. She asked me if it was okay that she stayed, and I said yes. I knew my dad would like more people that loved him around him. My sister didn't want to come in the room. She said she felt better in the meditation room. I didn't push her. My brother came too. We started telling stories as we all surrounded my dad. The palliative nurse asked us questions and engaged us and we had a good time talking about my dad and our family. I was thinking 'dad is liking this' – all the people around him, chatting about memories.

I saw my sister slip into the room and sit down next to my brother. I could see in her face she was struggling and exhausted. I was at my dad's side, and Shirlee and Maura were on the other side. Jessica, my dad's long-time caregiver, came in – I'm not sure if she came in first, or my sister, however, it was obvious my dad was waiting for both of them. He passed away not more than a few minutes after they came in the room. He was probably hovering above watching us all and thinking, 'There. This is a good time to go.'

There was a lot of crying in the room when we all realized my dad was gone. I wasn't crying anymore. I felt just like I did when my mom died. I felt a strong silence in the midst of all the emotion around me. It felt as if all the noise around me was on mute.

Just like with my mom, I did not want to be with my dad's body after he was gone. The nurses came in and started asking questions. There was so much busyness – much different than when my mom passed. She was at home and it was peaceful after. Here at the hospital there were forms and signatures needed and instructions needed. I was involved in some and my sister too.

Unfortunately for me, because of the small room we were in, I got a glimpse of my dad's body that I wish I hadn't. I'm glad I was far enough away that I didn't see too many details before I quickly looked away. I just had an aversion to seeing his lifeless body. I was happy that was the extent of it. I have many more memories of him alive and warm when he was in this world. My world now. He's somewhere new. Somewhere he's supposed to be now. And I'm where I'm supposed to be right now.

June 30, 2010

I realized as I was receiving some email responses to my last email that I may have given the impression that my dad's prognosis seemed better than it actually was. Although it was really good news that the respirator was able to be removed and he could talk to us again, we also knew that it was just a matter of time before the fluid collected again in his lungs, and he would require a respirator again – only my brother and sister and I had decided that we would not put him on one again (because his organs were failing, and we knew his wish was not to be on life support if he couldn't get better and go back home and in his wheelchair again). After meeting with the palliative care team, we realized that he wasn't getting stronger since being in the hospital, and it didn't appear that he would get stronger due to all his medical issues.

My dad passed away earlier this afternoon. My sister had called me around 11am, and my brother and I didn't think we would make it there on time, but we did. I was so relieved to be able to talk to my dad and hold his hand. He was alert until the very end. He knew that everyone was there. As soon as I walked in, I got really close to his face and told him that I was there and that I love him, and he opened his eyes and looked at me. He tried to talk to me, and I put my ear as close to him as I could get and I heard him say "I love you" by his breaths. Those were his last words.

I was able to tell him how proud I am of him, and that I love him. I told him he gets to see mom now, and I told him that I was excited for him about that. I said, "You know I'll be all right, right?" He nodded.

Shirlee was there (she was with us when my mom died also), which was such a blessing because she was able to get there fast to be with my sister who was alone with my dad at that point. Maura was there too (my dad's close friend from the VA), and Jessica (one of my dad's caregivers – the one who's been caring for him the longest). Shortly after Jessica had arrived, and my sister entered the room again, my dad passed away. It was just as he wanted.

I wanted to mention one more thing about this morning. Something that just shows how much the smallest things mean so much. The nurse on duty this morning, Marilyn, was especially attentive. She talked with my dad, asked if he want-

ed a shave, and he said yes. She asked if he wanted his teeth brushed, and he said yes. She freshened him up and made him comfortable. He asked what her name was, and she told him. He said, "Thank you, Marilyn. Now I can sleep. You are my angel." (Marilyn was also there when my dad passed away, and she is an angel).

Ever since my dad has been able to speak since the respirator was taken out, most of what he said were words of appreciation for everyone. He told me he was thinking a lot about mom, and how blessed he is to have us kids.

I am also so thankful that as sad as this time is and how heartbroken I am, I can't help but feel so much appreciation for my dad's peaceful passing and that he was surrounded by so much love...and that I was right there with him. I really savored the time.

I will email everyone information on the services for my dad. Because of the holiday, most likely it will be later next week, and most likely mid-morning. We'll have just one service, like we did for my mom. I'll let you know as soon as I know more – most likely this weekend.

I know this is a sad email, but I felt that you all would appreciate it, as I know you love my dad too.

Love always,
Lea

For many months after my dad died, I kept having visions of him peacefully floating in the ocean as if he were transitioning from this world to the next. The following poem came out of me, many months after my dad died. To me, it represents a glimpse of what his last year was like for him.

The Way It Is

and the water keeps rocking
and the trees are looming
and the petals have fallen
      and the beach is far, far away

and I want to keep going
and I want to give up
and I squint my eyes shut
      to stop
      what I don't want

I'm floating in the current
      openly
half open eyes to the sun
      glistening on my wet skin

      a glimpse of beauty

I'm a grieving husband
      with moments of laughter
      abandoned alive and pure
yet my sorrow has won
      with roots long and strong

my sadness is a tribute to my love
      who is gone
my happiness a betrayal

but I know better
      I'm holding her down
I'm not free but she needs to be

I breathe in the ocean air
        alone with my pain as I drift along
                on this fine day
                with my mind

I appreciate
I love
I am thankful
I am incredibly overwhelmingly sad

so my days get longer and my laughter less
my efforts fueled by knowledge lose effectiveness

I still try on a certain level as I did enjoy this life
        I don't want
        to disappoint
                anyone

my identity looms as an old man
        who is frail worried and distraught
I am cared for
I am loved
I am lonely

I try my best to get along
        with little enthusiasm
        to succeed

my body has responded to my incessant thoughts
        not pleasantly
        yet obviously

a natural progression

my focus has intensified on the physical

my care has turned palliative which I graciously receive
        as one thing I know for sure
                I don't want pain anymore…

and the water
        is gently rocking
                side to side
                        as I'm moved along
and the trees are rustling in awe
and my body is far, far away
and I'm welcomed to my new senses
        and I simply go forth
                flying with the angels
                        guiding me home…
                                on whose wings I travel with joy

Dedicated to Hank Gambina (1939-2010)

****

Funeral in the Tail Wind

I made the decision the morning of my dad's funeral not to wear eye makeup. I figured I'd be crying and my eyes would end up stinging and black smudges would be all over my face. Turns out I didn't cry that day. I was pretty much exhausted and plugging along for the benefit of those who came to say goodbye to my dad.

I was almost late to the service. I was just slow moving that day. I remember grabbing a bunch of pictures off my walls to set up at the church hall after. This was nothing like my mom's funeral as far as preparations. I did manage to throw together a digital photo album after my dad died – choosing as many digital pictures of him that I could find and allowing the software to place them wherever. The book didn't arrive in time though.

One thing I did manage to do the day before the funeral is look through my notes from those writing sessions I had with my dad in the summer prior.

The day before my dad's funeral, I put together the following words to share with all those that who came to say goodbye to my dad. I knew my dad would have loved to share some of his wisdom, and I also knew how much it would be appreciated by those who knew and loved him.

Hank Gambina's Thoughts on Oneness and Spirituality

There is a certain vitality that comes from focusing on the common denominator amongst us instead of what is dissimilar. The barrier to our natural connection to others is having a narrow definition of our spirituality, or having a lack of awareness of our inherent spirituality. Whenever we define our or others' beliefs or disbeliefs, which we all do, it is important to be aware that we're narrowing our view to the exclusion of others. We are noticing our <u>differences</u>, which serves no one. We don't have to take on another's belief or value, however, we don't have to demonize it either. When one refuses to look at another – to have compassion for another as a human being – all dialogue is halted, and any hope for unification is lost. Each person on this earth has needs and desires, hopes and dreams – they may be different than ours, but are no less important.

What is "Spirituality"? I have created my personal definition, although I believe words are insufficient to describe this divine Mystery. Here is my personal definition, to which

I hope will inspire others to create their own: Spirituality is within each of our core beings – our heart and soul – it's a connection to our inner selves that naturally emanates toward others in a loving way as it is recognized and acknowledged. It's an authentic expression of God's love. Regardless of a person's denomination, lack thereof, or specific beliefs or disbeliefs, there is a Oneness that seeks to unite rather than divide. The label of that "Oneness" or "God" is irrelevant to the spirituality that resides in each of us, as spirituality cannot be captured by a term or definition.

One may say, "I don't know if I believe in God or a Higher Power." My sense is that it doesn't matter if you know or even make a choice to believe in anything or nothing, however, it's my feeling that everyone believes in something – the question is "what is your experience in life?" At any time have you encountered, for example, a basic goodness in a person? My sense is that everyone has some experience or belief that is "spiritual", which sometimes lies dormant and is not yet recognized. What I'm suggesting is to stop, observe, feel – allow yourself to experience a moment – there is a point at which you sense a relief or letting go in even the most difficult times – pay attention to this feeling of relief, and recognize that this is coming from a place that is beyond your own efforts.

One may say, "I just don't feel the need for spiritual guidance." My sense of things is that we can only go so far in coping by using psychological or mental modes (such as affirmations, relaxation, and behavioral practices), and although some of these may help and "work" for a time, they will not bring a lasting sense of well-being and peace within you – and this is the point I'm trying to make. Whether one is aware of it or not, the richness of life comes from an inner sense of peace – that no matter what life brings, there is a basis and foundation within each of us that can be tapped into to provide the strength necessary to move beyond our difficulties and make a difference in this life. I say it's your spiritual side at work, sustained by the Goodness that exists in the world.

At 70 years old now, I've come full circle back to the Mystery. My experience in life tells me that there is more – much more. There is an Uncertainty despite knowledge. I do not comprehend the Mystery, but I rest assured. This is what I know for sure: There is a Goodness in life, and I am grateful.

Written by: Lea Gambina Pecora
(Based on conversations with dad in
the Summer of 2009)

In the entrance of the church, along with a stack of printouts of the above, I laid out the pictures I brought – my parents' wedding picture, some pictures of my dad. I think I also grabbed their wedding album. (I stopped short of putting out the small Buddha my dad had. After all, it was a Catholic Church, so I wanted to be considerate of people – even though in hindsight, my dad would have loved having his Buddha in the Catholic Church.)

I remember my brother, sister and I standing at the church entrance to greet people as they came in. My sister looked beautiful, and very fragile. She probably felt like I did – I just wanted to curl up and lie down. I felt this service wasn't for us – it was for everyone else. We had our long goodbye with my dad.

It was strange saying hello to all these people that we only saw with my parents around. I truly felt lost. I didn't have my bearings. I watched as our kids ran around outside laughing and playing.

It was time to walk in, and part of the procession was that we walk behind the casket as it was rolled up to the front of the church. I remember sitting in the front row, and I wish I thought to turn around and look at the congregation. I didn't see how many people were there. That would have been nice to see.

My dad would have liked the service. His good friend, Father Jim, led the service. It was very traditional, and I remember thinking my dad would have liked the part when Father Jim walked around his casket swinging the smoking incense. I believe my dad would have appreciated the way his ceremony was, just as much as I believe my mom would have appreciated hers. They were just right for each of them.

As we walked out of the church, once again behind the casket, Dominic said, "Now grandpa can walk." That blew my mind that he said that! I said, "Yes, Dominic, you are right. Grandpa can walk now."

I'm very glad Oliver and I decided to bring the kids to the service. My dad had a closed casket, which he wanted. (He casually mentioned this to me one day on our way to our usual lunch spot, then followed it up with a joke about a horse going to the doctor, and the doctor asking, "Why the long face?" Now, whenever I see a horse's face, I think of a casket.) Anyway, Dominic and Sophie experienced the entire service as did my sister's kids, Sara and Colby. I'm glad it was a closed casket because I wasn't sure how the kids would reconcile that part in their minds at the ages of 6 and 8 seeing an embalmed body.

Death is a natural part of life and something that I believe should be talked about around children appropriate to their age level. I allowed any and all questions the kids had for me, even though I wasn't sure how to respond sometimes. I remember Dominic asking if grandpa was in the casket. I explained that grandpa's body was in there, but grandpa was not. I explained that every person has a spirit, and when they no longer need their body, they leave and are with God with all the other people that left their bodies. (I didn't know how else to explain. How do you explain something no human being is capable of? Dominic seemed satisfied with my answer.)

We followed the hearse to the burial site and had another short service. I don't remember much about it, other than thinking it was a nice day out with a beautiful blue sky and California "golden" hills nearby. We headed back to the church for the reception.

The reception was catered by a casual Italian diner that my dad ate at a lot. This part of the service is when people got up and spoke. I stood up and walked to the front. I said something about what a good childhood I had. I just felt the heaviness and sadness in the room. I also didn't know what to really say, so I stood there a moment. I decided to sing a song I made up in childhood. It was a song that I would sing to my dad, and he enjoyed it so much (he thought it was hilarious), which inspired me to make many more verses when I was a kid.

I explained to everyone that my dad would get a real kick out of knowing that I sang this particular song at his funeral. I prefaced it by saying to please remember that I was in elementary school when I created these lyrics, and also that the name of the song is My Gross Song. I said I wouldn't put them through all the verses, and that I would just sing my dad's two most favorite. I noticed all the smiles from people in anticipation, and saw my kids and niece and nephew all dart under the table in embarrassment as I sang:

> *Great big boogers hanging out of someone's nose*
> *Only he alone knows*
> *About the stringy snotty hose.*
> *No one saw the shrivel of his nose*
> *when he began to blow*
> *But I could feel the spray!*

And for the finale, my dad's all-time favorite verse!

> *Great old man*
> *Sitting on a toilet seat*
> *Trying not to lift his feet*
> *Breathing very heavily*
> *We all knew what he was trying hard to start*
> *But all we heard was....[loud farting sound]*

"That was for you dad," I said, and that's how I ended my final words in tribute to my dad that day. I thought later about how I should have said this and that. Then I told myself it was just as it was supposed to be. Had I prepared for my speech, I highly doubt I would have ended up singing that song. Maybe I would, however, there is a good chance

I wouldn't have. People enjoyed it and I know my dad was laughing his butt off that I sang that song at his funeral. All is well.

One thing I know for sure is that my dad was happy with me.

It was so wonderful to hear about all the nice memories people had about my dad. I wish I recorded it all because I don't remember everything that was said. I do remember Lori saying that when she was a young graduate working at the VA, she admired my dad so much and really wanted to work with him. When there was a job opening in the Spinal Chord Injury Unit, she jumped at it and got the job.

I actually remember my dad talking to me about when Lori was first hired. He said that he sat down with her and told her that he spoke very highly of her to the supervisor, but that there was just one problem. He waited and watched Lori's reaction for a moment. (He loved to make people squirm). He then said that he told the supervisor, "She is too beautiful. That could be distracting for people." (My dad didn't really tell the supervisor this, however, it's true. Lori is very beautiful, and so very kind too.)

After the funeral, I remember walking outside and how strange it felt not to have to check and see if my dad needed anything, or to help get him home. My sister and brother and I were standing outside the hall. We were "free". We were free to just go. Yet we stood there. For 2 ½ years straight we were all used to making constant accommodations and constant considerations for my parents' needs, and their needs were extensive. We were all used to the constant emotional mood swings – the outbursts, the tears, the raw intensity of the ups and downs of the whole experience. It was over.

And the silence was so strong.

Part Seven

Alignment

There is a certain rhythm to grief. It comes and goes without warning. It's different for everyone. There is no right way to grieve. Eventually they'll be more good days than bad. I've read the pamphlets from Hospice. They were very helpful. I understood. What I didn't understand was that *understanding* does not have much of an effect on grief, other than having an awareness of what's going on. However, I thought that I "knew" about grief, so I should be able to rise above it to a certain extent. Wow. How arrogant was I?

My overall feeling was a sense that "the rug was pulled out from underneath me." I felt like I was flailing emotionally. I had no frame of reference to handle the death of someone close to me. I wasn't around illness or dying much. I do remember my grandparents being ill right before they died, however, I only recall seeing them once before they died in the advanced stages of their illness. It almost seemed a formality. I was "kept away". I remember attending funerals of family members when I was younger that I didn't know well and being nervous looking at their lifeless bodies in the open casket. My parents didn't talk about death, even though they experienced people close to them dying.

I recall having trouble sleeping the months following my dad's death. I remember during the day, feeling as though something was pressing down on my chest, and it made me want to sit or lie down. I was having trouble concentrating on things, and completely tasks – like balancing a checkbook – and taking a long time to do it, or putting it off. This was so unlike me. I remember asking myself, "Why can't I just balance this checkbook? It's right here and I just don't want to do it." It didn't make sense to me since the tasks I had been accomplishing prior to my parents' illnesses were 50 times more intense than balancing a checkbook. I wouldn't even have thought twice about a checkbook during that time, and it would have got balanced without me even thinking about it. I would just do it – literally in between other things.

"Sure," I thought, "I must be grieving." Okay. So what? So I'm grieving, but it's upsetting me that it's affecting my ability to manage my responsibilities. Then I'd look at that damn checkbook and think, "Who cares if it's balanced." Ahhhh! That thought made me very uncomfortable. I used to get great satisfaction over things like a balanced checkbook, an organized file cabinet, being caught up on laundry, and having a clean house. What does it mean if I don't care about these things anymore?

I had the ability to do what I was responsible for, but I noticed I would put things off until I ran up against a deadline. This was so completely not like me. I did not feel good about it. It's a terrible feeling to not feel like doing much. It's not much help to understand that perhaps the traumatic last few years and grief were playing a part. I just wanted to feel better.

I remember waking up with the thought, "I should be feeling better by now. After all, it's not like my dad dying was a surprise. My mom has been gone for even longer. The crisis time is over. I want to feel better." I felt an impatience. I was upset that my sleep was affected because that made me feel worse – being tired when I was already tired.

I decided to talk to a therapist. I chose the therapist that my dad used to see. It did help a little to talk to him. I do remember one thing he said that stuck with me. He knew what I had been through with my parents and all that my sister and I accomplished with their care and end of life experience. He used the word "heroic". I remember listening to him thinking, 'Yes, it was an extremely challenging time and we did perse-

vere.' Then I remembered one other statement. He said, "You're looking for something that is worthy of your time and abilities." Hmmmm.
At the time, I didn't feel like I was looking for anything. I just felt like
taking a nap.

****

What Is This All For?

My intense sadness and grief continued. Emotions are a tricky
thing. The mind says one thing and the heart has no reasoning. We just
feel. And we must. And there is nothing to *figure out* or *do* sometimes in
life. I've learned that one danger during grief is that it appears no choice
is worthwhile. I remember looking around at the world and thinking,
"What is everyone *doing*?" I saw faces of people laughing or angry; people walking around quickly going here and there as if what they were
moving towards was so important. I just didn't see the point in so many
things.

I don't know if it's dangerous or liberating not to care. I know I
did not feel danger and I didn't feel particularly liberated. I didn't feel
much, but I must have cared somewhat or maybe I just didn't want to
deal with the consequences of not performing. It seemed easy to do the
"most important" tasks, like taking care of the kids' needs and meeting
business deadlines because I could imagine what I'd have to deal with if
I stopped, and I just didn't want to deal with more.

I was lost in thought constantly. I was moving slower and sleeping
longer and waking up tired. I was aware that I was thinking about these
facts and I just had more thoughts about them, "Hmmm, I'm still tired
even though I slept soundly for 9 hours. Maybe I'm a bit depressed. Or
maybe I'm sad." I didn't feel the need to fix this "problem" anymore.

I usually prided myself on efficiency and I was in resistance to my
usual organizational and efficient tendencies. I was purposefully stopping myself from getting into task mode – even though that mode turned
my thoughts off. I didn't want to lose touch with myself. I really wanted
to notice what was going on with me. I don't know why. It was just real-

ly important to me to notice my feelings. Feelings like, "What is this all for? I guess I'm just biding time until it's over." I suppose I was contemplating the meaning of life.

I remember thinking it would be interesting watching Dominic and Sophie grow up, and if they got married, how interesting it would be to go to their wedding, and if they had kids, how interesting it would be to be a grandma. But it felt like someone else's life – almost like I would have been satisfied if I saw some pictures of those particular events in a crystal ball.

Oliver is a very busy man. He is someone who does not sit still. He ran our business, which took up a lot of his time. He talked a lot about work pressure. I tried to empathize and would suggest that he just stop the business if it's so stressful. I told him to just say the word and it would be fine with me. I just didn't see the point if it was so stressful. But then what? Okay – so I didn't have the future plan worked out and I didn't feel the need to. Thank God Oliver still had some stamina to think things through before reacting. His perseverance is incredible.

What kept me going day after day? I never really stayed in bed all day with covers over my head like I saw in the movies, although I could totally relate. I think I was just so conditioned to keep doing what needed to be done that I just did it – to a point.

I pinpointed one main shift I was experiencing. I had a loss of drive toward achievement. I didn't care as much about "accomplishing" and "achieving". I had an aversion to "goals". The goal itself wasn't enough to motivate me to action. I started making notes for this book during my mom's illness. Certain thoughts would just come to mind, very often. I would jot them down. Writing a book is an "achievement", however, the idea or vision of me completing the book and holding it in my hands, was not enough to inspire me to work on it. That vision fell flat and if I would think about it, I would actually be less inspired to write. This confused me. After all, wouldn't it be great to complete a book and perhaps help others as a result?

Even though literally every day I thought about "my book" and made notes often, I wasn't sure anymore what I was really writing about.

When my dad began having his issues, and he ended up dying too – well the book was changing. I also was changing a lot from when I first started writing. I got to a point when I realized that I didn't want to write a sad story. Because while the experience was sad, it was also bittersweet, and also joyful – it was all over the place. It was real, raw life, and an extremely powerful experience. I was writing from a sad place. I would get headaches after I worked on the book. I would cry when I would work on the book. I would stop writing for a while. Damn grief! Why couldn't it just pass?

****

Momentum

There came a point when I was ready to let go of the sadness theme of my life, yet I didn't know how. Ultimately, I declared to myself, "I am not going to live the rest of my life in sadness. There has got to be a way out of this." I began thinking about *momentum*. In my efforts to relax and de-stress from the trauma and chaos I experienced during the 2 ½ year journey with my parents, there was a tipping point where the lessening of activity began to gain momentum and it became really hard to do even simple things. I really noticed this. I realized that while I purposefully prevented myself from getting into task mode, I went too far.

With grief, there is growth, and life changes – forever. I saw two choices. I could look at this positively – that my life will continue, and I can grow and live on, or I could dig in my heels and resist (not even knowing it was resistance). I dangled in the balance of choosing to stop in life. Stop living. I wasn't suicidal, I was just comfortable in my misery. However, there came a point where I was so miserable being miserable, that I wasn't going to continue being in that state. Fortunately, I wasn't so depressed that I felt hopeless. At times I did have that feeling, and I'm grateful that I was able to reach out for help. I can now empathize more with others that experience depression. I really believe depression is not something a person can come out of on their own.

My thoughts would toggle between feelings of defeat, and feelings of "what can I do now?" I still felt that there was a way out of this dragging existence. I didn't like *not liking* anything. I didn't like sleeping so much. I didn't like not caring about things. I didn't like feeling like I was just existing and going through the motions. The thing is, I didn't like my "old life" either, and I didn't know what my "new life" would look like. Was this grief? At this point, I didn't care about any label or trying to figure it out so much anymore. I just wanted it to change. I wasn't going to live like this anymore.

I realized the answer was not less and less activity. I didn't know the answer. I just saw myself *going down*. I knew I didn't want to be sad so much of the time, even though I had gathered enough evidence to keep me there. At this point of revelation, it had been over a year since my dad died.

I looked back in my life to find something that I used to do that made me feel good. Besides eating chocolate chip cookies, the healthier answer was running for me. I remembered the feeling I had after my runs. It was a consistent feeling *each time* of "all is well" – even if my mind said it wasn't.

I told myself that I would run every day for one week. That was my only intention. I still met certain responsibilities during the week, but my sole focus was on running. It took all my effort to focus on running every day for just one week. The problem was, I didn't *want* to run *at all*. Even though I knew that once I started I would benefit from it and I would feel better. I still did not want to run. I wanted to *relax*. I wanted to curl up on my couch with my big, soft blanket in my beautiful living room. *This is what I really wanted to do and was being pulled to do.* But, instead, I chose to run because more than wanting to stay comfy on my couch, I wanted that feeling of *all is well*.

I gained momentum by the end of that week. Even though everything else in my life felt scattered, I accomplished what I set out to do with running. I then decided to join a running group and found one through my gym. I asked a friend of mine, Julie, to join me, and she did. I remember being so impressed because Julie was not a runner. She just made the choice to do it because she never participated in an organized run and it sounded fun to her.

This running group really helped me. It was awesome being around other people of all different ages and backgrounds – all with one purpose – to train for a 10k run. I had done dozens of these runs 15 years earlier, and this would be my first 10k since then. The training was a commitment of certain days in the week. It was challenging for me because I run best in the mornings and one of the training days was a Tuesday evening – the worst possible day for me because that was my longest work day.

I remember one Tuesday I was feeling so tired I decided to take a nap after work, even though I was supposed to meet the group soon to run. I set the timer for 15 minutes, curled up on the couch and slept instantly. The timer woke me up. I laid there and looked out my living room window to the valley view. It was all cloudy and rainy. I did not want to go meet the group. I wanted to stay there curled up on my couch. *I really, really wanted to stay there.*

I decided to stand up, and I did. I stood there looking outside. I decided to get my running clothes on, and I did. I decided to walk out my front door and get in my car, which I did, then I began driving to meet the group. I wasn't happy. I was actually feeling pretty miserable, but I kept driving.

I arrived and met the group and just by being there with them it distracted me from my feelings. As always, as soon as I started to run, I had no regrets and was absolutely happy after I completed yet another awesome run. The routine of doing this again and again, got me back in the habit of running. I am so thankful for this.

Fortunately, I do reach out to people. In grief, I found it's absolutely imperative to reach out and I became careful about how much time I spent by myself because it became so clear that I always felt worse feeling sad by myself than feeling sad with people who cared about me. Maybe it was a distraction, and it didn't really matter. What mattered is that I know it worked.

I told my sad self at different times and in different ways: "*Moment to moment. Don't rush. Be kind to yourself. Soak in the kindness of others. Know that it's not for you to make things better all by yourself. You're entering into a new life.*" I knew in my heart that behind great sadness is the capacity for great joy. I was going to experience this joy. I held on to this vision and started foreseeing joy in my life. I actually felt twinges of excitement in anticipation. I just had to be patient and keep going in this direction.

One thing that brought me great comfort was choosing a picture of my mom and one of my dad and getting them custom-framed. I had a bunch of pictures picked out, then decided to narrow it down because I didn't want a shrine. Also, as I looked at each picture to make my choice, I noticed that some made me smile and some made me feel sad. I narrowed them down to only the ones that made me smile. I wanted to feel good when I looked at my mom and my dad.

It was difficult, but I finally settled on the two pictures. One was a candid shot of my mom the day we all went to pick up her puppy, Yogi. I had it framed with a caption, and also with my Golden Boy poem.

The picture of my dad I chose was the one from my wedding day. I was sitting on his lap in my wedding dress during our "Father/Daughter Dance". It was also a candid shot and we were both smiling. I had this custom framed as well, with a caption, and a card that my dad gave me. (I had found this card months after my dad died. It was in the pocket of my work bag. What a great surprise it was to find it.) The words my dad wrote in this card expressed his appreciation for me.

I love these two custom frames and they are hanging in the hall-way in my home and I have the pleasure of seeing them every single day. They still make me smile.

****

Why Not?

Oliver mentioned a seminar he had heard about. It was a seminar on public speaking. I told him that I didn't want to be a public speaker. He said it's not just for public speakers, it's also for people who want to get comfortable with speaking in front of an audience. I did enjoy learning and going to various seminars, and I agreed to go, figuring it would force me to get out of the house and distract me. Did it ever! When we arrived, instantly I felt like a foreigner. I saw all these people who had ambition and who were in the midst of life and doing things. What had I been doing lately?

We were put into groups based on our experience with public speaking. I put "zero" experience (other than speaking at my parents' funerals, I hadn't had any experience speaking in front of large groups.) Our assignment was to each think of a topic to talk about – one that we were passionate about. It could be in alignment with our career, or anything else. Well, at this point, I really felt like I didn't belong. I thought to myself, "What I've been doing these last 3 years was dealing with illness and death."

I talked to the facilitator about my dilemma. I told her that I don't have a passion right now to talk about because I'm coming off a difficult journey. She thought talking about my journey was ideal. She said, "It's a story of hope." 'Really?' I thought. That was an interesting perspective for me at that time.

The first round of speeches started. Each group had their own rounds. It reminded me of the singing competition American Idol because there was a panel of judges that would give feedback. Every person that went on stage looked really nervous. All of us in the audience were very supportive, after all, we could feel their pain. When it was my turn, I fumbled around to find words. Afterward I was thinking, 'Why did I agree to this?' What was I thinking going from my low-key existence to a public speaking seminar? My stomach was a mess from nerves.

This was a 4-day course. The goal was to learn the realities of public speaking. The most important point was to be vulnerable and real, and to know that to be effective, you must truly care about the audience. The most challenging part of this course (besides standing up in front of a few hundred people), was that our speech was timed to two minutes. It was so challenging to make a point in 2 minutes.

We were videotaped and were able to view our video after. What I ended up saying wasn't what I had written down. I know I mentioned the story of walking into my parents' house, and my dad saying to me *'it's as if a light just entered the room'*. I also talked about how I learned what a gift it is to just "be" with someone – to connect and be real. After the 2 minutes was up, I was stunned at all the applause. I heard someone in the back shout my name and when I walked off the stage, people in the front row put their hands out to high-5 me. I thought to myself, 'Gosh, I was just talking about an experience.' I had no idea that it could be so impactful. Several people came up to me at the end of the day and said that I inspired them to call their parents, and to visit their parents when they returned home. Others came up to me to talk about the death of their parent. Even though I was really uncomfortable the entire time (I could barely eat for those 4 days because I was so nervous), I really value this experience. All the discomfort was worth it.

****

Anxiety Suction

Yes, I would become sad when I thought about my parents, however, the more overwhelming emotion I realized was that I was *scared*. I was really scared about death. I saw my dad, who was so spiritual, being so scared during that last year of his life. (Or was I projecting? Perhaps a little of both.) I realized that being spiritual doesn't mean that dying is an easy journey. After all, my dad was human, as we all are.

I definitely think there are people out there who have a good relationship with their own mortality. I'm just not there yet.

I figured out that I have an issue with the "not knowing" part, and the "not being in control" part. I don't know what the end of life will be for me. Neither does anyone else on the planet. Also, what is the point of life? Seriously, what is this all about? I think about how my parents lived a decent and courageous life. They were honest people who did their best. They overcame adversity. They helped others. Then their journey ended, in a way that involved much suffering, and they are not on this earth anymore.

As long as I live, I will not see them again, and neither will anyone else. I don't sound very uplifting, do I? That's because on the outside looking in, I'm just a woman in my 40's who grew up in Northern California, went to Catholic school, made friends, got my heart broken a few times, broke a few more, married, had two children, started a small business with my husband, had marital issues on and off, learned a few things, remodeled a house, sold it, moved into a "dream" house, had an active social life, was busy living "the good life"…then my parents got sick and died.

The person I was then is not the person I am now. I turned into a woman searching for answers to life's big questions. Everything in my world seemed insignificant compared to figuring out what this "life" is all about. Why? Because every single day I was bombarded with the thought that we are all on the same journey my parents were on. The only difference between us and my parents (and anyone else dealing with a terminal illness) is that we just don't currently have as much information as they did about their impending death, and the details on how it would most likely happen. But the fact is, we *are all going to die.* I couldn't get this fact out of my head. It compelled me to start seriously looking at how I was living, and consider what I really wanted in life.

My mindset after my experience with my parents is that I'm a *baby* in this game called life. The experience with my parents, being so engaged with them at the end of their lives, and holding their hands as they drew their last breaths – I realize how much I don't know. Everything I experienced seems to be sinking in slowly and changing me, whether I like it or not. It's very unsettling, yet I cannot "go back". As anxiety-provoking as this experience was, I wouldn't want to go back to my old life even if I could. I'm living with a different level of insight. I *know* more than ever before about how little I can control life, yet at the same time, I *know* how much I can impact it. It's like a paradox. I actually have more control than I thought – just in a different way – a more fluid way.

What is the point of life? I do not have a solid answer. Does anyone really? After all, we are all in this together as human beings. I can just say that for me, *celebration* is so much more important to me than ever before. When I focus on celebrating all that is a part of my life, I feel so grateful, and my fears of impending death subside and disappear. *Every time*…even if only for a moment. What I found though, is that if I commit to a practice of focusing on what I'm grateful for, I enjoy life more, I feel more, do more and love and appreciate people more. *I've found there is simply no downside to gratitude.*

Grief has the capacity to linger. It's driven by emotions – like many things we feel and do in life. What makes grief more unique is that it forced certain realities into my life. It reinforced the fact that *death is a part of life* in a way that, prior, I only intellectually understood. The reality that "I'm going to die" was a like a "smack in the head" clear realization that, in all seriousness, "I'm going to die." I don't know how. I don't know when. I just really understood for the first time ever that it's going to really happen. Also, people in my life are going to die. People that I love are going to die. I don't know when or how, but they will. Who will be first?

I didn't want to think about this, and it was futile anyway. So I didn't. But the thoughts were still there being pushed down every time they came up. I started having anxiety episodes. I've never felt anxiety attacks in my life. Let me tell you what I mean by anxiety. All of a sudden, out of the blue, in the middle of relaxing and watching a television show after a nice weekend away, my heart started racing and I started sweating, and I really thought I had to go to the hospital. I felt like I couldn't get air. It was the worst feeling I've ever had. I can honestly say, I'd rather go through child labor than have an anxiety attack. With anxiety, I didn't know when it was going to happen, and I had little to no control over it.

I had doctor appointments and psychologist appointments and read books and did research. I was not going to accept this in my life! It was horrible. Well, I started having insomnia too. I thought sarcastically, 'Yet another thing I can empathize with people about.' I've never had insomnia issues before. In fact, anyone that knows me would say that I'm able to fall asleep at the drop of a hat. What was worse? Insomnia or anxiety attacks? I think anxiety, even though insomnia is a horrible feeling too – that feeling of, 'I'm having trouble sleeping…I'm tired… if I don't sleep, I'll be foggy in the head tomorrow and I have so much to do…I want to work out too because if I don't, I will be irritable and not feel well and get a headache and it's not healthy to be so inactive after not sleeping all night long…and then I won't be able to sleep the next night either…then I'll get sick…and if I don't control this, I'll get a disease…" My mind would loop.

My doctor instantly prescribed sleeping pills, but I was so uncomfortable taking them. I did try them, and it seemed to help, although I'm not really sure if it was the placebo effect or if they really worked. It did feel good to be able to "do something" for the insomnia. But it seemed so unhealthy to me. It seemed like a temporary solution to an in-depth problem. I knew making sleeping pills part of my life wasn't the answer. I felt like it would be the start of a downward spiral. I wanted to take care of the core issue.

I would still call my doctor and I even went in for a few more appointments because again, the feeling of anxiety was so awful – like being in the middle of a heart attack. I was desperate for relief. During an anxiety attack, I really felt like I was going to die. It would be hard to breathe and I would feel tingling and pain in my left arm, and my breathing would be really shallow. Every time I called my doctor or went it, it was always the same thing, "It's anxiety. You need to get that under control. See the psychologist again."

I guess I'll live.

✱✱✱✱

Say Goodbye Stress Monster

One night – it was always at night for me – I started having an anxiety attack. "Noooo!" Was my first thought at the onset. Then I got mad. I got really mad. I said out loud, "Fine." I grabbed my pillow and stomped downstairs and got comfortable on the couch, slightly elevated with the pillows, and I thought to myself, "Okay, looks like I'm having an anxiety attack. That's all this is. No one ever died from anxiety." I then said, "Okay, so go for it. I don't care if I never sleep again. I'll just stay here all night and focus on my breathing for 8 hours straight. That's what I'm going to do." I focused my mind and was all set. I was so determined. I focused on my breathing, which was out of control. I could barely get air in because I was having trouble getting air out. I just stuck with it and focused on only that, not trying to breathe differently, just focusing on whatever my breathing was doing. I don't know when, but I fell asleep and didn't wake up until 7am the next morning.

I woke up and when I realized what happened – that I had solid sleep – I was so happy. I smiled and jumped up and ran upstairs to tell Oliver. This was so huge to me. I felt like I was able to somewhat control what was happening. I was so excited because I felt that now I knew something I could do – besides taking a pill – that could help me.

There are certain other things that I do to counteract anxiety. Writing this book is one thing. Reciting "The Serenity Prayer" is another. Also, regular exercise, yoga, meditation/stillness, eating a healthy diet with much less sugar, less gluten and processed foods, etc. (I actually cut out sugar for 90 days, and that made an incredible difference overall. I have much less of a taste for it now and have so much more energy.) I also make sure to go to bed at a reasonable hour, and I've found that if I'm in bed by 10pm most nights, I feel the best the next day.

I saw a Naturopathic doctor and was an excellent student and followed her instructions almost exactly. I weigh less now than before Dominic was born. With all these lifestyle ideals I follow them more days in the week than not. It's all about practice, and I find that the practice is well worth it. For me, taking the time and energy and being disciplined to practice a healthy lifestyle that works for me, is preferable to living with chronic stress and anxiety.

When I first started yoga, it seemed to just use up time and I didn't feel that much value from it. That was until I was disciplined enough to stay with it a while. I committed to doing yoga 3 times a week. I had a one-half hour DVD that Oliver put on my I-Pad for me. It was convenient and much easier than going to a yoga class, although I did that too. Once I let go of my preconceived notions of what yoga was about and simply did it based on the reality that much research has been done about the beneficial effects, and many people have gained so much peace of mind, I decided to get out of my own way.

I love yoga. I'm a baby at it still – meaning I still lean toward beginner sessions. I have to say though, when I get my yoga mat out, dress appropriately with yoga attire, and sit on my mat with my I-Pad propped up and press "play", I'm in another world. I'm aware of my whole body. I'm aware of the control I have of my breathing and my movements. I feel very empowered as I slowly move through the short 35 minute session.

When I do yoga, I get the sensation sometimes that I'm "stuck in my body" – meaning I sense that I'm really <u>not</u> my body. Yet I see the connection and importance of taking care of my body so I can feel most flexible and free. Yoga does bring me to a place of peace. I learned that Yoga is not a prescription. Meaning, if I'm feeling stressed or tense, doing Yoga doesn't relieve it. However, the *practice* of yoga does. Incorporating it as part of my lifestyle does wonders for helping me relax and releasing my mind to more easily explore a more peaceful state.

Something else that really helped me counteract anxiety was changing my attitude about stress and what it means. During one of my sessions with a psychologist that I saw a few times, I was talking about how my mom died and how I thought that stress had a lot to do with the onset of her illness. I told her that my mom had such a healthy lifestyle and that it's scary to think you could die young even with eating healthy and living a very active lifestyle. The psychologist looked me in the eye, and in the most calm and convincing voice said, "Your mom's life is not yours. Not even close." I looked at her. Wow. I hadn't thought of this fact, yet it sounded so obvious.

My life stress is nothing like my mom's life stress was. My life was not hers, or anyone else's for that matter. My line of thinking suddenly felt foolish. That statement really helped me shake the worry off and start thinking more strategically about things. I also started thinking differently about stress. I thought, "If I'm never stressed, then I'm probably dead, or close to it." I even started thinking about anxiety differently. I thought, "Anxiety – it's just a wake up call to pay attention to my life." I started taking stress and anxiety as signals to keep searching – keep knocking on doors. The strange thing was, I didn't know exactly what I was searching for. I just knew I had to keep moving and I would run into it.

****

Knocking on Doors

In the wake of my parents' deaths, I also was experiencing a lot of disappointment from friends. I wanted to spend more time with them than they had time for me. I realized that they hadn't changed in any way – I changed. With my parents' deaths, I lost a lot of social activity. I used to see my parents regularly and talk on the phone throughout the week. I didn't lose just one parent, I lost both, and there was a notice-able void. I wanted to connect with people. My friends were the logical choice to reach out to.

I got tired of feeling disappointment. I felt there was no point in talking to some of my friends about my feelings of disappointment be-cause they were doing nothing wrong. They were living their lives. I'm such a social person though. I missed having more interaction with peo-ple – and I don't mean going to parties. I wanted to connect with peo-ple on a deeper level.

I remember expressing to Oliver my boredom after coming home from certain parties. I would tell him that whenever I "got down to it" with people, most didn't reciprocate or would start talking about super-ficial things. Oliver said to me, "You know, Lea, not everyone wants to talk about deep things you know."

I said, "Really?"

He laughed at me, "Really!"

I thought about his point and of course, he's correct. Just because I'm interested in certain subjects and a certain lifestyle doesn't mean ev-eryone is interested in the same way. This didn't change the fact that I still wanted to connect and talk about *real* things. And I wanted to do this <u>every</u> day. I was sure there were people out there as interested in this as I was. After all, it didn't make sense that I would be the only one.

I remember one day sitting in my living room and no one was home. It was quiet. I was processing that disappointment feeling again from my friends and recognized I was feeling the void of my parents again. I said to myself, "I am not going to live the rest of my life without the type of connection I had with my parents." I really missed certain feelings that I had associated with them. I remembered their smiling faces being genuinely happy for me when I was in a good space. I felt accepted no matter how much I messed up. I knew that all I had to do was go to them and they would be there for me.

I started a new line of thinking. Yes, my parents were gone, but our level of relationship was not. After all, I am still here. I was part of the relationships I had with my parents. I had something to do with the creation of the relationships I had with them also. I wasn't just a bystander gaining. I was engaged with them and also gave to them. I suddenly felt that I could do something about the void I was feeling. I just didn't know what. I just knew I had to take some sort of action toward filling that void because the status quo was so incredibly dissatisfying, and I was experiencing real pain. There was a gnawing feeling of something missing.

I know a lot of people turn to God in moments like this. I do feel temporary comfort with prayer, however, I still had this strong feeling that I had to *do* something. God is a buddy of mine, but I wanted buddies in the flesh too – some other humans to pal around with on a deeper level. I knew I had to "put myself out there".

I know people say there is nothing like a parents' attention. Well, I finally resigned myself to the fact that this phase of life was over. My parents were loved and now gone – at least from this earth. I got to the place of being truly grateful that I had such great parents. I became ever more aware of the fact that many, many people cannot say the same. Many people have so much pain from their childhoods. I started thinking about how fortunate I was to have had relationships with my parents that I truly missed.

I decided to volunteer my time to the seminar company that had facilitated the public speaking seminar. After volunteering, I had the opportunity to participate in a 90-day course they offered. I really didn't want to do it. I knew people that had taken the course, including Oliver, and it sounded intense to me. The program involved being on a team with other people that I never met before, and set goals and work toward them. It was quite a commitment – 3 weekends, weekly meetings, daily coach calls, and surprise events, etc. It was designed so you "can't hide". "Who you are" shows up at some point in those 90 days, and "it's all about day 91". I was intrigued by the idea of getting to know some new people, working on myself, and getting to day 91.

I still didn't want to do it.

I was also continuing to experience a lot of sadness and bouts of anxiety. I thought maybe it wasn't a good time to take the course. However, the facilitator said it doesn't matter where you are in life because the course is about your life. I was at the point that I knew I wanted a change. I was tired of feeling like every day I was pulling myself up with great effort, which would sometimes "work" and sometimes not. I knew I needed to take action in something, which was why I volunteered at the company in the first place.

After feeling very uncomfortable and uncertain, deep inside I knew this was an opportunity, and I signed up for the 90 day course. My hand was actually shaking as I signed the registration form.

Day 91: Our team created something great in those 90 days. The connections we made and what we achieved together, and individually, was truly incredible. (The fact is, incredible things do happen when people are fully engaged in life.)

Courses such as this one nudge me – they remind me of what I already know, and offer me a safe practice ground to explore. I always remind myself that all courses, workshops, seminars – even religious institutions, schools, and entrepreneurial organizations – they are all designed and run by *people*. These people had an idea, purpose and mission, and many created something to share with the world, giving people the opportunity to benefit.

Like with any form of learning, I've found that the real value comes when I incorporate what resonates with me *into my actual life*. Part of this process involves being careful not to hide behind doctrine, certain concepts or compatible people – but really practicing what I'm learning "across the board" of my life. When things get particularly hard, it's tempting to "throw the baby out with the bath water." The challenge is in *keeping what resonates with me and leaving the rest*.

I think about my curiosity for learning in this way – I'm willing to open my eyes and search for the blossoms amongst all the weeds. One analogy to explain what I mean is this: I'm not working hard sifting through and pulling a bunch of weeds to find the blossoms. What I'm doing is keeping my focus on the blossoms, and by doing so, the weeds simply fade away in the background. The effort goes into changing my thoughts – into opening my mind to all the wonderful possibilities this life has to offer. I don't have to "pull the weeds" or spend energy "sifting through them" because I simply don't see them anymore. Why? Because of my focus on the blossoms. They become so bright that the weeds simply fade away in the background with no effort on my part. This is what I've discovered – whatever I focus on strengthens.

I can relay all the wise and beautiful words in the world as a result of all the things I've learned, but I realize it means nothing if I'm not speaking from the truth of who I am. This is the ultimate practice offering the most fulfillment.

> *"Who I am speaks so loudly, no one can hear a word I'm saying."*

> *(Quote by Ralph Waldo Emerson)*

****

Dream On

I've learned that I enjoy life much more when I allow myself to dream. I don't mean massive dreams of fame or fortune (although these certainly are dreams) – for me, I'm talking about simple dreams such as what I find beautiful and adding that to my life. Or, dreams of dancing more because I love music and moving my body. Or, dreams of eating together with my family more, because we are all together and interacting in a different way – a more intimate way.

I also learned the value of "true support". Meaning, having people in my life that I trust and love and who also trust and love me, and who want to learn and grow. These people know my dreams – my thoughts – and they support me by reminding me of what I say I want in life. They have the courage to point out when I'm helping myself in the direction of my dreams, or when I'm lying to myself.

These people allow me to be down and frustrated, and ask me how long I want to stay there. For example, they will say something like, "How long do you want to stay down? I'll be there with you to get it all out. Let's grumble and pout together, then let's shift." We're all about *awareness* – being observers instead of reactors. With the support of each other, we decide how we want to be in any given situation, then we *practice*. This is what I find very interesting in life – the abundance of opportunities that present themselves, daily, that I can use to practice. Not always welcome and pleasant, but always an adventure.

I still hold the vision of *connecting with people every day*. I want people in my life where it's normal to have *deep* conversations and not just something that occurs on occasion. I broached the idea of a Mastermind Group to the people that I developed a connection with during the 90-day program we all participated in. Seven of us came together, collaborated, and met with one purpose in mind:

> *To support each other in designing and living the life each of us say we want. To create and maintain an authentic bond with each other and share our dreams, challenges, and celebrate our wins. We become our "soft place" to fall and inspire each other to action. We participate with compassion, integrity, commitment, and vulnerability. We "have each others' backs". This group will support each member in staying in alignment with each of our individual life purposes in a balanced and inspiring way.*

We have a buddy system too. For example, my buddy, Emi, and I talk almost daily. We usually communicate over a walkie-talkie app on our cell phones, which works out great. We are accountability buddies, as well as "life buddies", and share our deepest thoughts and our journey through life together.

The logistics of our group will change, and have changed, as our group is meant to be fluid and collaborative. The kind of support we are able to offer each other is far from the "norm". I get to practice how I want to be in the loving presence of our team. This helps me have the courage to be me at all times, with all people – regardless of their belief systems. This feels very freeing to me, even though it's challenging. Our group is still together a year after forming. We're engaged in it right now and will be until we're not.

"All things are possible, and nothing is necessary."

(Author Unknown)

I've come to realize that the subject of "vision" is a big concept for a lot of people. I've found that often it's easier to set "goals", however, goals don't necessarily align to what is truly important to a person. There is nothing wrong with this. Many people get much satisfaction from achievement.

I'm working with concepts beyond achievement – determining value systems, acting from inspiration versus motivation, asking myself often, "Does what I'm doing really matter?" If not, then, "Is it at least getting me to what really matters?" And, then the big question, *"What is it that really matters?"*

Working on a life vision makes so much sense to me because I no longer want to waste even one day "going through the motions."

I'm really inspired by compassion. I believe that all people are the same at a human level and that we want the same things out of life, and our freedom comes when we're able to express it in our own way. Freedom comes from being who we are in the world. We are completely unique in our strengths and what we are able to offer to the world. When we practice using our strengths, we build evidence supporting the truth that WE MATTER.

Once we connect with our strengths and really "get" that we matter, we will automatically discover how we may use our strengths to live the life we want. By doing so, we will positively impact those we come into contact with, creating a ripple effect. We will actually impact humanity in a big way just by doing our part in our own lives. This is a process. I believe life is a journey and one way we can support each other is by recognizing the ups and downs, loving each other, and celebrating forward momentum in the direction of our dreams, despite setbacks.

****

What's Important to Me?

For me, without a life vision, it's so easy to just "go along" and wake up one day and realize what is truly important to me fell to the wayside. It's so easy to get caught up in emotions. During the time with my parents, it would have been very easy for my emotions to overtake me, leaving me unable to engage with what was happening. However, I believe what helped me during that time is that part of my vision *was to engage.* Even though the whole situation was extremely difficult, it didn't matter, because *I was more connected to the vision I held for the situation than I was to the challenges surrounding it.*

My experience with my parents is now over. I'm left with this nagging reality, a non-stop tap on the shoulder, that: *All of us are approaching the end of our lives.* I don't mean to be morbid or depressing, and this isn't about instilling a sense of worry. It's about instilling a sense of empowerment.

> *"You are a soul whose true nature is light, on a journey to ever-higher levels of consciousness and states of divine expression. Your vitality on that journey is directly proportion-*

ate to the vividness of your vision. If you don't have something challenging and fulfilling to awaken for in the morning, you won't rise and shine. Even with a clear purpose, you'll occasionally be distracted and uninspired. The only reason you are not inspired at those times is because you haven't linked what you are doing, to your purpose. Make a list of everything you do in a day and ask yourself: How does this help me fulfill my mission? Keep linking everything to your purpose. Anything you don't see as part of your purpose feels pointless and the ratio of pointlessness to purposefulness is how much 'hell or heaven' you have in your life. The truth is that everything you do is connected."

(Quote by Dr. John Demartini)

Why not apply the same logic of what's been proven to me through the journey with my parents – the power of vision – to my life? Why not figure out what's important to me in life and make my decisions in complete alignment with what I value? Why not practice accepting "what is" in all situations?

After all, the above worked wonders in the situation with my parents. There is no downside I see to putting effort into this direction. It's all about *practice* and having gratitude for our life *now*, instead of focusing on "arriving".

I don't have to view life as a journey with a destination. There is no destination. I don't have to view day-to-day living with a checklist of goals. I don't have to feel pressure in life. I'll buy into that being *uncomfortable* at times in life is unavoidable – because anything new will always feel uncomfortable – but *pressure* is something entirely different.

When I focus on my vision, on how I want to be based on who I really am, pressure disappears. When my actions are in alignment with my vision, pressure simply cannot co-exist. *I am approaching the end of my life.* I must decide how I want to live. I must decide what is important to me. My answers will be different than other people's answers to these questions.

> *"Oh, how the pressure lifts, when we live our essence and move only from the truth of who we are."*

(Quote by Lea Gambina Pecora)

I no longer put pressure on myself when I try new things. I move quicker. I approach ideas with the attitude, "Let me give this a try and see what happens." I practice disengaging with any result that I think I may want. I focus on the "new thing" I'm trying. This may sound contradictory to my idea of vision. After all, wasn't I saying it's important to have clarity of vision? To focus on vision?

Yes, clarity of vision is essential, however, it's easy to get "locked up" when trying new things if the focus is, "I'm doing this to realize my vision." If I think like this, then I feel pressure. In fact, for me, the point of vision is to become inspired to action. Also, vision is flexible and changes as I grow. It's not a destination – it's a way of living. Vision is my soft place to fall during all those times I fail to be how I want to be. It's my personal reminder of my true nature.

Back to the contradiction of not focusing on vision when trying new things. If I know my vision with clarity, that helps me decide what to do in life. If I determine that what I want to do is in alignment with my vision, then that's enough for me. I then shift my focus on the "new thing".

Let me give an example on how I successfully integrated yoga into my life. I've learned from others that practicing yoga can result in feelings of relaxation. I personally had no experience with yoga, yet, based on the results in other people's lives, it appeared to add great value in terms of feeling relaxed and peaceful. After talking with people who practice yoga, and getting to know them and feeling like "I want what they have" – that sense of serenity – I asked myself, "Would a yoga practice be in alignment with my vision?" The answer was 'yes'. Then I decided, "I will give it a try." No more talking about it. My focus was trying yoga, with first deciding what "trying" meant, i.e. different studios, types, lengths, etc. Deciding what "trying" meant was important to avoid stopping too soon without gaining an accurate picture so I could decide if I really wanted yoga in my life.

I reminded myself, "I don't *have* to do anything. I always have a choice. I *want* to do this, and I'm grateful that I *get* to do this." This helps relieve pressure that I put on myself when I try new things.

I went to a local yoga studio that practiced a specific type of yoga. I was curious. I went to 3 sessions. It wasn't quite "it", although it was interesting. I went to a local wellness center and signed up for 3 classes there. I liked how they also offered community events. The challenge was that the sessions were an hour and a half, and with the 15 minute commute each way, that was 2 hours out of my day. I enjoyed it and appreciated the help from the teacher, especially because I didn't know what I was doing.

A day or so later, I noticed a CD at my local grocery store with the most perfect title. "Yoga for Stress Relief & Flexibility". That's what I wanted. It was even on sale for $4.00. I bought it. That evening, after explaining to my family that I would like an hour to myself in my room with no interruptions, I rolled out my yoga mat and followed along to the CD. I felt awkward. I had no teacher to help me confirm that I was "doing it right". Then I just told myself, "I'm just going to finish it." I did. I liked the fact that it was only ½ hour. Less time-consuming than the 2 hr. experience going to a studio. That motivated me to try it again a couple of days later. Again, I felt awkward. It was a lot about breathing and I was having a hard time concentrating on breathing AND moving, but I was determined to finish the CD every time I began it. (I refused to give up on myself.)

My buddy accountability system worked great with this yoga commitment I made. Emi knew what I was doing and we made a pact. The commitment was that I would text her a certain amount of times during the week, and I would say, for example, "I did a yoga session", or "I didn't do a yoga session." No explanations. It was about being truthful and aware of what we were and were not doing. No judgment. (Emi would do the same with me – she would text me about her commitments.)

The fact was, just by declaring what we wanted to do, it was "out" in the world and not just a thought in our heads. Also, we could not ignore the constant reminder of our commitment, which kept it in the forefront of our minds, so we couldn't easily (or conveniently) forget.

Once the new habit of yoga was incorporated into my life, I no longer needed the accountability system as much, and I would use it only during those weeks when I felt I was getting off track. Emi and I start each week with a new round of commitments – action items that are always in alignment with our bigger visions. For example, this week I committed to: no sugar sweets 5 days; hide love notes for family 2 days; work on book 4 days. Another example, one week I committed to: alone time one evening from 8pm on; go to lab for annual blood work; ask Oliver to plan out date night.

I think about goals totally differently now. I heard someone paraphrasing a mentor they had worked with who said something to the effect of: *"It's not about the goal. It's about who you have to become in order to reach the goal."* Wow. This made total sense to me. This explained why the idea of achievement wasn't motivating me anymore. However, focusing on 'who I will become' was very inspiring. For example, with my book writing I thought to myself, 'When I have my book done, who will I be?' Instinctively I felt I would be more *me*. I would be living more authentically…more free. I was inspired to action because of *my vision*, not my goal.

****

A Vision in the Making

I'm well aware that many people do not live with a clear, written vision for their life. First, it's important to understand the value of having a vision.

I have a suggestion. Think about the end of your life, when you simply are at that point that we will all get to – you have no more time to explore or participate on this earth. Ask yourself, "Did my life matter?" I believe that by living according to a vision, the answer to this question will be a most definite, "Yes." We will have no regrets. When we become clear about who we are, we automatically start living life more purposefully.

Another practice is to dream. We used to do this as children. This practice isn't about ignoring the reality of the world. It's a practice to open up our minds. What is the value in that? It's huge. It helps the mind think in terms of *possibilities* that you can choose among, versus stopping your mind from dreaming further. Think about when we say, "Well, that's not likely to happen because…" Just by thinking along those lines, it becomes more difficult to continue thought patterns in alignment with a desire or dream. Instead, if we say, "Imagine if I… then imagine how wonderful it would feel if…" This opens the mind to start streaming more thoughts that match possibilities. *It's a mindset practice.*

Vision is about *clarity*, so if a person does not have a vision for their life, then perhaps they are devoting energy to things that don't really matter to them. Perhaps they experience chaos in certain areas that can otherwise be avoidable, to a certain extent.

When we look at certain areas of our lives that are running smoothly, we are most likely in alignment with our values and expending energy on things that are more meaningful to us. The clearer we are, the easier our life will be in many ways. We also become more courageous because we know "why" we want to make certain changes. As such, we are better able to set firm boundaries with people in our lives without being swayed. Why is this? Because when setting boundaries, oftentimes people don't react well when we shake up the "status-quo" and it's hard to deal with the initial reactions of others. When we're clear on our "why", we aren't as emotionally affected by reactions because of our confidence in our decisions. We understand that the other person is just catching up to a new level of understanding. We become more patient.

Compassion helps here. As much as we would like, people don't always react the way we wish they did. Sometimes it's hard to put ourselves in another's place because we aren't experiencing struggle with their particular challenge. For example, I'm naturally "up-beat". I don't struggle to get out of bad moods. I realize though that other people have a harder time with this. When they are down, it's not so easy for them to shift. To relate to them better, what I do is imagine what I struggle with most in my life (which is being reactive when I allow myself to be triggered by those closest to me). Then I remember that the challenge I feel in my attempts to remain calm is the <u>same exact feeling</u> that a person has when they are attempting to shift out of a bad mood. This understanding allows my compassion to flow toward them. After all, pain is pain. Struggle is struggle. We all know what this feels like.

Having compassion doesn't mean putting up with the darkest sides of people. Often when people are acting out in mean ways, they are in pain. They are struggling. (I know when I'm acting mean, I'm in pain.) Compassion is simply recognizing this, remaining calm, and sending loving thoughts to them, or ourselves. Once we're aware and acting from a loving place, we then can make a more effective decision.

I've learned that it's okay to remove myself from hurtful situations. *I don't deserve to be "punished"* – even when I mess up – even when I'm acting mean – and especially when I'm enforcing a personal boundary. By punishment, I mean at the most basic level, being treated unkindly by others – including being unkind toward myself. Other people don't deserve punishment either. Does punishment even "work" anyway? We can express our feelings if we feel the need to and set personal boundaries, but who are we to judge and punish? Life offers natural consequences.

Vision is also about utilizing our strengths. It's important to value those strengths. If I think about it, I tend to admire people who have certain strengths that I feel I don't have, and I tend to downplay my own strengths because they seem so easy to me. A mind-shift here is powerful. Imagine if every human being knew and valued their own strengths just as much as they valued the strengths they witness in others. Then imagine if we all make changes in our lives around utilization of our strengths, and understand that we are contributing in such a big way by doing so – even though it seems *too easy* sometimes. We would no longer downplay our contributions. I've noticed that when I embrace my strengths – such as writing and relating to people – I have so much more energy and my creativity soars. Life is easier and more fulfilling.

I looked at my own personal vision statement, and came up with the following suggestions for anyone who wishes to create one of their own. Reciting my vision statement every day helps ground me and I am comforted because I have something to fall back on whenever life throws a curveball. I know that I just need to remind myself of my vision and keep taking actions in support of it, and all is well. It's pretty amazing actually how it works.

How I Created My Life Vision

Having a "life vision" has simplified my life. It's a reference point for every single thing that happens in my life, for every single emotion I feel, for every interaction I have. It grounds me. Having a life vision helps me with all that comes with being human.

"Our deepest fear is not that we are inadequate. Our deepest fear is that we are powerful beyond measure. It is our light, not our darkness that most frightens us. We ask ourselves, 'Who am I to be brilliant, gorgeous, talented, fabulous?' Actually, who are you not to be? Your playing small does not serve the world. There is nothing enlightened about shrinking so that other people won't feel insecure around you. We are all meant to shine, as children do. It's not just in some of us; it's in everyone. And as we let our own light shine, we unconsciously give other people permission to do the same. As we are liberated from our own fear, our presence automatically liberates others."

(Quote by Marianne Williamson)

Here are some suggestions that I've put together to help anyone interested in creating a life vision:

*A. **"Life Vision" is about knowing who you are and owning it**. Ask yourself: "Who am I?" What character traits are most important to me? How do I want to show up in the world? This is about believing in the importance of a human being's character in all facets of life.*

*B. **"Life Vision" is about the type of world we each want to live in. It's something to strive for even if we never achieve it. It's an ideal.** Ask yourself: "What would an ideal world look like? How would people act in an ideal world? How would people feel?" This image of the world should bring tears to your eyes. When thinking about this world, you should feel, "Wow. Wouldn't that be awesome? Wouldn't that be heaven on earth?"*

It doesn't matter if you think it's not possible. This is about creativity and imagination. This is about learning what inspires you, and by doing so, you automatically act in the direction of your dreams.

*C. **"Life Vision" is about what you commit to.** Ask yourself: "What am I willing to commit to that supports the kind of world I want to live in?" This is important. This is about your contribution, your effort toward making your ideal into a reality. This is about "beingness". This isn't about detailed action steps.*

This step of "commitment" is the practice of reminding yourself that you are powerful and that you make a difference simply by being you. This is about believing that who you are not only matters, it's your greatest gift to the world.

This is also about "surrendering" to the downfalls of humanity. By connecting with your life vision, choosing how to be in any given situation gets easier. More and more your effort to "be" simply becomes a part of you.

Your "beingness" evolves until one day, you're at a new starting point, and the cycle continues. Your vision of the world evolves. Instead of becoming stagnant and cynical about life, you keep living, more fully and more peacefully, until the day you die.

BUILDING MY LIFE VISION, as an example:

 My answer to "Who am I?" is: *"Compassionate and Courageous". Many other character traits speak to me, however, these 2 traits I connect with the most. (You may choose others such as "loving" "vibrant" "powerful" "confident" "bold" "graceful", etc.)*

 My answer to "What would an ideal world look like?" is: *"People would be kind to each other." This image brings tears to my eyes because I imagine a world where everyone is kind to each person. To me, something so simple would have such a dramatic effect. To me, that would be awesome. To me, that would be heaven on earth.*

Do I think it's possible that in every interaction people would be kind? No, and it doesn't matter. Why? Because what matters is knowing how I want to live, and knowing that when I'm living true to myself I create a ripple effect. (You may connect more with "freedom" "abundance" "joy" "peace" "unity", etc.)

 My answer to "What am I willing to commit to that supports the kind of world I want to live in?" is: *I will "engage openly and playfully; I will be myself; I will surrender; I will be an expression of love, integrity and gratitude." (Notice how these aren't "to-do's?" It's how I'm choosing to be.*

You may connect more with being "accepting" "supportive" "joyful", "inspiring" etc.)

Simplifying thoughts is a process. There are an abundance of ideals and character traits to consider before honing in on the few that speak most to you. <u>The main point is that you are connected with a statement, that YOU create, to support the ideal life that YOU want to live, knowing by living your life from the essence of who you are, you will impact the world in a positive and long-lasting way – you will leave a true legacy.</u> At the end of your life when you ask yourself the question, "Did my life matter?" You can sincerely and gratefully answer, "Yes" – with no regrets.

HERE IS MY LIFE VISION at this point in my life:

"I am a compassionate and courageous woman, committed to engaging with people in an open and playful way, having faith that through God's grace, and surrendering to his guidance, the lives I touch with love, integrity and gratitude will bring forth the peace and humanity within each of us, creating a ripple effect of kindness and joy."

****

Gateway to Freedom

The experience with my parents at the end of their lives was intense. Nothing I was experiencing in the couple of years after that point came close to compare. I didn't want to live "back to normal". I simply couldn't do that. But I didn't know what I wanted to do. Then I thought, "What if life isn't about 'doing'?" I was so used to doing. Was I taking a lazy path by not focusing on what I do or not do? No, I didn't think so. Was I depressed because I wasn't interested in accomplishing? Maybe a little. I just kept having this nagging feeling that it's not about what I'm "doing". Life isn't about doing. Then what is it about?

I thought to myself that what's more important is how I'm "being". Even my life vision statement had more to do with "being" than it did with doing. I realized that how I'm "being" impacts my life and the people in my life in a huge way. This is what most impacted my parents. I had evidence of this – it was a combination of how I was being and the actions I was taking. *Taking action without regard to how I was being no longer gave me satisfaction.* If I wasn't acting in alignment with a vision, I no longer was motivated to action. I was simply uninspired. My life vision was helpful as I could maintain a certain mindset that kept me open and empowered to handle what came my way.

I still experienced bouts of grief that would scream out for comfort. I no longer felt permeating sadness, but a part of me still felt that sense of loss.

I came across this passage from Ram Daas that brought me much solace. It was a letter he wrote to a family who lost their child. To me, it's a universal hug to comfort anyone in times of grief. I put my parents name in place of the original name to personalize it for me, and took out one part that was specific to the family this original letter was intended. Thank you for this letter, Ram Daas:

> *"Brenda and Hank finished their work on earth and left the stage in a manner that leaves those of us left behind with a cry of agony in our heart as the fragile thread of our faith is dealt with so unexpectedly. Is anyone strong enough to stay conscious through such teachings as you are receiving?*
>
> *I can't assuage your pain with any words, nor should I. For your pain is Hank and Brenda's legacy to you, not that they or I would inflict such pain by choice, but there it is. And it must burn its purifying way to completion, for something in you dies when you bear the unbearable. It is only in that dark night of the soul that you are prepared to see as God sees, and to love as God loves.*

Now is the time to let your grief find expression, no falses. Now is the time to sit quietly and speak to Hank and Brenda and thank them for being with you for these years and encourage them to go on with whatever their work is. Knowing that you will grow in compassion and wisdom from this experience. In my heart I know that you and they will meet again and again and recognize the many ways in which you have known each other, and when you meet you will know in a flash what now it is not given to you to know: why this had to be the way it was.

Our rational minds can never understand what has happened, but our hearts if we keep them open to God will find their own intuitive way. Hank and Brenda came to do their work on earth, which includes their manner of death. Now their souls are free and the love that you can share with them is invulnerable to the winds of changing time and space, in that deep love, include me.

In love,
Ram Dass"

****

A New Kind of Free

The memories I hold of my parents comfort me. Some memories make me laugh out loud as I share them. Some make me cry. I do experience my parents through my memories. Once I saw the famous actor, Sidney Poitier, giving an interview. He was 83 years old at the time. Halfway through the interview, he spoke of when he was a boy. He spoke of his parents and their guidance. He had tears in his eyes as he remembered his parents. I was so inspired by this. The fact that at 83 years old, he still felt such a connection with his parents that it brought tears to his eyes. This gave me hope. I also can remember my parents and feel close to them – even 40 years from now!

Yes, there is the reality that there will be no more new memories created with my parents now that they are no longer here on earth. They are gone. However, I AM STILL HERE. My parents live on through me. I carry a piece of my mother and father in me and I have the privilege of sharing them with the world as I share myself. We are in this together. Then I take it one step further: *We are all in this together – all of the wonderful human beings on this earth.*

Am I thinking this because I'm searching for something to bring me comfort? I do know that I'm attempting to make sense of this thing called life. What is missing in my life now that my parents are gone? The family times we had together. There will be no more get-togethers at my parents' home, the home I grew up in. I will not hear another joke from my father or see another exasperated smile from my mother as she relented and allowed herself to be coaxed out of a bad mood. I wouldn't be able to go running with my mom anymore on those cool and crisp early mornings.

The biggest void is that I would no longer have the absolute acceptance I enjoyed from my parents – that feeling of knowing that they had my back no matter what happened in life. I won't be able to look at them anymore and appreciate what I see. Yet, I can still appreciate them. I won't be able to care for them anymore. Yet, I'm forever comforted by the care I gave to them. I won't be able to make them smile. Yet, I receive great comfort in my memories.

My parents were human beings. My mom gave birth to me, and my parents raised me. My parents lived their lives to the best of their ability, as we all do. My parents' journey on earth came to an end, and I was privileged to accompany them during it and while they each took their last breath. I accepted this early on, yet emotionally I had not. I didn't want to miss them.

I think about the song by Al Green called "How Do We Mend a Broken Heart". I was feeling as he described toward the end of the song when he soulfully sang, '...*help me mend...my broken heart...I think I...I know I...I believe I....I know I...I feel like I got to...I feel like I'm going to LIVE again...*'

I recall driving down the freeway one day, and I had so much energy running through me. It felt like I was bursting from the inside out. I was moving around and wanted to scream. I had this intuitive feeling. It was as if I was being told, "Go, go, go!" And I wanted to go in a direction, yet I didn't know where or what. It was an eerie feeling. That rug that I felt was pulled out from under me – that unsteady feeling I had been experiencing for a long time had shifted. It was still unsteady, yet it was as if the shaky ground was my new base. I embraced it that day in the car in an unexpected flash of a moment. I felt like, "This is it." And I felt okay with it, even excited about it.

I was free.

The best way I can explain it is that I was free of that weighted feeling I was carrying. I felt lighter and I had a sudden awareness of *possibilities* in life. There was no longer a feeling of something constantly tugging at me to remind me of what I've lost. My mind was more open and hopeful.

It was as if I started dancing freely across logs floating in a river, instead of stopping on each one in fear of falling. The logs, which felt so steady underneath me when my parents were alive, had broken loose after their death. The shift that I felt was that I no longer wanted, or expected, those logs to lock back into place. I had a sudden understanding that they will forever move beneath me, and that my freedom comes when I lift my head up and see that I can 'dance' across those logs as I journey toward the other side – if I choose to. I understood in that flash of a moment that fulfillment in life comes when I look up far and wide and decide to move from the depths of my soul…*no matter what*. And I could even have fun while doing it.

One of my all-time favorite quotes came from my nephew, Colby Thomas, when he was just 6 years old. My sister asked him one day, "So, Colby, what do you think of this thing called life? Are you enjoying yourself?"

Colby thought for a moment and answered:

> *"If life wasn't fun, then God wouldn't even make people."*

(Quote by Colby Thomas, age 6)

Part Eight

Light

This is not a fairytale ending. My happiness comes and goes. Yet I must say, I'm enjoying life much more than I ever have before. *Each day* is filled with enjoyment at some level. I create it because, again, I do not want even one day to pass realizing that I've just "gone through the motions." I focus much more on what I'm grateful for in my life and much less on things that don't bring me joy. When I love, I feel the love. I don't have to wait for that powerful feeling to come to me. I can choose to be loving or joyful or happy or sad.

When I feel certain emotions that I'd rather not feel, I acknowledge them and shift, more quickly than ever before. For example, I say to myself, "I don't like this. I'm so angry right now!" Or, "I'm scared. I don't like what's happening." Or, "I feel hurt. I'm so disappointed." Then I say, "Okay. Now what?" And I choose. It's often a messy process, but the fact is, I do get to choose.

I'm not always successful in being how I want to be in any given moment, however, that's okay. It's a paradox. On the one hand, for example, it's not okay to yell at my kids, and on the other hand, if that's in fact what I did, then I can choose what I do next. I can sincerely apologize. I can tell my kids that I love them and my yelling has nothing to do with them. I can take the time to explain to them what's really going on with me. *I do not punish myself when I mess up.* I practice treating myself with the same loving kindness I envision treating other people.

I know I'm human and I will behave in ways that I wish I hadn't, and it's okay. I believe that because I <u>know</u> it's okay to mess up in life, I can create that space I want to live in much faster than ever before. Self-care is so essential for me. I grew up watching my mother "do it all" with a disabled husband and three kids. She rarely asked for support. I modeled after her. I'm very self-sufficient and it can be exhausting. The fact is, I want to be softer. I want to embrace my femininity. Self-care helps me create that space within myself.

I want to do my part in this world and allow everyone else to do their part, if they so choose. I can only control what I do *and this is such a relief to know*. I don't have to try to change others because, first of all, who am I to assume that I know what's best for someone else? Also, even if I do have a suggestion or insight for someone, I've learned through trial and error that it's best to only depart my so-called wisdom when asked, or when I feel a person may be on the road to being receptive, or if my intuition tells me to "go for it" - because I care enough about others to put my best self forward and not shy away from uncomfortable situations.

It's enough for me to live my life on my own terms, according to a vision that supports humanity and those I love. It makes sense to me to focus on how I'm being and what I'm doing in the world. I'm not able to, however, if I'm not my biggest advocate in taking care of myself. For me, this means making some alone time a priority in my life. Quiet space feeds my soul and enables me to naturally rejuvenate.

Allowing is also a practice – just stopping and observing instead of impulsively intervening. Engaging in life is very important to me too. I find that it's the key to fulfillment – just "choose in" and participate in life. My thinking too much often holds me back. I wish I had a button to shut off my mind sometimes.

Dreams come true, that's what they do. The only variable is when.

For the slow approach: Resist. Attach. Insist. Deny. Stop. Second guess. Whine. Argue. Defend. Protest. Cry. Struggle. And ask others, when you know the answer yourself.

For the quick approach: Visualize. Pretend. Prepare. Dodge. Roll. Serpentine. Do not waiver over intentions, but over methods. Show up, even when nothing happens. And give thanks in advance.

You knew that,
> *The Universe*

(Quote by Mike Dooley)

****

Food for Thought

I created a document called "Lea's Life". I read it almost every day because it's true for me. It came from inside me, then out, and back in again. I edit it from time to time as I grow and learn. As simplified as it may seem, it took quite an effort to get this summary down. Even though I've worked with a written life vision for quite some time, I found it helpful to break things down even more.

The below document helps me stay in alignment with what I want in life. (The original document is very colorful with stickers and other art which makes it more fun to look at and helps me connect with it on a deeper level.) I created this document (art piece) because I want to be *aware* day-to-day and remind myself of what is most important to me in my life. I also feel it's important to know whether or not I'm taking actions in alignment with what's important or not – for no other reason than to know – because if I don't know, then I'm not able to make true choices. I would then start living by default, which I personally do not want to do because of my deep understanding that life is truly precious and very short.

What I put first on my art piece are some sayings that I've heard said in different ways that inspire me. I read these almost daily.

Next on my document is my principle statement (my vision of who I am and what impact I have while I'm on this earth).

Then there is my simple measuring stick – how do I know I'm in alignment?

Next, I broke things down further and created a vision for each main area of life.

Lastly, and most importantly, I thought of action steps in alignment with my vision. These action items are not set in stone. I do not feel pressure to *do* because I focus on my small steps and I celebrate with people in my corner – people who "get me". It's truly awesome. What's awesome is the effect of working in synergy with others that are focusing on *living*. To be able to focus on living fully, we must know *who we are* and *how we're being*, and *what we want in life*. Otherwise, living feels more like moving sporadically in a cloud, or swirling in chaos, or like we're being held down by the weight of the world.

Lea's Life

What I focus on strengthens.
There are reasons and results. Forget the reasons.
"This isn't it" IS it! Enjoy where I am and <u>stay in motion</u>.
If it's to be, it starts with me.
I change and the world changes.
People don't remember what I say,
they remember how I make them feel.
I am responsible for my life.
Everything is perfect. (I just may not see it yet.)

Lea's Vision Statement *(who I am and the impact I make on humanity):*

    I am a compassionate and courageous woman, committed to engaging with people in an open and playful way, having faith that with God's grace, and surrendering to his guidance, the lives I touch with love, integrity, and gratitude, will bring forth the peace and humanity within each of us, creating a ripple effect of kindness and joy.

How do I know whether or not I'm living in alignment with my vision? *My energy level.*

Actions to Support Me in Living my Vision: *(I imagine the woman I will become by taking these actions):*

Spiritual Vision: **I am lovable, relaxed and peaceful.**
    Actions: *-Meditate 4+ days a week, for minimum of 10 min.*
        -Yoga 3+ days a week
        -Focus on gratitude 5+ days a week, i.e. gratitude lists, voicing appreciation to people, giving hugs and affection
        -receive massage once a month
        -no viewing electronics after 9pm
        -alone time at least once a week from 8pm on
        -practice surrender
        -be kind to myself

Physical Vision: **I am healthy, fit and vibrant.**
    Actions: *-Vary exercise routine 4+ days a week, i.e. run, bike, stretch, strength train, walk, dance, yoga.*

-Focus on nutrition 5+ days a week, i.e. eat
primarily whole foods, take nutritional supplements/vitamins, minimally eat sugar and gluten, drink a lot of water throughout day
-Eat consciously and slowly. Enjoy my food – all food I choose to eat.

Relationship Vision: I am loving and experience intimate relationships, connecting with people every day.

Actions: -Focus on gratitude 5+ days a week, i.e. gratitude lists, voicing appreciation to people, giving hugs and affection
-Family dance parties 3+ days a week (dance to 4+ songs)
-eating dinner as a family 3+ days a week
-hide "love note" for each family member 1+ times per week
-receive massage once a month
-date night with Oliver at least once every other week (allow him to plan and practice "receiving")
-connect with friends in some way 4+ days a week
-welcome friends into my family life
-alone time once a week from 8pm on
-practice being curious and truly listening to people
-be on time or early to every event with a set start time, re-aligning when necessary
-be conscious of the people I engage with and adjust when necessary

Vocational Vision: *I am a leader, living in abundance and creativity.*

Actions: -*go to outside location, i.e. coffee shop, and work on book 2 times per week until habit is created for home routine*
-*continue meeting my business responsibilities*
-*continue keeping finances organized*
-*work with tools learned in various work shops focusing on an abundant mindset and/or vision*
-*attend various courses in alignment with my vision, a minimum of once per year*
-*read a book in alignment with my vision, a minimum of once per month*

One note on the gauge I use to know whether or not I'm living in alignment with my vision. I list above that I observe "*my energy level*". I'm not saying, for example, that if I feel tired that it means I'm not living in alignment with my vision. What I mean is that I know the difference between feeling tired because I am stressed, versus feeling tired because of an active day writing. I know when I'm tired from giving to the point of martyrdom, versus tired from enjoying a day volunteering for my child's class field trip. (Something I consciously chose in alignment with my vision).

There's a difference between feeling overwhelmed and exhausted from meaningless tasks, versus feeling spent from a day working on what I value most. I also recognize when my energy level is elevated due to anxious feelings from worrying, versus elevated due to living fully and creatively. I've experienced time and again that when I expend energy moving toward my dreams, it creates a surge of even more energy. I may have trouble sleeping because I'm feeling so much enthusiasm, versus having trouble sleeping because I'm feeling anxious.

My energy level is a personal barometer that I use because when I pay attention, I always know the truth of what's *really* going on inside me, and this truth manifests itself physically. It's the perfect measuring stick for me. It's a clear reminder to make an adjustment to how I'm being and how I'm living each day.

I'm under no such expectation that I will "arrive" at my life vision. What I do expect, and what I intend, and what I know to be, is that by practicing, I feel free and light. I feel that anything is possible because each time I take some sort of action in the direction of what is important to me in life, I build more and more evidence of what is possible. I become more and more confident that I am capable. I feel more and more gratitude for my life and for everyone and everything in it.

> *"Enthusiasm is the element of success in everything. It is the light that leads and the strength that lifts people on and up in the great struggles of scientific pursuits and of professional labor. It robs endurance of difficulty, and makes pleasure of duty."*
>
> *(Quote by Bishop Doane)*

It's all about the practice and not the destination. The <u>practice</u> is the power. It makes life interesting because when I get up each day anticipating the adventures to come and all the circumstances that will present themselves that will give me the opportunity to practice, life is never boring. I have seen many results in my life from my practices, but *I've found no use focusing on the results* because the details of them are never within my control. In fact, often by disconnecting with a specific result, I experience an outcome much more amazing than I could ever think up myself.

****

If We Only Knew

I think about life's big questions. Is there a God? Where do we go when we die?

God?

How awesome it would be
               if it were true.
      A spirit that oversees all.
      A being in supreme control.
      A savior of our souls.

How secure our lives would be
               knowing we'll be set free.
Our sins would be forgiven, no matter what degree.

What a comfort to our soul
          to <u>know</u>
             a paradise awaits.
Life after death without pain, worries or wants.
            A life of eternal peace and serenity.
              Could this really be?

I want proof for these beliefs.
            I admit it - I want to <u>see</u>.
Show me and I'll believe.

Faith? I understand what that means.
            Why is it so hard for me?

Does God really exist?
    Is he here beside me as I speak?
        Is he all I imagine him to be?

        I really wish - I truly want to believe.

    I do believe in God – in a power greater than me. I do believe there is something more – something so much more that to even attempt to decipher the possibilities of the universe are futile. I don't believe our human brains could even understand the vastness.

The Discovery

Three seconds:
    My mother
    I love her.
        My brother
        When did we last speak?
            My husband.
            Will I see him again?
                Me
            I'm not ready yet.
Impact
    Sky Asphalt Sky Asphalt
The End.

Amidst the noise and confusion
    on that spot of the earth
    that spec of the universe,
    cradling arms, invisible to the human eye
    scoop her up into the sky
        lightening fast through the atmosphere
    leaving her body behind.

She is no longer alive, but acutely aware.

Absolutely no fear.

She reaches her destination, with no sense of time.

> Questions wither through her and dissipate,
> but two linger in her mind.
> > Why was she taken so soon?
> > Wasn't there more for her to do?

She is surrounded by the awesome answers
> to her final thoughts of confusion,
> > and peace flows through her as the realization of
> > > God's plan seeps into her soul.

Now she knows.
> Her discovery cannot be explained.

Humans struggle daily with the whys of the world
> and all the answers come at the end.
She finally understands.

She now knows the meaning of life which mankind
> will never truly be able to comprehend.

There is the concept of "surrender". I hear it often – how surrender-ing brings peace of mind. This idea is part of my vision also, "...*hav-ing faith that through God's grace and surrendering to his guidance...*" I've been there. Many times during my parents' illnesses I surrendered. I recited the Serenity Prayer often. I did feel peace in those moments. What about the moments following? I believe there comes a time when the foot has to come out and a step has to be taken. Some sort of move-ment is required to get from one moment to the next – *if we want some-thing different in life.* We must move.

The people I surround myself with are my angels on earth and through them I see glimpses of what may be beyond this life, when we no longer need to experience being in our bodies. Even with the huge mystery looming around all of us about what happens next, I feel empowered knowing that I get to choose how I want to be and what I want to do leading up to that point of transition from this life to the next. I've learned to embrace and appreciate <u>real</u>, <u>raw</u> <u>life</u> – living in acceptance with all the pain and all the joy.

I've come to realize ever more that every person wears a "mask" to protect them from this "harsh world". This mask is different for every person and can be displayed through words and behaviors, sometimes hurtful ones. The masks can be smiling when they want to cry. They can be screaming in anger when they're hurting deep inside. While each mask is different, the purpose is the same – to mask what's *really* going on for them – their pain or suffering, their dreams they don't dare say, the hopes they've given up on.

We all have ups and downs, joys and sorrows, excitements and disappointments. To connect is to know this – to know that we are all the same – no one is immune to what goes along with being human. It doesn't matter how successful someone appears to be or what they look like or how they act or what they say. We don't always behave as we would like. Knowing this makes it easier to engage with others compassionately and on a deeper level. Why connect in this way? Because we are hard-wired as human beings to care. It's the meaning we put to the trials and tribulations in this world, and our mindsets, that we suffer from.

I recently had a brief yet memorable experience with my daughter, Sophie, one morning when she was 9 years old. I climbed into her bed to cuddle her awake. She yawned and said as she stretched, "You know what, Mommy?"

"What?" I replied.

She finished her stretch and laid there on her bed, relaxed, with her arms sprawled above her head.

"I'm awesome," she sighed.

As I laid there next to her, taking in the moment, I replied with the utmost confidence, "*Yes, you are.*"

Now just imagine…if everyone in this world felt the same way about themselves…in those precious waking moments each day. What a different world we'd be living in. We wouldn't feel the need to tear others down, to compete, or control, because we would be at peace within ourselves. That peaceful feeling would emanate toward others. How could we then hate? It would be impossible.

I'm not saying peace is an attainable state 100% of the time. It cannot be, because we are human. However, if we felt good inside our bodies, like Sophie does inside hers, we can shift back to a peaceful state much more easily during times of challenge.

We are all awesome. Many of us have just forgotten how it feels to connect with our source. How can we begin to recognize who we are? I believe the very first step is to *treat ourselves with kindness.* It's important to take time out to assess how we really treat ourselves. Why? Because as much as we may want to or try to, we are simply not capable of treating others any differently than we treat ourselves. We can never live in alignment with who we are if we are not loving toward ourselves.

How do we begin to treat ourselves kindly? Create space for ourselves to just "be" and allow ourselves to embrace whatever it is that is important to us in life. Admit it, get clear on it, take action toward it, knowing that it's not about the goal and all about the progress. Practice dreaming.

> "*Imagination is more important than knowledge. For knowledge is limited to all we now know and understand, while imagination embraces the entire world, and all there ever will be to know and understand.*"
>
> *(Quote by Albert Einstein)*

Often in life, we stop caring about ourselves enough. We expend so much energy "out there". There comes a time when we must reel ourselves back in and break that shell we've encased ourselves in. After all, *it's our life we're living*. No one else will ever have the experience of being in our body. No other human being can go with us the moment it's time for us to leave this world – that flash of a moment when we leave our body is ours to fly alone. Let's be our own best friend, right here, right now.

We Have Fear

we have boundaries
we have fear
      but we don't know why we're scared

are we babies – no not babies
but we cry in the night just the same

woman so strong
so smart and real
      think more to see what's there

move beyond to reach your potential
live through the walls that glare

soothe the baby in you
wipe her tears
      but don't give her away
            never give her away

you have already?
reel her back in
      anchor her in place
            don't let the fear throw her

love the baby in you
she's done nothing but ride the storm

don't fault her for screaming out
in discomfort and pain

be those rainbows
that come out after the rain

fill up her scary nights
while she's in her shadowy crib
      with rays of constant sunshine

and sing the sweetest lullabies
using the softest most gentle sounds
      it will help her in the night and through the day
        help her not be so afraid

****

The Little Child Within Us

"All is well. You did not come here to fix a broken world. The world is not broken. You came here to live a wonderful life. And if you can learn to relax a little and let it all in, you will begin to see the universe present you with all that you have asked for."

(Quote by Esther Hicks)

When I get scared and I feel down from the images of a world that is less than perfect – a world that I see filled with pain and suffering and I think, "What's the use?", I remind myself of the choice I have to live with an open and loving heart. Not only do I feel like this is all I can do sometimes, I realize that when I succeed in this quest, it does make a difference – the energy shift has a ripple effect.

In addition to living with an open and loving heart, I believe in the power of "lightening up". I think the power of fun is greatly underestimated. Why not incorporate a spirit of fun in everything I do? Why not decide to celebrate and enjoy life more? I was told once, "Suffering is optional." I believe this is true.

> *Young souls, play hard to get.*
> *Mature souls, play hard.*
> *But old souls, just play...*

> *La, la, la -*
> *The Universe*

> *(Quote by Mike Dooley)*

The one thing we can count on in life is change, so why not embrace it as quickly as possible. I use dancing as a simple tool. It's so easy to turn on music and start dancing if I want to lift my mood. And then there are those times when I want to stew a while about something, and I allow myself to – for a certain amount of time – then I shift. I simply don't want to stay in that hardened place for long. It's a choice I make, and often that choice is difficult – that's why one easy way to shift is to focus on simple steps, such as focusing on turning on the stereo... then focusing on starting to dance...then focusing on letting go and allowing the music to move me.

I think about children. The same little girl I once was is still a part of me.

I imagine letting her back out instead of holding her as a distant memory. I believe adults have just as much energy as kids, we just use it differently (focusing on bills, rushing from task to task, holding onto the past, living by "shoulds", worrying, resisting, etc.) We lock ourselves up and *it's exhausting*.

I think about how young children live:

Kids feel their emotions and move on.
Kids live in the moment.
Kids are active and energetic.
Kids are resilient.
Kids are creative.
Kids are persistent.
Kids take risks.
Kids are loving.
Kids are playful.
Kids are enthusiastic.
Kids laugh wholeheartedly.
Kids dream big.

If we surrender to the spirit of that little child within us, imagine how our experience of life would change. Just imagine the possibilities. When I really think about, life doesn't have to be so complex - or so serious. Now, while embracing that child within us, think about our wisdom – our life experiences – which are unique and incomparable to anyone else. No one lives the same life.

Think about what we each have to offer simply by sharing our stories with people. Our stories offer a basis for understanding each other better. They offer the realization that we are united in both our joys and our fears because happiness and pain are felt by all. We may have different stories, but no one is immune from the emotions that come from being human.

Here is a poem I wrote about emotions and the moment of decision. It's the only other poem I found in my mom's file folder after her death. Coincidence?

Emotions

Upset - very

      Angry
      No

Depressed
sad

          Tears
          longing

Expectation

D i s a p p o i n t m e n t

      Want wish plead
          nothing

      Think try
          nothing

Hope
Yes

      possible
      slight

dream
      comfort

      longing
      waiting

          living?

do

move

strength

accept

continue

Life

While life doesn't always have to be hard, the fact is, it is at times. When life is smooth, we take action with a lot less effort. In contrast, during those painful times, just getting out of bed is the most action we feel like we are capable of sometimes. We do need support during these times. We don't have to do it all ourselves. With each step we take (action), we receive more and more support to get the momentum going, and we will climb out of the hole. The momentum will get us out.

When I allow me – my raw presence and vulnerability – to be shown, I am giving a gift to others, as others give the same to me when they are being *real*. We are giving each other gifts that inspire us to act. Actions born from inspiration take a lot less effort than action based on our thoughts and mental efforts alone. Vulnerability is about taking that step, that action. Vulnerability feels shaky and imperfect, and the outcome is unknown. Move anyway. Say it anyway. If you mess up, clean it up. The outcome does not matter. What matters is being willing to make the effort from a place of pure intention. Results are just feedback to be observed to help guide us in our future choices.

It's about taking a step, then another and another, which builds natural momentum.

*"Muddling through in life and growing is more fulfilling
than executing all our neatly packaged plans and renditions."*

(Quote by Lea Gambina Pecora)

Plans and strategies help tremendously in life, yet without being willing to muddle through – to keep taking steps during those times of uncertainty and pain, we miss out on the true beauty in life. The real beauty and fulfillment comes when we "show up" and *engage* in life from the depths of who we are, *regardless of circumstances.*

Then there's the stillness. I discovered a paradox. While I learned the extreme value of taking action, no matter how slight, there is something of equal value, and that is non-action. Being still. Some people may say meditation, however, it's the simple act of sitting quietly that may be more easy to understand. When we first pause to "be still", I think about the analogy of listening to music. If music didn't have pauses in the midst of a song, we couldn't enjoy it. Those pauses provide an anticipation of what's to come, and also offers the opportunity to soak in the experience of what was last heard. Such is the experience of life.

The real magic comes during those moments when our minds are silent. This is when we get to know ourselves - who we really are. It's also at these precious times when we invite wisdom to come into our lives more easily. The "monkeys" in our mind quiet down, and the answers we struggle so hard to figure out suddenly have a straight shot to us if we're open and willing to receive them. We may not realize them at that exact moment, yet they will surely come…serendipities, coincidences, grace…

As I mentioned earlier, I find that when I focus on how I want to *be* or my *beingness*, my path to joy is much shorter. The pressure is lifted, and I can move with more ease. I suppose what is happening is that my actions come from a place of inspiration instead of a means to an end. I suppose this is what is meant by "moment to moment" living. Each moment is the focus, and each moment gets strung together with the next, and all the moments make up a life.

I ask myself, "How do I want to be in this moment?" The more often I ask myself this question, and the more often I shift to be how I want to be, the more free I am – because I'm allowing myself to be *me*. I'm not talking about acting based on how I'm *feeling*, I'm talking about acting *despite* how I'm feeling. It's a tough practice – being who I am regardless of how I'm feeling. However, every time I make the shift and choose *love*, I become more and more courageous…more and more free.

****

Signing Off

Dominic and Sophie are my children. They have fun – every day. They also get upset – every day. They are wonderful. They are human. They make mistakes and they shine and they learn through it all. They inhabit the qualities I listed earlier that I see in most children. Some day, most likely before them, my journey in this life will come to an end. I hope this book will provide comfort to them because they will know that they will be okay. They will come to a point when they have to decide how they will continue in life when faced with hardship. I want them to know that there are always more great things to come if they keep their eyes open and let their curiosity get the best of them.

In the darkest of times…move…even if you just open your door and walk one block, and keep doing that process of making a decision toward action then following through. Don't ever give up on yourself, and know that a force greater than you – the Grace of God, the Power of the Universe – is always supporting you, whether your human mind sees it that way or not.

Don't worry about the future – trust that even the smallest of actions is enough to gain momentum toward living life – *really living*. Then watch the support surround you…that was always there and you just couldn't see it. You couldn't see it because your mind was blocked to it until you took that first step. Each step requires a moment of decision. That's all you have to do. Decide – again and again – to take each small step in the direction of where you want to go and wish to be. And as you're coming through the darkness, and your heart is opening once again, be that light – that support – for someone else.

Keep in motion and allow your heart to do what it was created to do - *love*.

We will forever be in changing shades of dark and light through-out this journey. Let's be there for each other during it all, and trust the light more than the darkness. With enough of us trusting, *we can change the world.*

As for my life, right now, at 45 years old, I say, "Goodbye, mom and dad. THANK YOU!! BIG hugs and kisses for you! XOXO I'll see you later. Until then…I'm going to be happy and I'm going to be sad. I'm going to work and I'm going to play. I'm going to be courageous and yes, afraid. I'm going to live life as a lovable human being – in all my glory and all my flaws. After all, I'm wonderfully human, and while I'm on this earth, I'll be playing in the field of *real, raw life.*

Want to join me?

Love, always,
    Lea

P.S. – Thank you for reading my story. I'd love to hear from you!
Lea@WonderfullyHuman.com

BONUS POEM
(published in "A 4th Course of Chicken Soup of the Soul")

Inspiration

He stares out the window
    to the children below
    who were playing so freely,
    laughing.
He sits in the dim room on the second floor
confined - but in his mind.
Each day, he's there.
Rarely does he move from his chair.
    It's just too much effort
    to use the cane.

The laughter - what sweetness to his ears.
Was he ever young like that?
Did he play in the street?
Was he ever free of worry?
They are - so obviously.

A little boy notices him one day
    just watching them play.
The boy gives him a toothless grin,
    and he does the same -
    It is so strange for his face
    to crease in that long forgotten way.

His friend pays him a visit,
    riddled with scolds and advice.
"You're just waiting aren't you? Waiting to die."
He makes no motion and does not turn from the window
    transfixed on the children below.

His friend leaves.
       He doesn't notice when,
       and he doesn't recall what was said
       except for one thought -
            Was he?
            Was he waiting to die?
He never thinks with any level of depth.
He never thinks about much
since the time
the time he keeps out of his mind
the time his wife died.

They push, they play
their laughter is fresh.
He lifts from his chair and leans
       against the window beam.
       He stands, watching the children.
The toothless boy looks up searchingly.
       The boy sees him
       and waves with excitement.
            He waves back.
He walks now with his cane
       around the small room.
What inspired him to do so?
He does not know.

"Hi," says a voice behind him.
With effort he turns around.
The toothless boy is smiling,
       his little arms swinging.
Perspiration collects on his forehead.
He slowly wipes his face with his free hand,
       leaning heavily on his cane.
"How are you, Sir?"
He nods.
"Would you like to come outside and play?"
"Play?" he says softly.

"Yes! It's stickball today."
"No - no. I can't play."
"Why, Sir?" The boy is confused.
"I'm too old to play."
"It's okay if you're slower than us. We all agreed.
　　　　It's funner to play than watch all the time - don't you think?"
"I - I suppose."

The boy quickly goes to his side
　　　　and leads him to the door.

He goes.

The boy helps him down the stairs
　　　　and opens the door to the outside -
His face feels the winter cold
His eyes feel the morning light.
He trembles a little, and the boy
　　　　holds his hand firmly.
His cane slips from his grasp
　　　　the boy steadies it securely.
He coughs twice, his body begins to shake.
The boy looks up at him in concern, "Are you all right?"
He nods, and meets the boys eyes -
　　　　the eyes of youth, sparkling and alive.
"Hey, everyone! This is -, uh, Sir, what is your name?"
"Donald."
"This is Donald, and he's going to play!"

ACKNOWLEDGMENTS

I'd like to acknowledge a few people who helped me make this book a reality. It goes without saying that the relationship I had with my parents had such an influence on who I am today. Their example of simply being *willing* in life, helped support me in being willing to do what it took to write and publish this book.

A special thanks to my friend, Diana Romanovska, who met me once a week at a coffee shop in Berkeley, California, for 4 months straight simply to support me in creating the space and rhythm of writing consistently. After that 4 months, I was off and running and able to adhere to a regular writing schedule which was a tremendous support in getting this book done. Thank you!

Many friends supported me in this book project through their encouragement and enthusiasm at the mere idea of it. I would like to acknowledge 3 of them in particular because of their impact on keeping me inspired to write more consistently. Emi Navas, Maureen Linder and Wendy Cepeda simply asked me, in regular intervals, about how my book was coming along. They expressed interest and curiosity in the subject matter, and left me feeling as though they couldn't wait to read it. This is my first book and while I had a vision for it, I felt a bit isolated during the writing process and it took quite a bit of discipline to work on the book through conclusion. Emi, Maureen and Wendy made me feel not so alone in my efforts and inspired me to pick up the pace in my writing. Thank you!

My husband, Oliver Pecora, helped me in so many ways. He is a true entrepreneur with a "can do" attitude. He gets excited by ideas and enthusiastically dreams them into fruition. What I mean by this is that he lets his mind go toward all the possibilities starting from an initial idea. He doesn't block his thoughts about things and is quite inspiring. He wrote a book called Up A Notch: Why Some Entrepreneurs Stay Stuck and Others Persevere with Passion. Oliver, who is not a prolific writer, and German being his first language, did what it took and utilized many resources to write and publish his book. I know a lot of people have written books, but by watching Oliver go through it, the idea of doing one myself seemed not only possible, but a natural next step and just a matter of time. He was very encouraging and supportive. He also has a talent for design. I gave him the picture of my parents that I envisioned being on the front of the book, and he created the book cover. Oliver also designed the layout of the pages of the book. We worked closely together and he helped make my vision for the look and feel of the book a reality. I am so grateful to him for all he does and for who he is.

ABOUT THE AUTHOR

Lea Gambina Pecora has enjoyed writing since childhood. Her professional background spans 17 years in the legal field. She achieved her Paralegal Certification through CSUH. Lea married Oliver Pecora, and utilizing their individual skills and strengths, they created a successful IT business, SIC Consulting, Inc.

Much of Lea's time is spent with her husband and their two children, Dominic and Sophie, in Northern California. They travel together often. Lea enjoys her family immensely and engages in a variety of creative pursuits in support of each family member's areas of interest. She also enjoys close friendships and spending time with those she loves. Lea's passions include living a healthy lifestyle, creative writing, learning, and connecting with people daily on a deep and meaningful level.

Her journey alongside her parents up until their deaths, and the aftermath, impacted her tremendously. She found herself jotting down notes for several years, sometimes daily, as insights began to flow through her. Lea's first book Wonderfully Human is an outpouring from her heart, and was pivotal to her healing and personal growth. Her true story of love, loss and freedom is an inspiring offering to all those experiencing the pain of hardship and loss.

CPSIA information can be obtained at www.ICGtesting.com
Printed in the USA
BVOW04s1915150215

387432BV00003B/7/P